"*Holiness in the Letters of Paul* provides a helpful treatment of a neglected topic. He shows clearly the importance of holiness in Paul's theology and ethics. Adewuya demonstrates how pervasive talk of holiness is within the Pauline corpus, even as he argues that the contemporary church needs to give more and better attention to it. This book's construction of holiness in Paul should stimulate further work on this important topic."

—JERRY L. SUMNEY
Professor of Biblical Studies, Lexington Theological Seminary

"All too often scholars neglect the topic of holiness in the study of Paul, and yet it is clearly a fixture in his thought and vocabulary. Adewuya fills an important gap in scholarship by carefully examining Paul's holiness language in the context of each of his letters. Both Adewuya's exegetical and synthetic work offer clarity and fresh insight. Given his career-long dedication to this topic, Adewuya serves as the perfect guide."

— NIJAY K. GUPTA
George Fox Evangelical Seminary

Holiness in the Letters of Paul

Holiness in the Letters of Paul

The Necessary Response to the Gospel

J. AYODEJI ADEWUYA

CASCADE *Books* • Eugene, Oregon

HOLINESS IN THE LETTERS OF PAUL
The Necessary Response to the Gospel

Copyright © 2016 J. Ayodeji Adewuya. All rights reserved. Except for brief quotations in critical publications or reviews, no part of this book may be reproduced in any manner without prior written permission from the publisher. Write: Permissions, Wipf and Stock Publishers, 199 W. 8th Ave., Suite 3, Eugene, OR 97401.

Cascade Books
An Imprint of Wipf and Stock Publishers
199 W. 8th Ave., Suite 3
Eugene, OR 97401

www.wipfandstock.com

PAPERBACK ISBN: 978-1-4982-9454-6
HARDCOVER ISBN: 978-1-4982-9456-0
EBOOK ISBN: 978-1-4982-9455-3

Cataloguing-in-Publication data:

Names: Adewuya, J. Ayodeji.

Title: Holiness in the letters of Paul : the necessary response to the gospel / J. Ayodeji Adewuya.

Description: Eugene, OR: Cascade Books, 2016 | Includes bibliographical references and index.

Identifiers: ISBN 978-1-4982-9454-6(paperback) | ISBN 978-1-4982-9456-0 (hardcover) | ISBN 978-1-4982-9455-3 (ebook)

Subjects: LCSH: Holiness—Biblical teaching | Sanctification—Biblical teaching | Bible. Epistles of Paul—Criticism, interpretation, etc.

Classification: BS2545.S27 A2 2016 (paperback) | BS2545.S27 (ebook)

Manufactured in the U.S.A.   10/06/16

Scripture quotations from the Revised Standard Version of the Bible, copyright © 1946, 1952, and 1971 the Division of Christian Education of the National Council of the Churches of Christ in the United States of America. Used by permission. All rights reserved.

Scripture taken from the NEW AMERICAN STANDARD BIBLE®, Copyright © 1960,1962,1963,1968,1971,1972,1973,1975,1977,1995 by The Lockman Foundation. Used by permission.

To the one and holy God who calls his people unto holiness.

Contents

Preface | ix
Acknowledgments | xiii
Abbreviations | xiv

Chapter 1
The Starting Point | 1

Chapter 2
Holiness in Romans | 20

Chapter 3
Holiness in 1 Corinthians | 39

Chapter 4
Holiness in 2 Corinthians | 63

Chapter 5
Holiness in Galatians | 86

Chapter 6
Holiness in Ephesians | 99

Chapter 7
Holiness in Philippians | 110

Chapter 8
Holiness in Colossians and Philemon | 122

Chapter 9
Holiness in 1 and 2 Thessalonians | 137

Chapter 10
Holiness in the Pastoral Epistles | 148

Chapter 11
Putting It All Together | 159

Bibliography | 165
Index of Biblical References and Other Ancient Literature | 177

Preface

Every book has its own story—just like every person. My upbringing in the Wesleyan-holiness tradition is an important aspect of my life journey, and one that has kept me interested in the subject of holiness. My academic interest in the subject was initially aroused during my pursuit of an advanced academic degree in Biblical Studies. My plan was to write a thesis on the use of the word *hagios* ("holy") and its cognates (similarly related words) in the letters of Paul, something that I later abandoned. Nevertheless, this initial research led me to the awareness of the absence of a book that provides an overview of Paul's thought on holiness or sanctification. Instead, published materials, more often than not, have portrayed the subject simply as an addendum to the subject of justification, and come under such headings as "Christian living," "righteousness," "morality," or "ethics," that is, somewhat incidental to Paul's theology. Or, at best it is treated as part of Paul's broad teaching on salvation.[1] Ultimately, the discussions of Paul's understanding of sanctification or holiness are only to be found in studies of broader application.

Given the fact that several of the biblical texts on holiness in the New Testament are to be found in the Pauline corpus, the subject demands a special treatment and more attention than has been given to it to date.[2] However, I must hasten to add that the importance of this study is not in its comprehensiveness but in its heuristic value.

---

1. Perhaps the closest one could find concerning Paul's thought in this area will be entries in theological dictionaries.

2. This is not to suggest that there are no treatments of the subject of holiness in individual books within the Pauline corpus. I have been privileged to author two of such. My contention is that holiness needs to be addressed as a stand-alone category in Paul's thought and demands as much attention as the other topics.

While it is true that sanctification/holiness is related to morality and ethics, such a relationship should be put in the proper perspective. Sanctification is to morality and ethics what a foundation is to a building. Therefore sanctification should not be confused with either or both—*it is more*.

The main thrust of Paul's letters is his concern for holiness, as well as his desire to stress, in very clear terms, the significance of what it means to be the people of God, and, consequently, to live as such.[3] Paul's concerns may be seen as involving both the *intra* (within) and *inter* (between) aspects of Christian relationships. Thus, this book sets out to examine what is considered to be Paul's underlying, as well as recurrent, motif in the canonical letters ascribed to Paul.[4]

Paul provides us with a number of facets of the nature of holiness. And as we will see, there is undoubtedly a link in Pauline thinking between holiness and separation. Holiness, while ultimately God's characteristic, is also both a characteristic and a calling of the people of God.

WHAT DOES "HOLINESS" MEAN?

One of the main questions that the discussion of holiness always generates relates to what it means. Different emphasis had been laid on different aspects. The interpretation of holiness is based on theological presuppositions and the faith traditions of interpreters. As succinctly stated by Petersen,

> Writers have often been preoccupied with establishing the place of sanctification within the framework of a given theological system rather than letting the biblical evidence speak for itself. For many, sanctification has become such a broad concept that its particular New Testament meaning has been obscured.[5]

However, such approaches have always led to an unclear articulation of holiness leading to a false dichotomy, being understood either as a status or a state. On the one hand, understood as a status, personal worthiness or the ethical component of holiness is minimized. On the other hand, understood as a state, the ethical aspect of holiness predominates, sometimes facing the danger of tending toward legalism. In this regard, the stress is placed on an individualistic, subjective experience of sanctification. As we

---

3. 2 Cor 11:2; Col 1:27.

4. I am not only aware of, but also engaged in, the continuing conversations on the lack of consensus concerning the authorship of some of the canonical letters ascribed to Paul, specifically Ephesians, Colossians, the Pastoral Epistles and 2 Thessalonians. This book is not the place for that discussion.

5. Peterson, *Possessed by God*, 16.

will see, holiness, although personal, is certainly never individualistic—it is not just about "me" and "myself." It is relational.

While it is incontestable that the holiness of God and his relationship with them both form the basis of the believers' holiness, one must not assume that one aspect is primary and the other secondary. Rather, while on the one hand, the definitive aspect is dominant in some places, on the other hand, the dynamic is dominant in other places. Even then, this still seems to be a false choice that flies in the face of Scriptural evidence. Both of the definitive and dynamic aspects are crucial and essential.

Rightly understood therefore, holiness should be conceived of as a definitive-dynamic experience, that is a dynamic, ongoing relationship. Positional and ethical holiness are not mutually exclusive. It is far from Paul's thought to suggest that it is possible to be relationally holy, without also being ethically holy. This is, at best, a false dichotomy, which runs contrary to Paul's thought. A concept of holiness that stresses the individualistic and personal experience over and against the communal is not only myopic but does a great injustice to the thought of the apostle Paul on sanctification, particularly in light of his exhortations to the various congregations to which he addressed his letters.

Paul's understanding of holiness, as here suggested, is primarily communal. As Mackay rightly observes, "we become related to Christ singly, but we cannot live 'in Christ' solitarily." God is not just making individuals holy, which he certainly does, but he is making a people holy.[6]

Holiness is multidimensional. Paul's teaching on holiness has different aspects, each of which should not be considered as a stand-alone. As such, an interpreter must avoid the temptation of "making a part to become the whole."

HOW TO PROCEED

As we examine the concept of holiness in the Pauline corpus, there are three important factors to consider, each of which plays an important role in how one proceeds. First is a clear recognition of the fact that Paul's letters were not written in a vacuum. They were specific responses or instructions to specific people with specific needs, and in specific places. As such, although there are certain common words and vocabularies that are employed in conveying Paul's message of holiness to the churches, there are different nuances as well as various specific concepts that are tailored both to the needs and particularities of each community to which Paul wrote.

---

6. As quoted by Hunter, *Interpreting Paul's Gospel*, 100.

Second, one must take note of the use of varied terminologies, concepts, and motifs. The use of different terminologies not only presents the difficulty of how they relate to one another, but also highlights the need and presents an opportunity to proffer a coherent picture of what "holiness" might mean within the Pauline corpus.

Third, the presence of a common vocabulary such as *hagios* ("holy") and its cognates dictates that the interpreter should examine Paul's usage in different contexts where its use is prominent, and see how it helps in analyzing Paul's understanding of holiness. With this new knowledge, we can see how a study limited only to texts in which the word commonly translated "holiness" occurs would be both incomplete and contrived, because holiness or sanctification is often implied where the holiness group of words may be absent.

Therefore, a more comprehensive approach is to include those texts dealing with the *concept* of holiness, not just the *word*. This is the task before us as we focus on the concept of holiness in canonical books of Paul—holiness that is predicated on—and has its "starting point" as—the holiness of God as revealed in the Old Testament.

Some of the chapters of this book have appeared in earlier form in other publishing venues, although revised here to one extent or another. Part of Chapter 2 is based on my earlier book, *Transformed by Grace: Paul's Understanding of Holiness in Romans 6–8* (Eugene, Oregon: Cascade, 2004). Parts of Chapters 1, 3, and 4 are based on my book *Holiness and Community in 2 Corinthians 6:14—7:1: Paul's View of Communal Holiness in the Corinthian Correspondence* (New York: Peter Lang, 2001) and my essay "Holiness in 2 Corinthians: The People of God in A Pluralistic Society," in *Holiness and Ecclesiology in the New Testament*, edited by Kent Brower and Andy Johnson. (Grand Rapids: Eerdmans, 2007, 201–18). The arguments in Chapter 5 were first published in my essay "Paul, Crucifixion and Sanctification in Galatians," in *Passover, Pentecost, & Parousia: Studies in Celebration of the Life and Ministry of R. Hollis Gause,* (JPTSS 35, 2010, 90–105), although the argumentation presented here takes account of more recent scholarship and, consequently, is more compelling than the earlier version.

Acknowledgments

MANY PEOPLE HAVE HELPED to make this book possible. I am grateful to the administration of the Pentecostal Theological Seminary for granting me a six-month sabbatical while I was doing the research for the book. I am also thankful to the Manchester Wesley Research Centre, Didsbury, for the privilege to make use of the facility for my research. I cannot thank my students at the Pentecostal Theological Seminary enough for allowing me to "road-test" the book with them while teaching a course on "Holiness in Paul." They helped in sharpening my thinking about the subject as we dialogued and discussed many issues on holiness.

Special appreciation goes to a number of individuals who have read part, or all, of the book. They include Daniel Darko, Brian Tucker, Michael Gorman, Lee Roy Martin, Craig Keener, Tony Richie, Terry Jensen, and Jerry Sumney. Without the incisive comments of these readers, the end product might have turned out poorer. Yet, I take responsibility for the contents, as well as the mistakes that may remain in the book.

I would also like to express my profound gratitude to Asbury Theological Seminary both for providing me with free accommodation and full access to the library as a visiting scholar during my research for this book.

It would border on travesty to fail to mention my thankfulness to and for my wife, Grace, and children Toluwalope, Iyanuloluwa, Ruth, and Jonathan. Our daughter-in-law, Kellie, also deserves mention. Each has been a tremendous source of encouragement. Their involvement made a big difference.

Abbreviations

ACNT	Augsburg Commentaries on the New Testament
BAGD	Walter Bauer, Frederick W. Danker, W. F. Arndt, and F .W. Gingrich, *A Greek-English Lexicon of the New Testament Other Early Christian Literature,* 3rd ed. Chicago: University of Chicago Press, 2000.
BETL	Bibliotheca Ephemeridum Theologicarum Lovaniensium
BJS	Brown Judaic Studies
BNTC	Black's New Testament Commentaries
BZAW	Beihefte zur Zeitschrift für die alttestamentliche Wissenschaft
EDNT	Exegetical Dictionary of the New Testament
HNTC	Harper's New Testament Commentary
ICC	International Critical Commentary
JBL	*Journal of Biblical Literature*
JPTS	*Journal of Pentecostal Theology Supplement Series*
JSNT	*Journal for the Study of the New Testament*
JSNTS	*Journal for the Study of the New Testament Supplement Series*
JSOT	*Journal for the Study of the Old Testament*
JSOTS	*Journal for the Study of the Old Testament Supplement Series*
LHBOTS	Library of Hebrew Bible/Old Testament Studies
LNTS	Library of New Testament Studies
LXX	The Septuagint
MNTC	The Moffatt New Testament Commentary

ABBREVIATIONS

MT	The Masoretic Text
NICNT	New International Commentary on the New Testament
NIGTC	New International Greek Testament Commentary
NTD	Das Neue Testament Deutsch
NTS	*New Testament Studies*
OTL	Old Testament Library
RSV	Revised Standard Version
SNTSMS	Society for New Testament Studies Monograph Series
TDNT	Theological Dictionary of the New Testament
TNTC	Tyndale New Testament Commentaries
WBC	Word Biblical Commentary
ZAW	Zeitschrift für die alttestamentliche Wissenschaft
ZNW	Zeitschrift für die neutestamentliche Wissenschaft

Chapter 1

The Starting Point

PAUL'S LIFE, MINISTRY, AND theology did not take place in a vacuum. Yet oftentimes we become oblivious to the obvious. In this case, to fully understand his message, we should examine the religious and socio-cultural influences that shaped Paul's thought with regards to holiness.

Paul was a Jew who lived in a Greco-Roman world, during the period of Second Temple Judaism. As a Jew, his theology has its point of departure from the Old Testament Scriptures. Generally, references to the Scripture are weighty in Paul's view and he assumes that his converts will grant them authority. Scripture is, therefore, a significant part of what he and his followers know and are expected to acknowledge. Paul grounds his exhortations and doctrinal instruction in Old Testament soil by covering a score of topics intended to reflect—either explicitly or implicitly—its influence. Holiness is one of those themes.

For Paul, the same God was working in both ages (both OT and NT), and the patterns of God's past activity were prototypes of his present and future acts. Thus, when Paul used the Old Testament to illustrate God's present and future works, he was following the example of the Old Testament itself. Take, for instance, the Exodus from Egypt, which sets the pattern for the return from captivity—the New Exodus (see Isa 43:16–20). To Paul, the Scripture is central and formative, rather than merely peripheral or illustrative.

The Old Testament is important for its inspired record of God's creative, elective, and redemptive activity. As Richard Hays succinctly states, "the vocabulary and cadences of Scripture—particularly of the LXX—are imprinted deeply on Paul's mind, and the great stories of Israel continue to serve for him as a fund of symbols and metaphors that condition his perception of the world, of God's promised deliverance of his people, and of his own identity and calling. His faith, in short, is one whose articulation is intertextual in character, and Israel's Scripture is the 'determinate subject that plays a constitutive role' in shaping his literary production."[1]

As an important feature of Paul's Diaspora Judaism, the Septuagint (commonly referred to as LXX) was everyone's Bible. While retaining some of its Hebrew flavor, the Septuagint, composed in the ordinary Greek of the day, was generally understood by those who heard it read or cited in synagogue settings. It appears that Paul, whose missionary activity concentrated on predominantly Gentile congregations in Asia Minor and Greece, normally read and cited Scripture in Greek—a common language of the eastern empire in his time. It is not surprising then that most of Paul's quotations of the OT are from the Septuagint.[2]

Whenever Paul cites the Old Testament in his letters, he does so from the LXX, modifying his lessons and messages as he sees the need. Further, Paul's usage of the *hagios* word group (holy, holiness, sanctification, etc.) in his letters is essentially the same as how it is used in the Septuagint, which in turn, is patterned after the Old Testament usage of the Hebrew word for holy (*qodesh*).[3]

In the Septuagint, as in the Old Testament, *hagios* is used in various ways. It is sometimes used with a qualitative significance, such as in the sense of "what is holy," in contrast to the profane (see Ezek 22:26; 44:23). At other times it may simply imply belongingness. Israel is holy as God's chosen people (see Jer 2:3). Although caution must be taken in putting all the meaning of holiness in one particular word,[4] it is important to note that the primary vocabulary of holiness in the OT is the word *qodesh*, translated as *hagios* in the Septuagint and in the New Testament.[5]

---

1. Hays, *Echoes of Scripture*, 17.

2. Ibid., xi. See also, Silva, "Old Testament in Paul," 630–42. Having listed all Old Testament citations in Paul against LXX and MT backgrounds, he also observes that, "more frequently, Paul follows the LXX over against the Hebrew."

3. Cf. Gehman, "Αγιος in the Septuagint," 337–48. See Chapter 5.

4. Brower, *Holiness in the Gospels*, 16, rightly notes that, "the concept of holiness is too big for word study alone. Holiness is a people-of-God language, a notion that defines the essential character of the people of God."

5. The word is not found in Galatians. However, it will be wrong to suggest that there nothing is related to holiness in the book. Cf. Brower, *Holiness in the Gospels*, 16, writing on the search for key words like "holiness" and "sanctification" in the Gospels rightly concludes that . . . "the absence of the word does not imply the absence of the

A study of the *hagios* word group in the LXX reveals that the concept of holiness conveys more than a set-apartness. Instead, what we find are varied nuances when the word is used with reference to God, people, places, and things. The concept of holiness in Paul's letters is varied both in language and expression in the same manner as in the Old Testament. It even has an ethical nuance. Therefore, we must turn to the Old Testament to examine the meaning and significance of holiness as conveyed by the word *qodesh*.

HOLINESS IN THE OLD TESTAMENT

As rightly noted by many scholars, the New Testament inherited the categories and concepts of holiness that were established in the Old Testament.[6] Since Paul grounded his teachings in the Old Testament, we must briefly explore the notion of holiness as it pertains to God and his people in the Old Testament.[7]

The Holiness of God

A study on holiness must begin with the holiness of God. As Lipka observes and states so well, "Holiness in the Hebrew Bible is intrinsically connected to God. God is the holy one *par excellence*, with the exclusive power to confer holiness unto others."[8] She goes further to say that, "Not only is God the source of all holiness, but human bodies require holiness in order to be in proximity to the deity."[9] However, we must begin by asking what it means when we say that *God is holy*.

---

thought." This is true of all other New Testament writings.

6. Harrington, *Holiness*, 12. See Purkiser, *Exploring Christian Holiness*, 33: "No important biblical doctrine finds its complete expression in the Old Testament. On the other hand, no important biblical doctrine is without Old Testament foundations. We cannot read back into the Old Testament the full meaning of the New Testament. But we should never ignore the Old Testament basis of the Christian faith."

7. On in-depth and exhaustive study on the nature of holiness in the Old Testament, see (among many others) Gammie, *Holiness in Israel*; Jenson, *Graded Holiness*; Neusner, *The Idea of Purity in Ancient Judaism*, which includes "Critique and Commentary" by Mary Douglas, 137–42; Eilberg-Schwartz, *Savage in Judaism*, 177–216; Houston, *Purity and Monotheism*; Sawyer, *Reading Leviticus*.

8. Lipka, "Profaning the Body," 90.

9. Ibid. Her primary contention on the connection between personal holiness and the use of the body are similar to Paul's in several places in his writings. See for example, 1 Cor 6:12–20; 1 Thess 4:5.

In several places in the Pentateuch, God refers to his name and himself as holy. Furthermore, there are incidents that show a clear violation of his holiness, either by individuals or a group. The affirmation "God is holy" is a basic declaration regarding his most essential being.[10] The question then is how one expresses what the declaration means, but there is no easy answer, because no selection of the Pentateuch offers any comment regarding the meaning of "God is holy." Instead what we have is a demonstration of God's holy nature.

The holy God is known by how he acts and what he expects of his people. The imprecision of the word, particularly its relation to purity, has led many scholars to restrict its meaning to "otherness," thus removing any moral or ethical nuance.[11] However, as recent studies have shown, holiness, even when applied to God, has always had an ethical notion.[12] For example, based on various injunctions in Leviticus 19, one could suggest that God's holiness involves justice. As Vriezen writes,

> That the holiness of God is closely linked up with the demand for justice in the priestly literature as well appears most emphatically from Lev Xix. "Ye shall be holy, for I am holy" is the introduction to, and the conclusion of a great number of commandments, mostly moral in character . . .[13]

In restricting the meaning of holiness to "otherness," Snaith states, "God is holy" means that God is "the only true God, separate, different

---

10. As Eichrodt, *Theology of the Old Testament*, 274 says, holy " . . . comes to mean that which is distinctively characteristic of God, that which constitutes His nature."

11. Cf. Ringgren, *Prophetical Conception of Holiness*, 3; Whitehouse, "Holiness: Semitic," 758: "The conception of holiness when traced to its historic origins among Semitic people is stripped of all the ethical qualities. . . . The ethical elements which have become absorbed into its content have become absorbed into its content entered at a much later stage in the evolution of idea which became attached to the term." This was further developed by Otto, *Idea of the* Holy. For a recent analysis and critique of Otto's work, see Raphael, *Rudolf Otto*.

12. Cf. Harrington, *Holiness*, 11–44; Raphael, *Rudolf Otto*, 130; Hrobon, *Ethical Dimension of the Cult*, 43: "The incorporation of the ethical notion into the concept of holiness did not result from the prophetic transformation of the idea of God, but more likely from the prophetic rejuvenation of the idea of the proper human response to the holiness of God."

13. Vriezen, *Old Testament Theology*, 159. So also Jensen, *Ethical Dimensions*, 29. He rightly suggests that if one were to consider the dimension of the Law as horizontal and that of ethics as vertical, "the vertical and the horizontal dimensions go together, equally expressions of God's will; and this in turn means that where the horizontal dimension (social justice, etc.) is lacking, the vertical dimension (worship, sacrifice) is impossible.

and distinct."[14] When Lev 18:1–5 or 20:22–26 is read, such a conclusion is a natural inference from his commands that Israel be a separate, different, and distinct people. Such an approach, nevertheless, is profitable only to the degree that it expresses that which characterizes God's holiness. By this approach one cannot say, "'holy' regarding God is. . . ." In fact, in the Pentateuch, *holy* with reference to God is absolute; that is to say, holy as a modifier of God is not relative to any thing or person. He affirms, "I am holy" without elaboration. He simply asserts his holiness—it is undefined, not categorized, and is wholly lacking in circumscription. Such can no more be done of God's holiness than of himself. For, as E. Jacob suggests, "holiness is not one divine quality among others, even the chiefest, for it expresses what is characteristic of God and corresponds precisely to his deity."[15] Even when the writings of the prophets are examined, holy with reference to God still resists any explicit definition, other than to say "holy is deity."

A second series of references to God as holy is found in Lev 10:3, where God not only asserts that, "I will show myself holy among those who are near me" but also in Deut 32:51 and Num 20:12, 27:14, where God condemns Moses's failure "to revere me as holy in the midst of the people of Israel." Leviticus 10:1ff. recounts that Nadab and Abihu "offered unholy fire"[16] contrary to the instructions of the Lord, an action that precipitated their untimely death by fire.

Moses quoted God who said, "I will show Myself holy." The context suggests the issue is the question of explicit obedience—what God has commanded his servants to do has no exception (see Lev 18:4–30; 22:9).[17] If we pay attention to the stress in verses Lev 10:6, 9–11, and 12–15 on obedience to God's commands, God's concern is not only for Aaron and the remaining priests to be faithful to his ordinances, but likewise for the whole people to hear and obey what he commands in its entirety (see Lev 10:11). Those who fail to obey must be prepared to bear the consequences of their disobedience.

Whereas these two Israelites thought they could safely act other than in accordance with God's instructions, he shows himself determined to

---

14. Snaith, *Leviticus and Numbers*, 122.

15. Jacob, *Theology of the Old Testament*, 86. Cf. Eichrodt, *Old Testament Theology*, 274: holy ". . . comes to mean that which is distinctively characteristic of God, that which constitutes His nature."

16. Lev 10:1 RSV; MT = "strange": *tsarah*.

17. As Jenson, *Graded Holiness*, 121–122, noted, "The sons of the high priest shared some of his pre-eminence and were given certain responsibilities." He goes further to say that "the death of Nadab and Abihu [Lev 10.1–3] stressed that these responsibilities entailed strict disobedience, and disobedience would evoke divine sanctions."

make himself clearly known as one whose demands may not be compromised without the offender being punished.[18] When God says, "I will show Myself holy," he is declaring that his nature is such that he knows neither equivocation nor fluctuation within himself, relative to his expectations of this chosen people to fulfill his commands. He is revealing to Israel that because he is the holy God, his decrees shall not be abrogated.[19]

The pertinent question regarding the second set of passages is "What does it mean 'to revere me as holy in the sight of Israel'?" Various suggestions have been proposed as to the nature of Moses's sin and failure to treat God as holy.[20] Snaith,[21] summarizing various views, adds that some translate Moses's statement as "can we bring forth water . . ." or "must we bring forth . . ." showing either doubt or unwillingness in respect to the command of God. Yet this is quite unlikely because there is no indication either in the passage or elsewhere that Moses entertained any doubts in God's ability or power to supply water to the famishing Israelites.

Furthermore, Moses had previously seen God manifest his power to deliver Israel in too many ways for him to doubt at this point. Likewise Moses's words do not reflect embarrassment. At the most, his use of the word *hamorim* ("you rebels") could be seen as a blunt statement, which most likely reflects a degree of loss of temper. But even then, one must add that Moses did not speak amiss. Israel was indeed rebelling (Num 20:3–5) and Moses was only acknowledging reality.

Probably then, Moses's sin was not in what he said, but in how he said it, along with how he acted—that is, in a moment of uncontrolled temper. The point is that, what God commands is what God expects and his servants are not free to elaborate upon or modify his commands even slightly; they are only free to fulfill them. By acting contrary to God's directive, Moses failed to communicate to the people the nature of God as the ever-constant

---

18. As Hartley, *Leviticus*, 308, observes, "God is to be treated as holy in the midst of his people by their enthusiastic, wholehearted observance of these decrees (19:12b). Faithful observance honors God. When the people honor God, he is in their midst sanctifying them (20:8; 21:8). Since he sets his name in the midst of his people, they must conduct themselves in a way that will not defile it. For whenever they transgress any of God's laws, they shame his name, i.e., tarnish his reputation."

19. Cf. Marsh, "Numbers," 272: "Once obedience to God is accepted as a necessary human duty, the leaders of religion must conform to the highest standards. Any lessening in demand would derogate, not enhance, the authority of God" and, it may be added, the holiness of God.

20. Cole, *Numbers*, 327–29.

21. Marsh, *Numbers*, 239.

faithful partner in covenant with his people, and as God who demanded an unqualified obedience from all his people.[22]

In Leviticus 10, Numbers 20 and 27, and Deuteronomy 32, the picture of the holy God is one that does not allow any deviation from his ordinances or assumption of his authority by his followers. Nadab and Abihu acted at the wrong time and did what they were not commissioned to do. Moses both acted wrongly (by striking the rock when he had been commanded to speak) and he spoke wrongly (by speaking condemningly to the people when he had not been given that task).[23]

God, who had promised to care for Israel, manifested his holiness by two things. First, he provided the water in spite of Moses's disobedience. Thus, holiness in this case is demonstrated by the "goodness of God" in providing for the needs of his people. As Harrington notes, "holiness without active goodness, or righteousness, is not holiness."[24] Second, he punished Moses for his disobedience. By these two acts, the narrative states, God "showed Himself holy among them" (Num 20:13b). His demonstration of his ability and willingness to provide for Israel's needs and his refusal to allow disobedience to go unchastized constituted God's "showing Himself holy."[25]

In Lev 22:2, 32; 20:3, God warns against acts that might "profane My holy name." The name by which God has chosen to reveal himself to Israel ("the Lord" YHWH) is a special name reserved only for himself, and is to be used for and by no other. More is expressed in this phrase ("My Holy Name") than in the title of "God," which is reserved for Israel's God alone. Here God is saying, "You shall not profane Me, the One who is holy." In Old Testament thought, one's name is the same as the person named.[26] It implies

22. Moriarty, "Numbers," 93, suggests that if Moses had followed God's instructions, he would have shown God's command over nature and "God's unfailing providence." Instead, in their anger and sarcasm ". . . the two leaders had changed the whole character of the event as it was intended by God. Instead of making the occasion a joyful manifestation of God's effortless control over nature, they had turned it into a scene of bitter denunciation."

23. Arden, "How Moses Failed God," 50–52, suggests that Moses assumed that God was angry with the Israelites, an assumption that is not supported by the text. Arden's suggestion that Moses's sin is one of blasphemy may have some merit if the "we" of 20:10 refers to Moses and God as Arden argues, rather than to Moses and Aaron, which not only appears to be the natural reading of the text but also as I would interpret it.

24. Harrington, *Holiness*, 27.

25. Cole, *Numbers*, 329: "God's mercy and grace were evidenced when the waters gushed forth from the rocky crag, in spite of Moses's actions. He fulfilled his promise to provide ample water for the people, and Moses was used as an agent in the miracle."

26. Cf. von Rad, *Old Testament Theology*, 181: "According to ancient ideas, a name was not just 'noise and smoke': instead, there was a close and essential relationship

the character of the one so named. Consequently, God is designating not just his name, but also his own self as holy. This is shown most clearly in the assertion by God that "I the Lord am holy" (e.g., Lev 11:44; 19:2; 20:26; 21:8).

In summary, the Pentateuch reveals two strands of thought regarding God as holy. First is that God declares himself as holy; this is an expression of his most absolute being. It is not a declaration of what God is like; it is a declaration of what and who he is. Second, the word *holy* is not used in an absolute sense but as an expression of God's nature as he communicates it to his people. Holy in this sense denotes his unfailing and unrelenting self-consistency.

Holiness: The Basic Notion

The portion of the Old Testament literature usually designated as "the Former Prophets"—that is, Joshua, Judges, 1 and 2 Samuel, and 1 and 2 Kings—presents examples of *qodesh-hagios* that reflect no uniformity in the actual application of the *qodesh* concept itself, although there is uniformity in the basic notion of what constitutes *qodesh*. Several passages deal with *holy* and the system of worship with the same meaning as in the Pentateuch: holy is that which is set apart to encounter God or a divine manifestation, and that is also set apart for God's possession and use.

Among the things designated as holy is the "bread of the Presence" (1 Sam 21:4, 6). The bread was food for God's priests and, therefore holy. Joshua, when demanding of Israel a commitment for or against God, joins together the following ideas in an effort to describe him: "He is a holy God; He is a jealous God; He will not forgive your transgressions or your sins" (Josh 24:19; see 24:15 LXX). "Holy" and "jealous," with reference to God, are two fundamental aspects of God's nature, according to Joshua. Whereas "holy" has been described earlier as expressive of his absolute being, here the two terms convey both God's demand for a people who are unequivocally separated to himself from foreign gods and wholly loyal and submissive to him, and his nature as God who brings divine punishment and non-forgiveness upon sinful Israel, that is, those serving foreign gods rather than living in fidelity to God.

This and passages such as Josh 24:19; 1 Sam 6:19–21; and 2 Sam 6:7 may be contrasted with 1 Sam 2:2, the song of Hannah. In the former, God

---

between it and its subject." Eichrodt, *Old Testament Theology*, 178: "If the saying *nomina sunt realia* is valid in any context, it is surely that of the divine name in the ancient world."

as the Holy One is separated, unapproachable, and to be feared. In the song, Hannah praises God, acknowledging by her use of "holy" that he is separated and distinct from any other gods, but no element of fear is present. Such a contrast may be readily explained if one observes that Hannah was, in fact, a faithful worshiper and servant of God who had cause to reflect, not on the wrathful jealous nature of God, but on his beneficent fidelity to his people.

Joshua 24, on the other hand, was spoken before the assembly of the Lord's people whose fathers had served other gods (see Josh 24:14) and among whom there were foreign gods present (see Josh 24:23). This passage may be compared with others where a Deuteronomic theme is prevalent: the people are reminded again and again that the rebelliousness of former ages must not be repeated, and the particular form of rebelliousness that is singled out is idolatry. God abhors idols; he is not represented by idols; he claims Israel as his possession (Deut 4:20, *qodesh* [this refers to the word holy] does not appear, but the thought that Israel is holy is clear; see 7:6 and 14:2); his possession, therefore, should not be involved in idolatry. The consequence of such involvement will be the outpouring of the devouring fire of God because God is a jealous God.[27]

In the use of *holy* to refer to people, of Elisha, the Shunammite woman declares, "this is a holy man of God" (2 Kgs 4:9). Although there is no indication of how or why she perceived him to be such, her use of the title "man of God" suggests that perhaps he was viewed as a cultic prophet, in which case he would have been considered a holy person.[28] The act of designating a person as the recipient of a given task in the service of God, or as a participant in certain activities of approaching God, is expressed by the word *sanctify* in the Former Prophets (Joshua, Judges, 1 and 2 Samuel, and 1 and 2 Kings).

After the battle of Jericho, because Achan kept some of the *cherem* (devoted) treasures reserved for God, Joshua is told, "Up, sanctify the people, and say 'Sanctify yourselves for tomorrow'" (7:13), when God will render judgment upon Israel. The idea conveyed by *sanctify* is one of preparation for a special day of confrontation with God, for which the people are admonished to be ready (see Num 16:16 LXX; Joel 1:14; 2:15, 16).

When Samuel went to anoint the son of Jesse, the approaching elders of Bethlehem were told "sanctify yourselves and come with me to the sacrifice" (1 Sam 16:5a). Samuel "sanctified Jesse and his sons, and invited them to the sacrifice" (1 Sam 16:5b). Although this passage and Josh 7:13 are reminiscent of Exod 19:10, 14f., and its preparation for encountering God

---

27. See Deut 4:5-24; 5:9 [cf. Exod 20:5; 34:14; 6:10-15; 29:16-24).
28. Cf. Rowley, *Worship in Ancient Israel*, 151, 159.

by means of personal, ceremonial cleansing, no indication of the nature of the rites is given. It is noteworthy though that the act is performed by God's prophet-priest upon the chosen family.

When the ark returned to Israel (1 Sam 6) the men of Kiriathjearim brought it to the house of Abinadab of Judah and . . . sanctified his son, Eleazar, to have charge of the ark of the Lord" (1 Sam 7:1). Again, no record of the rite or process of consecration is given; Eleazar is simply given the task of being the caretaker of God's ark. To the priest of Nob, David declares that the young men who fight with him have kept their vessels holy (1 Sam 21:4f.) in response to the statement, "there is holy bread [which you may have]; if only the young men have kept themselves from women." David euphemistically was responding that they have abstained from sexual intercourse, and are ceremonially clean.

Holiness as Separation

The preceding examples of the use of *qodesh* provide excellent illustration of the notion that "holy" in earliest Israel bore no moral connotation. These persons who are "sanctified" are separated to serve or to encounter God or a divine manifestation, but there is no indication of any qualifying factor(s) that they must meet in order to be reckoned holy or to be sanctified, except in the case of David's young men.

An examination of the use of *qodesh* within the context of the prophetic movement reveals a basic consistency in its meaning, albeit with a certain fluctuation in the application of the term, depending upon the circumstances of the era. This basic consistency is observed in the use of *qodesh* to designate that which is separated to God for his possession or use.

The eighth-century prophets significantly enrich the notion of *qodesh* in comparison with the Former Prophets (Joshua, Judges, Samuel, and Kings) in their linking it to the name of God and the moral realm. Among the pre-exilic prophets of the eighth century, only Isaiah and Micah refer to things as holy, by which they mean "things of which God and/or His people make use." Zion, God's dwelling place, which is referred to as the holy city or mountain (Isa 11:9; 27:13), is one of these.

Throughout its history, Israel confessed that God made himself known to his people at certain places, e.g., Bethel, Shiloh, Gilgal, Sinai, etc. More than any other site in the Promised Land, Jerusalem became the place *par excellence* of God's self-revelation to humanity. As such, it was holy. Zion received its holy status through being the site where God manifested himself to David (2 Sam 24:15ff.). Subsequently, Solomon built the temple of the Lord there (see 2 Chron 3:1) as the place where Israel should celebrate its religious rites and offer its prayers to God. Isreal testified to Jerusalem, a place chosen by God, adn the temple as the dwelling place of God (1 Kgs 8:16 [LXX]; 9:3; 11:32, 36). To be clear, Israel recognized that God himself did not *physically* dwell in the temple; his name did. His abode was heaven (see 1 Kgs 8:27, 29). Nevertheless de Vaux's comment well states the prevalent view: "To the Semitic mind, the name expressed and represented the person: God was present in a special way wherever the 'Name of God' was."[29] Consequently because of such a role, Jerusalem and the temple were holy.[30] Likewise, God's heavenly temple (Mic 1:2); the pathway upon which "the ransomed of the LORD" will walk, called "the Holy Way" (Isa 35:8—a road with no "uncleanness"); the merchandise of Tyre that will be used by the Lord's people (Isa 23:18); a sword of the Lord used to slay Leviathan (Isa 27:1 [LXX]; and a particular feast kept in the night (Isa 30:29) are all considered holy.

The most significant idea of the prophets for this study is the connection they show between God's personal nature and his demand that Israel—as his possession—be of a certain prescribed character or else bear punishment for its disobedience. Exodus, in the same manner as Leviticus, is content to present God's demand "You shall serve the Lord your God" (Exod 23:25a) together with numerous commandments regarding various subjects, without establishing any reason for Israel's obedience, in terms of God's personal nature.

Holiness of Israel

In Exod 19:3-8, Israel is summoned to a special relationship with God, described by three phrases: a special possession among all peoples, a kingdom of priests, and a holy nation. Israel is to be God's own people, set apart from other nations for his own service, just as priests were set apart from other men and marked by a quality of life commensurate with the holiness of their covenant with God.[31] Also, as Deut 7:6-8 makes clear, "people of God" is to be understood as Israel, which, according to God's will, is to distinguish itself from all the other peoples of the earth.

---

29. De Vaux, *Ancient Israel*, 327.

30. Cf. Ackroyd, *Exile and Restoration*, 249n61 for a discussion and references regarding the historical process of selection and the development of Jerusalem as the holy city.

31. Childs, *Book of Exodus*, 367.

The people's conduct must correspond to the liberating action of God who chose Israel from all nations and saved it from Egypt. Israel is to be a holy people with a social order, which distinguishes it from other nations. In the words of Deut 7:11: "You shall therefore be careful to do the commandment and the statutes, and the ordinances, which I command you this day."

Thus, Israel's holiness is predicated upon two grounds: First, there is the electing love of God who chose Israel from all nations to be his own people. As Jospe succinctly states: "It is precisely because of the special, intimate relationship that Israel has with God that it can be held accountable for its wrongdoing. Others may seek to excuse their behaviour because they did not realize what they were doing. Israel can make no such excuse; the Jewish people should know better."[32] The covenant set Israel apart from the other nations. They were expected to be "a kingdom of priests and a holy nation" in the words of Exod 19:6. Holiness denotes something distinctive, different, or special. In relational terms, it denotes exclusivity, a situation in which those related are "special" to each other and "different" from others.

In Deuteronomy, Israel's holy status is found precisely in her being the people whom God chose out of all nations of the earth to be his special possession (see 7:6; 14:2) and to be his sons (14:1). As a consequence of belonging to God, Israel is to be separated from the nations and people she encounters in Canaan, and she is to be totally obedient to God (see 7:9–14). That is to say, Israel's obedience does not constitute her holiness; rather her obedience is to spring from her holiness—her being the possession of God.[33] Second, Israel's holiness also depends on whether she really lives in accordance with the social order God has given her, a social order that stands in sharp distinction against those of all other nations. This connection is expressed trenchantly in Leviticus.[34]

The Book of Leviticus is a book of regulations covering a broad spectrum of issues relating to sacrifice, priesthood, and purity.[35] Leviticus spells

---

32. Jospe, "Concept of the Chosen People," 139. See also Hogan, *Biblical Vision*, 297.

33. Clements, *God's Chosen People*, 32: "Israel is holy by virtue of the specially tight bond which binds it to God." That is to say that Israel's holiness is based on its relationship to God. However, as Clements notes, "Israel is to keep the law because it is the holy people."

34. Trevaskis, *Holiness, Ethics and Ritual in Leviticus,* challenges the view that holiness in the so-called "priestly" (P) segment of Leviticus (chs. 1–16) lacks the kind of ethical dimension that characterizes the concept in the "holiness" (H) portions of the book (mainly chs. 17–26). He contends that P and H agree that holiness must include ethics; the difference is that in P the requirement is implicit, but in H it becomes explicit.

35. There is a close connection between holiness and purity. As Gammie, *Holiness in Israel*, 195, has persuasively argued, "holiness summoned Israel to cleanness throughout the entire Hebrew Scriptures."

out in detail what holiness entails and, as such, articulates the means by which the relationship established by God with his people Israel is to be maintained.[36] The fact that the Levitical purity system is not a series of suggestions, but codified regulations, is seen in the punishments attached to many of the offences. For some of the purity violations, the offender is identified as "guilty" and requires purgation (e.g., 5:6). But for more serious offences, one could be "cut off" (excommunicated, socially banned; e.g., 18:29) or even executed (20:9).

Leviticus 26 lists a number of group punishments enacted by God for failing to maintain this system: disease, defeat in war, drought, fruitless land, plagues, wild beasts, famine, exile, and fear. Thus threats of social exclusion, death, and disaster provided the negative motivation for adhering strictly to the purity code. The code functions as a map of conformity/deviance, as well as identifying the danger points to the individual, the society, and the sanctuary. But the recurring positive motivation to holiness and purity derives from God's nature, and the conceptualization of the Israelites as God's people: "And consecrate yourselves and be holy, because I am God, your God. And keep my statutes and perform them; I am God, who sanctifies you" (20:7-8). Thus purity consists of concrete actions performed by the people, but also entails God's reciprocal action. It consequently has personal, social, and cosmic dimensions.

The Holiness Code

When examining the Holiness Code (HC),[37] the section of the Pentateuch that most clearly and emphatically sounds the call for Israel to be a holy people, it is pertinent to consider the grounds for Israel's call to holiness. The most characteristic feature of the HC is its repeated assertion that God is holy; indeed "holy" and its derivatives appear nowhere in the OT more consistently as an attribute of God than in the HC. Typical is the refrain, "Do this or that, because I the Lord your God am holy," while references to God's sanctuary, God's holy name, and to God's sanctification of people and

---

36. Cf. Clines, *The Theme of the Pentateuch*, 50. He suggests that holiness is the theme of Leviticus as the book spells out in detail the means by which the relationship between God and Israel was to be maintained.

37. The "Holiness Code" consists of Leviticus 17-26. The ethical imperative of the covenant requires a sense of being special or distinctive: behavior that may be permitted or tolerated in others is unacceptable in someone special. Therefore the Holiness Code begins with the Israelites being told: "You be holy, for I, the Lord your God, am holy." Holiness, for example, is the only rationale explicitly mentioned in the Torah in connection with the system of kashrut (dietary laws).

objects abound. Conversely, the HC warns against the danger of profaning God's holiness and holy things (Lev 20:3; 21:6; 12).

It is in Lev 20:26 that God expresses his own inmost nature and his expectations of the people of Israel whom he is claiming. Of himself, God says 1) I am holy (20:26a); 2) I have separated you from the nations (20:26b); 3) I claim you for myself (11:45a; 20:26b). The same argument is to be found in Lev 11:44–45[38] but with two additional thoughts: "I am the Lord your God" (11:44a), and "I have rescued you" (11:45). In sum, as a logical consequence of who he is, what he has done, and the relationship that exists between himself and this people, God tells Israel what it is to be and do; namely, Israel is to imitate its master—it is to be holy. The text of Lev 11:45b emphatically grounds God's demand in his own nature—that of holiness—and it provides both the basis and the standard for his expectation concerning the nature-to-be of this people whom he is claiming for himself.

Nevertheless, Israel was not physically separated from the peoples in the sense that all the surrounding nations had been obliterated. As Israel was to experience for the remainder of her history, there were numerous peoples and nations still in her midst. What God means when he says he has separated Israel from the nations (v. 26b) is that Israel, at the time of God's command, was not intermingling with the nations and, moreover, Israel was to continue neither intermingling with the nations nor adopting the customs and practices of these nations (see 20:23). God says he abhorred any such intermixing; it was thoroughly abominable to him. Involvement in these foreign customs would be disobedience resulting in ritual contamination, or disobedience with respect to the religious and moral commands of God. The apartness (v. 26a) called for by God is an obedience to God's commands—ritual, ethical, and religious (see 20:8a; 22:31)—and their positive assertions of what God desires.

The basis of Hebrew conduct, even in the ritualistic setting of Leviticus, is clear; the teachings are done because they are the will of their Savior God. It can be emphatically agreed that God's will is the *basis* for the commands of Leviticus 17–26. Nonetheless it must be insisted that many of the requirements of Leviticus 17–26 are ethical in content and that consequently, the one who is holy is one who not only is possessed by God and who performs certain ritual acts, but who also is living according to certain God-enunciated ethical standards in his or her relationships with others. Various ethical demands that deal with personal human relationships, societal norms, and familial relationships are prefaced or summarized by the command, "You

---

38. As Houston, *Purity and Monotheism*, 238, notes, "Leviticus 20:24–27 is like 11:44–45, part of the stream of theological reflection that has made the dietary rules symbols of the holiness of Israel."

shall be holy."³⁹ While the commands are all concerned with ethics, they do not demand ritual or cultic cleanness.⁴⁰ Instead they stem directly from the Decalogue (Ten Commandments) and, as such, clearly express the highest ethical imperatives that are found in the Old Testament.

Consequently, in the Holiness Code, God's command that Israel be holy is a demand that Israel participate in a life in which one's ethical and religious behavior is determined by God. Such a God-determined life must be characterized by those standards that God sets forth as expressive of his own will and desires for the people whom he is creating and sustaining.⁴¹ No pattern of behavior distilled from the practices of the worshipers of any other god would suffice as the source of the behavioral pattern for his people. To the contrary, the mind of God in the Holiness Code is set forth in regards to the interpersonal behavioral pattern of his covenant people in a much wider scope than the strictly cultic sphere.⁴² This God-originated, directed, and motivated life includes social justice, compassion, and care for the aliens and the underprivileged. Thus, it is evident in the HC that for Israel, holiness is both a relationship and a responsibility—relational and required.

In Deuteronomy, the basis for God's expectation that Israel be holy is expressed.⁴³ It is found in Moses's affirmation that "you are the children of the Lord your God" (14:1), a statement which finds parallel in the Old

---

39. See Lev 19:2, 11, 13, 15f., 17–18, 33, 35f.; 20:7, 10, 11, 13, 14, 17, 19f.

40. Cf. Harrington, *Holiness*, 12: "The command to Israel to be holy as God is holy (Lev 19:2) is not simply an instruction to be 'other,' nor is it a command to be mighty."

41. Note that between Lev 20:7a "Sanctify yourselves therefore and be holy . . ." and 20:8b ". . . I am the Lord who sanctifies you" is the command "Keep my statutes and do them . . . ." (20:8a).

42. Eichrodt, *Old Testament Theology*, 17: ". . . Holiness itself . . . becomes a condition, a personal quality. The man who belongs to God must possess a particular kind of nature, which by comprising at once outward and inward, ritual and moral purity will correspond to the nature of the holy God (Lev 19.2 . . . Lev 17–26)." Cf. Jacob, *Theology of the Old Testament*, 92: "Following the example for divine holiness (cf. Lev 19:2—20:7; 21:8; 22:9, 31), man is to be holy, which . . . implies cultic duties as well as a personal attitude . . . ."

43. Cf. Childs, *Biblical Theology*, 139: "The theology of Israel as the people of God is most thoroughly developed in the book of Deuteronomy. The emphasis falls on the solidarity of 'all Israel', both when addressed in the singular or plural form. This people has been chosen by God to be distinct from the nations, to be holy to God." So also Wright, *People of God*, 261: "The book of Deuteronomy is the major work of covenant theology which stands at the head of a long line of subsequent writings on this theme . . . . The emphases throughout are on the promises made to Abraham, blessing as the consequence of covenant fidelity, the land as the gift of Israel's god to his people, and Israel as holding the place of honour among nations."

Testament only in both Exod 4:22 and Hos 11:1.[44] As children of God, Israel can share no closer relationship to him and in this relationship, Israel should express the same character as that of her father.[45]

As clearly expressed in Deut 26:1–19, a necessary consequence of Israel claiming God as her God is that Israel submit to God's regulations. In covenant together, God will exalt Israel as his special possession; but Israel, for her part, must bring exaltation to God through obedience to him. By conforming to God's ways, keeping his statutes, his commandments, and his laws, and obeying him (see 26:16), Israel fulfills her role as God's holy people. The call of Israel to holiness is that which affects all phases of her life in the same way the Deuteronomic code addresses all of Israel's life. All of Israel is to be obedient to God's directives, which affect the Israelites' relations with their fellow Israelites, strangers, and foreigners; with God and the priests of the cult; and in their relations to their surrounding environment.

Israel's Conditions to Fulfill

In Deuteronomy 28, Moses continues his sermon by stating certain conditions Israel must fulfill in order to receive the blessings of God. Verse 9 in its entirety indicates that the condition for Israel to become "a people holy to the Lord" is its obedience and conformity to his ways. Whereas in 7:6 and 14:2, 21, the holy status of Israel was the basis for the charge to be obedient. Here obedience is the condition for becoming holy. Israel is set apart from the nations as the possession of the Lord. In that respect she is holy. In addition, Deuteronomy warns that as the set-apart nation, Israel must fulfill all the demands of its owner God. Only by such obedience will Israel express in practice what she is in theory.[46]

Based on all of this, it's safe to suggest that Israel's holiness is a complex whole, comprising of different aspects. It is first and foremost, relational. The ground of Israel's holiness is her deliverance from Egypt and her call as God's own people. Israel is holy because she is called by God as his own people. However, it must be understood that Israel's relationship with God has serious implications. Israel's holiness is not only based on her

---

44. So von Rad, *Deuteronomy*, 100.

45. Cf. Deut 32:1–7 (NIV) a song in which Moses calls God their father (vs. 6b): "Praise the greatness of our God, his works are perfect . . . ." (vv. 3b, 4a), but who contradict themselves by being a generation who "have acted corruptly towards him . . . a warped and crooked generation" (v. 5).

46. Israel is called to fulfill God's commandments, all of which ". . . point out the way by which Israel can become in practical expression, what it already is in theological affirmation." Cf. Clements, *God's Chosen People*, 32.

relationship with God as a separate, distinct people, but also on the actualization of that holiness in its relationship with strangers, the poor, and the surrounding nations. This calls for a dynamic, ongoing relationship with God—a relationship, which, in turn, is to govern Israel's conduct, relationship with surrounding nations, and members of its own community (see Lev 19:1–37). As such, Israel's holiness is to be a responsible (or required) one, and Israel was to be actively and intensely committed to God in loving obedience and trust.

Furthermore, the call of Israel was to a people with a common goal and destiny and not just individuals. The way to holiness, in other words, was for the Israelites, individually and collectively, to emulate God's attributes.[47] As Levine rightly notes, "Holiness . . . could not be achieved through purity and proper worship alone; it had an important place in the realm of societal experience."[48] Therefore, Israel's holiness is to be understood as having a communal dimension. It is to be manifested in social relationships.

MULTIFACETED HOLINESS

In summing up the understanding of holiness in the Old Testament, a few observations can be made. First, God is the source of holiness. Second, in the Old Testament, the term *holiness* is applied to God in two senses. On the one hand, God is separate, set above all which is created. Yet, it is God who calls us to an ethical purity. On the other hand, the holiness of things or people is derived. In other words, things are regarded holy because of their connection with God—holy ground, holy Sabbath, holy place. God's holiness permeates anything touched by him, especially humans. Third, holy may also be used to describe someone or something that God has "set apart" for special purposes. Fourth, the Old Testament witness testifies to God's holiness, understood as God's "otherness" and "purity," as well as to God's prerogative to set people and things apart for his own purposes, together with the resulting godliness in the lives of those whom he declares and commands to be holy.

Lastly, the discussion on Israel's holiness suggests that it, as presented in the OT, is multifaceted. It is therefore plausible to suggest that in Israel there are various aspects of holiness, though none of the aspects is a "stand-alone." Rather it should be understood that any claim to holiness should exhibit the various aspects.

47. Ibid.
48. Levine, *Leviticus*, 257.

First, relational holiness—personal holiness—is based on a relationship to the Holy God. Second, it seems both anachronistic and unthinkable, as far as Israel's holiness is concerned, to talk of personal holiness without communal holiness, that is, holiness that is manifested in social relationships. In this regard, holiness is not just a quality or power associated with God. Instead, as Leviticus 19 shows, holiness is enacted in, by, and through the life of the community. Therefore the divine life, understood in relational terms, is manifest in relationships characterized by integrity, honesty, faithfulness, and love. Therefore, the call for Israel to be holy is the call for the community to concretize the divine life in the world.

Israel was to be a model of God among the nations. How were the nations that surrounded her to know the God of Israel? One may suggest that it was to be by a close observation of the life of Israel. Thus Israel's holiness has a missionary purpose of revealing God to the nations. As Gordon Tomas succinctly states,

> in their shared living Israel is called to model the life of the Godhead, to live out the love and goodness and justice of God for the nations to see and be drawn to. But they can only be a kingdom of priests insofar as they are also a holy nation. If they are undistinguishable from their neighbors in their spiritual, sexual, and social conduct, the mission of God is "dead in the water."[49]

Israel's holiness also involved separation. People committed to keeping God's law and being organized for his service are not the same as other people. They should be distinguishable because they are God's people.

There are two aspects to the matter of separation, and God made provision for his people to practice both aspects. In the first place, they were to be separated from all that was defiling (see Num 5:1–4). Every kind of defilement, from the purely physical to the emotional and spiritual, was under God's ban. That such separation worked in the physical realm made a good picture of what he expected in the spiritual. But just as carefully as they were to remove any physical contagion from among them, so they were equally bound to remove the contagion of sin. Understood in this light, Israel's "separateness" is not to be understood merely in terms of isolationism and external behavior, although the latter is surely included, but in terms of attitudes and morals (Lev 19:1–36).

Israel's separation from the nations implies distinctiveness in terms of religion and social values and modeling God's attractive holiness to the people of the nations. The letters of Paul, although very different, consist of pastoral letters to churches and are primarily concerned with the welfare of

---

49. Thomas, "A Holy God," 59–60.

the members. But, while Paul's letters to the churches are pastoral and hortatory rather than regulatory, they still operate with purity assumptions that stem from those of the Old Testament. In the same way that the Old Testament spells out the requirements of maintaining the relationship between God and his people, the letters of Paul deal with the specifics of Christian living in practical terms—that is, how the Christian life ought to be lived.

Chapter 2

Holiness in Romans

ALTHOUGH IDENTIFYING THE UNIFYING theology of Romans may be elusive and remains a matter of debate, it is nevertheless clear that in the same manner as Paul's other letters, the book is a result of everyday life issues, and is concerned with Christian living.

The introduction to the book highlights the theme of holiness. Right from 1:6–7, Paul highlights the call of the Romans as God's holy people and, as Oakes rightly notes, the call is not an aspiration but a current reality. They are called saints (*klētois hagiois*) by virtue of God's call.[1]

The New Testament understands all believers to be "saints," that is, "holy ones" or "sanctified" (*hagioi*; see Rom 15:25–26, 31; 16:2, 15). The basic idea of sainthood is separation. The saints or "holy ones" are those people God has separated "from all the people on earth to be his very own" (Deut 7:6; see 1 Kgs 8:53; 1 Pet 2:9–10). In this sense, the Roman Christians were "holy." They were no longer simply Gentiles or Jews; they had been called to belong to Jesus Christ (Rom 1:6). God had claimed them for himself.[2] As such, Paul expects believers to be "holy," not only in the sense of being set apart, but also in the sense of being pure and blameless (see Rom 12:1; 1 Cor 7:34; Eph 1:4; 5:3, 27; Col 1:22; 1 Thess 3:13).[3]

---

1. Godet, *St. Paul's Epistle to the Romans*, 74.
2. Greathouse and Lyons, *Romans 1–8*, 45.
3. Kruse, *Paul's Letter to the Romans*, 54–55.

Holiness, Sin, and Humanity

A broader discussion on holiness must look at the concept within the broader context of the book. In the opening chapters of Romans, Paul deals with the problem of sin as it relates to humanity. He begins the epistle with one of the most graphic pictures of sinful humanity found in the Scriptures. As Paul's argument in the entire section of 3:1–20, and particularly in 1:18–32 shows, the problem that brought the wrath of a loving God upon his creatures is sin. Paul maintains that sin, in whatever forms or shades, is a serious issue. He characterizes sin as deliberate rebellion against God's truth and his revealed righteousness.

Humanity began their downward plunge by not honoring God as God; "they became futile in their thinking and their senseless minds were darkened" (Rom 1:21). In their willful disobedience "God gave them up in the lusts of their hearts to impurity," "He gave them up to dishonorable passions," and he "gave them up to a base mind and to improper conduct" (Rom 1:24, 26, 28). Paul's picture of the human situation, that is, of sin and its consequences, is unmistakable. With a fine brush—in Rom 3:9–23, especially—Paul highlights the human dilemma, showing the horridness of sin as well as its universality. Humanity outside Christ—regardless of social status, gender, genealogy, geography, creed, or religion—stood condemned. And as Paul painstakingly argues, sin must be judged.

Thankfully, there is hope for humanity, and Paul speaks of justification. God has made provision for forgiveness and reconciliation. Paul's emphasis on solidarity, particularly in Rom 1:16—3:20, is striking. Paul obviously thinks of humanity in solidarity rather than humanity as individuals, although the latter is not excluded. One must therefore grant the possibility that Paul understands justification of the ungodly to be relational and to involve a strong corporate nuance.

The passage brings the Gentile and Jewish strands together—both are guilty; neither is righteous. Even though the Jews may be the only ones who recognize the Old Testament sources of the scriptures that Paul recites here, the metaphors are plain and powerful. Paul closes with a statement, which he will develop further: the purpose of the Law is to make us aware of sin.

At various points in Romans 1–3, Paul argues that God's righteousness is a gift from God conditioned upon acceptance by faith, and he provides a detailed explanation in Rom 3:21–26. First, God's righteousness is a gift to sinful humanity, by which he sets them right with himself. Second, the gift of righteousness is to be received only through faith and not through any good works that humans may do (vv. 22, 28). Third, God's gift of righteousness abolishes the distinction between Jew and Gentile, not only because all alike have sinned and turned against God, but also because all can be—and are to be—accepted by faith alone (vv. 22, 23, 27, 30). Fourth, God's gift of righteousness is available to humanity because of Christ's death. Lastly, the teaching on justification is found in the Old Testament but is clearly revealed in Christ (vv. 21, 25, 26). Paul continues to narrow the differences between his Gentile and Jewish listeners. He works through the fact that both groups have only one path to justification—through Christ (Rom 3:21–4:25).

In chapters 4–5, drawing on an aspect of the story of Abraham substantiated with a quotation from the Psalms (Ps 32:1–2), Paul presents the reader with an example of how God justifies the sinner. Because of human failure to attain to God's standard of righteousness, God had to provide the way of salvation as illustrated in the life of Abraham whose "faith is reckoned as righteousness." "God reckons righteousness apart from works" (Rom 4:5, 6), and the only way to get right with God is by faith. Paul argues that Abraham's righteousness came by faith, vv. 1–5; David's righteousness did not come from his own works, vv. 6–8; Abraham's righteousness did not come from circumcision, vv. 9–12; and Abraham's righteousness did not come as a result of his obedience to the Law, vv. 13–17. As a minister once said, "We contribute nothing to our own salvation except the sin from which we are saved." And the gift of righteousness can be received only by faith (Eph 2:8, 9; Titus 3:5). Abraham's faith demonstrates that faith is more than simply believing about God or accepting what he says. It means and involves a reliance on him and a deliberate commitment to him. It involves faithfulness.

Righteousness Versus Holiness

What exactly is righteousness? The theme has elicited much discussion and examination by many scholars.[4] Yet there is an intricate connection between holiness and righteousness, and the latter may be understood not only in relational, covenantal, or judicial terms but also with moral and ethical connotation.

As noted in the previous chapter, Paul's view of holiness derives from the Old Testament. In this respect, one must note that one of the great contributions of eighth-century prophets is the association of holiness with righteousness. Holiness refers to moral and spiritual purity, not only ritual. "Righteousness" is no abstraction: it means a "righteous act" and is one of many "righteous acts" or "triumphs" (Judg 5:11), in which "the Holy One of

---

4. An exhaustive study of the meaning of righteousness in Paul is not only unnecessary but also falls outside the purview of this book.

Israel" transforms history into a means of divine revelation for "those who have eyes to see and ears to hear."[5] By executing this righteous judgment on Jerusalem, the holy God shows his holiness.[6] Verse 16 is often regarded as summing up the connection between holiness and righteousness in Isaiah.[7]

God's separateness from human beings is not only ontological but also moral; his holiness is not a simple synonym for his majesty (though majesty is an element in it; cf., e.g., Exod 15:11) but more—the basis is his eternal character of his righteous judgments on sinners. The moral nature of divine holiness finds one of its most awesome expressions in Isaiah 6.[8] God's righteousness or justice is the natural expression of his holiness—he consistently acts in accord with his own character, and his actions are always right and fair.

Because the holy God is infinitely pure, he is opposed to all sin, and that opposition to sin must be demonstrated in his treatment of both sin and those who commit sin. God will be exalted because he acts with justice and righteousness to demonstrate his holiness (5:16). This holy character of God is not just an abstract concept that defines God's nature or being; it was something Isaiah himself personally experienced in chapter 6. God's holiness describes his glorious divinity and the justice with which he rules the world and deals with humanity. Although he punishes his people because of their sins, his ultimate goal is to use every providential act to cause his holiness to infiltrate all of creation. This happens both through God's acts of dire judgment and through his grace. Ultimately, God, who will always be holy, will finally be seen as holy. In the end, the world will all be holy, too (4:3–4); then God will be glorified. Every person and nation must ask, *Is it better to experience God's holy judgment, or join those righteous people who glorify his holy name?*[9]

Chapters 6–8 of Romans provide the most exhaustive treatment of holiness in the book, as Paul employs different motifs in describing the same reality. In Romans 6, one faces important questions: How does sin relate to the believer? If an end has been made to morality—morality that is not grounded on Christ's sacrifice—and grace alone is effectual, why not continue sinning? If, after all, it does not depend on our own actions, what does it matter how we live? What are the implications of justification? What are we to do with our new freedom in Christ?

5. Sawyer, *Isaiah*, 58.
6. Spence-Jones, *Isaiah*, 80.
7. Snaith, *Distinctive Ideas of the Old Testament*, 51, 53.
8. Grogan, *Isaiah*, 502.
9. Smith, *Isaiah 1–39*, 176.

Paul answers these questions in three ways, which divide the chapter into three natural sections (viz., 6:1–11, 12–14; 15–23). In the first section, Paul considers the believers' new situation, that is, the indicatives, using concepts such as "died to sin" (6:2), "baptized into Christ" (6:3a), "baptized into his death" (6:3b), "buried with Him through baptism" (6:4), "our old self crucified so that the body of sin might be destroyed" (v. 6), and "died with Christ" (v. 8). Specifically, in 6:1–11, Paul draws out the implications of the believers' faith-union with Christ, the outward expression of which was baptism. In these verses, Paul was not saying what Christians *ought to* be like; he was simply describing what Christians *are like*. Our first responsibility, then, is to understand the facts of who we are in Christ upon conversion and baptism.

In the second section, Paul challenges the believers not just to take some specific actions, but to become in life what they are in Christ—to live up to the reality of their new existence as part of God's holy people. The duty of believers is to live the kind of life that is suitable for the kind of people they now are.

Third, Paul uses the slavery metaphor to show the absurdity of a believer remaining under the control of sin. The believer's life is described both as a life of freedom and slavery simultaneously. Paul's overriding concern here is ethical. Instead of offering a theoretical explanation of a believer's relation to sin, he focuses on the experienced fact of sinning, and of living a sinful life. He is about to show the incompatibility of sin with the new life in Christ (grace). Because sin and grace are shown to be mutually exclusive, his intention is to lead the Roman Christians to the realization that the gospel of grace, rightly understood and properly interpreted, leads not to licentiousness (far from it!) but to righteousness.

Are We Slaves of Sin?

In this chapter, Paul has consistently spoken of the believers' status prior to their conversion as "slaves of sin." In these passages, although Paul does not explicitly formulate the notion of "sin" in such a fashion, it nevertheless has essentially been personified. Man can live in sin, just as he can live in Christ (6:2). Sin may possess and reign in the body (6:6, 12, 13, 16–18, 20, 22). One may live "to sin" (6:11). One either receives the wage of death from sin (6:23a) or the free gift of eternal life from God (6:23b). No persons are free; none is his/her own master. All serve either sin or God. Nevertheless it must be remembered that it is to people whom Paul describes as enslaved that he speaks words of ethical exhortation. More precisely, he exhorts Christians to submit themselves to God, rather than to sin (see Rom 6:13, 16; 12:1–2).

Paul clearly saw the Christian as one who had—within the framework of his being enslaved to God—freedom either to obey, or not to obey, the master. Consequently, there was need for the exhortation. Such freedom is not explicitly or implicitly attributed to the one enslaved to sin. For that person there were no alternatives. The one enslaved to sin yielded himself to a sinful life; the only consequence was sin.

In verse 19, however, Paul says the former slavery was "to uncleanness and lawlessness," rather than to sin directly. Romans 1:24, Gal 5:19, and Eph 4:19 give reason to suggest that "uncleanness" is not so much the designation of that to which one was enslaved, as it is denoting the power of being enslaved to sin.

While living in bondage to sin, one is characterized by uncleanness and lawlessness. The consequence of such a life is that one becomes what one has done. If one has lived in lawlessness, one has become the personification of lawlessness. Verse 19b posits that the believers had previously given themselves over to be slaves to uncleanness and lawlessness.

Paul evidently is recalling the entire manner of life in which these people once lived, though he does not imply that now they do such. It is quite significant to note Paul's assertion that the Roman Christians presented themselves as slaves rather than saying that they were enslaved. In other words, Paul attributes to the believers at Rome the responsibility for what they had previously done, and he implies that they could be charged with the responsibility to follow a new lifestyle.

In verse 19c, Paul repeats himself in the clause "present your members as slaves" in the context of a contrast with verse 19b. Those who are now new persons who have experienced the death of the "old self" and are living, not under law, but under grace (v. 14) must begin presenting themselves as slaves to righteousness (v. 19c), just as those who were under law presented themselves as slaves to sin. But, it must be observed, Paul has just asserted in verse 18 that "you were made slaves to righteousness."

In verse 18, Paul has not slipped to "sub-Christian" thought[10] when he claims the believer is enslaved "to righteousness," rather than "to God."

---

10. Such is the suggestion of Dodd, *Epistle of Paul to the Romans*, 98. Dodd's critical question, "Would not that ['slavery to righteousness'] more aptly describe life under the Law than the condition of Christian freedom?" may *in this context* be emphatically answered in the negative. Paul's argument is partially grounded on the contention that the Law brings in its wake sin leading to condemnation, not slavery to righteousness (cf. 3:19–21; 5:20a; 7:11, 13). In the present context Paul is simply using a form of words to present the antithesis to "slavery to sin."

In order to give all the more impact to his declaration that the Christian is not to sin because he is under grace, he expresses the new slavery in terms not of the new master—God (as he does in v. 22)—but of the character of the new master. Note that he is not using "righteousness" as a synonym for God; he is emphasizing that to be enslaved to God is to be enslaved to one whose character is that of righteousness and in whose kingdom sin has no legitimate role.

Paul, from a theological standpoint, can affirm that the Christian is enslaved to righteousness because Christ Jesus has become, for the Christian's benefit, the embodiment of God's righteousness (1 Cor 1:30) and because the Christian is united with Christ through the baptismal death and renewal of life. Consequently, in union with Christ, the believer is within the dominion of God's righteousness (see 2 Cor 5:21).

The Process of Sanctification

Although the believer has been enslaved through union with Christ to God's righteousness or to God, there still remains the necessity—as the Corinthians had all too clearly demonstrated—of coming to be like the one to whom they are enslaved. Enslavement does not of itself bring submission, and even submission may not transform one's personal character, regardless of how restrictive or oppressive enslavement may be. For Paul, transformation of personal character requires the positive co-operation of the individual. The people who have been enslaved must now serve their new master with acceptance of their new status, so that they may reflect the character of their owner in their own character. As those who are enslaved to God—not to sin—the believers must begin doing that which they have not previously done: they must present their members as slaves to God and his righteousness. When they do so, they will achieve their own personal sanctification and, ultimately, eternal life (vv. 19b, 22).

When the believers regularly commit themselves as slaves to God and his righteousness, their behavioral patterns will begin changing. Their former lifestyle of enslavement to sin was bringing (v. 21) only things of which they could now be ashamed. Their transformation is the process of sanctification, of being made holy. This new life in which the person is experiencing personal sanctification comes into being through the Christian's continuing to accept the reality that he is dead to sin's enslavement (see 6:11a) and that he is alive as a slave of God (see 6:11b), together with his continued keeping himself or his members within the dominion of Christ Jesus his Lord and the Holy Spirit (see Rom 8:4, 5b, 10). Sanctification, the emerging fruit of the Christian's submission to God (6:22), is the process of becoming like Christ Jesus; one has been transferred from the dominion of sin and has become a new creation (see 6:1–11; 2 Cor 5:11). Together with the Holy Spirit, the believer's new life is being manifested (see Gal 2:20; Rom 8:11).

Some observations regarding the use of the noun, *hagiasmos* ("sanctification"), are in order. A definition of sanctification in this context as "persons set apart or consecrated for God's use" is inappropriate. In the present context (Rom 6:19, 22) the persons addressed are those who are already set apart for God's use. Rather than using the image of being set apart to God, in Romans 6, Paul has used the image of being enslaved to God. The two amount essentially to the same thing—those who died to sin's dominion and who began to walk in newness of life as God's slaves should live in conformity to God's character, as made known through Christ Jesus, not that they should be his possession.

The Law of the Spirit

In chapter 7, Paul has stripped away every aspect of the privileges the Jews may claim to have—as the Torah law of Rom 7:1 gradually shifts to the "law of the Spirit" (Rom 8:2). Jews and Gentiles stand together as ones who have "no condemnation for those who are in Christ Jesus" (Rom 8:1). Rom 7:14–25 is atypical of Paul's portrayal of the life of faith and, therefore, should never be considered as the centerpiece of Paul's view of the Christian life. However, one thing is clear: the meaning of the passage cannot be decided solely by grammar. The passage is to be understood as the description of an unregenerate person viewed from the vantage point of faith. There is a continuity of theme across the supposed division between Rom 7:7–13 and 7:13–25. In other words, 7:7–25 should be read as a whole.

The experience Paul describes in 7:7–13 is exactly the same experience he describes in 7:14–25. It is an experience of failure, despite one's best efforts. The only change, apart from tense, is perhaps a move from a specific personal example to the general condition of those seeking to serve by the written code. Unfortunately, many people, through the past centuries and until the present, have attempted to produce doctrines based upon their own experiences, and the lament of the "wretched man" in Rom 7:14–25 has comforted many people as they yield to various temptations to sin.

However, the life of constant defeat shown in this passage is completely contrary to the believer's new life as portrayed in chapters 6–8. Specifically Rom 6:1—7:6 shows that believers are free from sin and the Law through their participation in the death and resurrection of Jesus Christ. Within the immediate context and its focus on the Law, the passage of 7:14–25 emphasizes the plight of searching for sanctification without faith and highlights the frustration of seeking freedom by the Law.

In conclusion, the idea that the Christian is powerless and does the very thing he or she hates is to be seen as not only repugnant, and therefore to be *rejected*, but also is contrary to Christ's call for repentance, discipleship, and holy living. Indeed no Christian, such as is portrayed in chapter 6, would cry, "Wretched man that I am!"

Romans 7 should not be understood either as a description or prescriptive norm of the Christian life. If that is the kind of Christian life we have, then it is non-Pauline and substandard. Verses 14–25 are more than a mere moral frustration. Instead, what we have is a moral failure, which does not sound or look like a life transformed by grace and led by the Spirit as we find in chapters 6–8.

Based upon Paul's extensive use of literary devices in his rhetorical writings and the bridge of solidarity he was extending to the Jews, it appears that Paul used the present tense "I am" in an effort to strengthen his solidarity with the Jews and for its dramatic effect. Paul is emphasizing the struggle with sin and with being under the Law before gaining victory "in Christ."

Unfortunately, many people do not want to hear that they can live without sin; however, it is inaccurate to use the passage of 7:14–25 to validate an unrighteous lifestyle. Christians are not consigned to wallow in sin, but are instead challenged and encouraged through Paul's writing to live within their hopeful Christian existence because they are no longer condemned to a life of struggling with sin.

The Argument for Sanctification

Full weight must now be given to chapter 8. In many ways, it caps the whole argument on sanctification in the three chapters,[11] as it gathers up the central intent of the two previous chapters and takes the key points further.[12] It shows the connection between the newness of life that characterizes the one who has died to sin with the Spirit and, at the same time, by connecting the fulfilment of the Law with the Spirit.

As Paul would argue, Christ's saving work does not nullify the call of God to live a holy life—quite the contrary: because of the Spirit, God brings

---

11. Godet, *Epistle to the Romans*, 295 quotes Spener as saying that "if the holy Scripture was a ring, and the Epistle to the Romans its precious stone, chapter 8 would be the sparkling point of the jewel."

12. Kaylor, *Paul's Covenant Community*, 141–42.

to fulfilment in the community of faith the "just requirements of the Law" (8:1–5). The unquestionable emphasis in this chapter, then, is upon the life that is lived by the power of the Holy Spirit.[13]

It is significant to note that prior to this point in Romans, there are only four references (Rom 1:4; 2:29; 5:5; 7:6) to the Holy Spirit, compared to twenty-one in this chapter—Rom 8:2, 4, 5 (two times), 6, 9 (three times), 10, 11 (two times), 13, 14, 15 (two times), 16 (two times), 23, 26 (two times)—more than in any other chapter in the whole Bible. As Fee succinctly states,

> This section (Rom 8:1–39) climaxes the soteriological dimension of the argument that began in 1:18 and one can scarcely miss the crucial role played by the Holy Spirit. Even though it is never said quite in this way, the Spirit is the life-giving linchpin to everything that has been argued up to this point . . . nonetheless the Spirit is the experiential key to the whole: God in love is creating a people for his name, apart from the Law. . . . All of this is actualized in the church (and in the believer as well, of course) by the Spirit whom God has given.[14]

Furthermore, in contrast to Romans 7, Paul shows that the solution to the human problem of sin is not through the Law, and through legalistic regulations, but is a life lived under the discipline, guidance, and direction of the Holy Spirit.[15] A life in the Spirit is one where God's will is fulfilled, a life that bears the promise of resurrection and eternal life; it is a life that is lived in hope, and a life that experiences the victory of God in the midst of the adverse circumstances of life. It is therefore clear that Romans 8 describes the ministry of the Holy Spirit in relationship to the believer.

A cursory reading of these verses also reveals Paul's concern about the relationship of the Holy Spirit to his ethics. The Christian life is not to be lived by one's own efforts and strength. Rather, Paul is about to show that an adequate provision for Christian living is to be seen in the person, presence, and power of the Holy Spirit.

Most scholars and commentators would agree that Rom 8:1–4 begins Paul's description of what may be termed life in the Spirit—the sanctified life. The verses link directly with Rom 7:6.[16] Verses 1–4 are chiefly a summary of

---

13. Fee, *God's Empowering Presence*, 517 comments on Rom 5:1—8:39: ". . . nonetheless the Spirit is the experiential key to the whole: God in love is creating a people for his name, apart from the Law . . . . All of this is actualized in the church (and in the believer as well, of course) by the Spirit whom God has given."

14. Ibid., 516–17.

15. Howard, *Newness of Life*, 160.

16. Romans 7:6 is the essential presupposition of Romans 8, for it is clear that the perspective of faith that Paul develops in Romans 8 was already the foundation of his

what the Christian has become, as a result of having died to the Law (Rom 7:6).[17] Paul starts his arguments in the chapter with the inferential particle "therefore" to show that the discussion that follows is a consequence of his preceding arguments. The opening words of the chapter echo the themes of 5:1: those who have been "justified through faith" are now "those in Christ Jesus." The benefit of "peace with God" (see Rom 5:1) is now expressed as freedom from condemnation.

Condemnation, as Paul would stress, is completely out of the question, as suggested by the emphatic use of the word *ouden* ("none"). It is significant to note that Paul uses the same Greek noun for "condemnation" (*katakrima*) in Rom 8:1 that he uses in Rom 5:16 and 18. Moreover, it is also important to note that those who are free from condemnation are those who are "in Christ Jesus."

In verse 1, Paul brings back his readers to the "now" and to his description of the benefits of justification. It is important to note that Paul uses the word "now" many times in his letter to the Romans (see 3:21, 24; 5:9; 6:19; 21). In such passages he refers to blessings that Christians already experience. As Adam Clarke rightly notes, "the *now* therefore, in the text must refer more to the happy transition from darkness to light, from condemnation to pardon, which the believer now enjoys."[18] On the one hand, the word "now" is temporal and distinguishes the Christian from the pre-Christian period of life. However, on the other hand, it may be understood as eschatological. In the latter sense, "now" means after Christ, thus depicting something bigger than what is happening in any individual's life.

In vv. 2–3, Paul continues by describing the present reality of believers. Verse 2 provides the basic truth with regards to deliverance from sin. Christians have been "set free" from the law of sin and death. The breakthrough or liberation is grounded upon Christ's redemptive act—Christ has removed the believers' guilt by means of his sacrificial death on Calvary.

Far-Reaching Freedom

One may ask, "How deep and far-reaching is the freedom that Paul speaks about here?" Let's answer the question with a story: A man who had been a hard drinker was saved, and at once he dropped the liquor habit. One day he was going down the street past a tavern he formerly patronized regularly. Seeing him go by, the owner called out, "What's wrong, Charlie? Why do

---

argument in Romans 7.

17. Bowen, *Guide to Romans*, 102.

18. Clarke, "Romans," 93.

you keep going past instead of coming in?" Charlie paused a brief moment; then he finally replied, "It's not just me who goes past now. We go past—the Lord and I." Where sin had once abounded, grace now much more abounds (Rom 5:20).

Only the saving acts of God in Jesus Christ, consummated through the Spirit, can free human beings from their hopeless situation (Rom 8:2–3). Humanity, outside the saving and sanctifying grace of God and the power of the Spirit, does not possess the strength for victory. But with Christ and the Holy Spirit, victory over sin is possible. As Paul starts to lay out the contrast between living according to the flesh and living according to the Spirit, he boldly affirms that the pivot between these two ways of existing is redemption through Christ Jesus. Although Paul in the first two verses returns to the sacrificial death of Christ on the cross, he quickly shifts his focus toward a new image and dimension of the Christian experience—life in the Spirit. Paul argues that, "Christ condemned sin in the flesh in order that the requirement of the Law might be fulfilled in us, who do not walk according to the flesh, but according to the Spirit."

From the onset, Paul appears to be addressing a two-fold problem with relation to sin. The first is that of assurance, and the second of day-to-day, Spirit-filled, holy living. With regard to the first, Paul unequivocally maintains that for all who are in Christ by faith, there is no condemnation for sin, but rather the condemnation of sin in the flesh. The Christian does not need to be overcome by guilt or by fear, due to his or her sins. The cross of Jesus Christ is the solution, and the death that Christ died was for all the sins of the one who receives his work by faith. Paul's arguments in 3:1—4:25 have now come full circle: The forgiveness of sins Paul describes in that section of the book applies to all the sins of the one who trusts in Christ. There is no condemnation! Even more so, Christ's death at Calvary delivered believers from condemnation of sin, and also dealt a severe blow to sin, delivering it to condemnation as well.

Paul simply declares the fact of the believer's deliverance and accepts by faith that no condemnation and no bondage remains for those who have died and risen with Christ. The victory of the believer is sure and certain, for it is made possible by the Spirit. What could never be accomplished in the power of the flesh—fulfilling the righteous demand of the Law, which is holiness and righteousness—is now possible through the power of the Spirit. Walking by the Spirit, Christians share the result of Christ's victory and are able to do the good things the Law really wanted.

Paul's Prophetic Call to Christians

Undoubtedly, Paul's teaching in Rom 8:1–4 is central to the Christian life, and it is very likely that Paul must have had in mind the actual obedience of believers. First, the use of the passive "has been fulfilled" coupled with the prepositional phrase "in us," points in the direction that the obedience described in Rom 8:4 is the work of God. Second, it is also hard to explain how the participle "the ones who are walking," which means to conduct one's life, could refer to anything less than an actual experience of the believers. Furthermore, it is unlikely that Paul's radical antithesis of flesh and spirit is merely to be perceived or applied individualistically but also communally. The passage, although it could describe individual or group behaviors, does more than that. It is Paul's prophetic call to the Roman Christians, both to a decisive commitment and to be witnesses in the society in which they lived. Kaylor sums it up well:

> The Spirit produces transformed living in which God's will comes to fulfillment in those who walk no longer according to the flesh but according to the Spirit. . . . The Spirit effects a life through renewed relationships more than a life of piety expressed in religious activity. The new life created and given by the Spirit is to be expressed in concrete living. It is not a prize possession to be placed in a case and admired, nor an insurance policy to be kept in a safe deposit-box. Rather, the new life involves a new set of relationships in which self and community are freed for life of faith expressing itself in love.[19]

In Rom 12:1–2, Paul summarily states the ethical response the Christian is to make to God in view of God's mercies, which is the possibility to respond positively to such a gift. For the non-Christian, there is the need to become a believer and then to present himself/herself a living sacrifice.

This passage, as well as Rom 15:15–16, has several terms common to the Old Testament sacrificial cultus: *present, sacrifice, holy,* and *acceptable*. In these verses it is possible to see how Paul uses terms of the Mosaic Covenant, but gives them a new orientation so they are expressive of the new relationship with Christ. "Paul's exhortation that the Christians present their bodies as a sacrifice gives ultimate personalization to the sacrificial act, thereby transforming it and giving the Christian sacrifice a radically new content."[20] In the Pentateuchal sources that address the question of sacrifice, none required that the offering should be the same as the offerer, or the one

---

19. Kaylor, *Paul's Covenant Community*, 150.
20. Hewet, *Hagios*, 258.

presenting the offerings. Instead, the worshipper brought some prescribed personal possession. By contrast, Paul indicates that for the Christian, the proper sacrifice is one's own body.

Certainly Paul does not designate by his use of *sōma* ("body") something that is not essential to humanness. Moreover Rom 6:12, 16, 19, illustrate how Paul can alternate between body (*sōma*), members (*melē*), and yourselves (*heautous*), while referring to the total person. It may be suggested that when in 12:1 he uses *sōmata*, he has chosen that term not simply to express "yourselves," but to express with unequivocal emphasis that the physical body of the believer is to be holy. By using *bodies* Paul designates "the whole person," but his primary emphasis falls on the physical being—although the other faculties that comprise a person (e.g., the mind, conscience, and spirit) are not excluded. As aspects of humanity, these faculties cannot be separated from the *body* so that only the latter is presented to God. If a person has presented his or her *body* to God, then because of a human's constitutive character, a person has presented all of himself or herself. By choosing *bodies* Paul has guarded himself against a mistaken interpretation that might have asserted that either the *body* was irrelevant (or incapable of such dedication to God) or that the Christian must commit himself or herself only with respect to the "inner self."

Furthermore it should be observed that when Paul exhorts the Christians to be transformed by the renewal of their minds (Rom 12:2), it is due to his belief that the metamorphosis of the physical organism designated by *body* will not occur until the Parousia (arrival) of Christ (see 1 Cor 15:20–23, 44, 51–53; Phil 3:20f.). It would therefore have been a theological impossibility for him to say, "be transformed in the renewal of your physical bodies," the same physical bodies he describes by the terms "perishable," "dishonor," and "weakness" (1 Cor 15:42f.; see Phil 3:21). As Jewett suggests, "the transformation Paul has in view here is shaped by the recovery of a realistic appraisal of ethical choices in the light of the converted community's experience of the 'new creation' brought by Christ."[21]

What Paul urges is not merely a change of appearance and behavior, but a change of essence. This is not a matter of *acting* a part, but of *being* completely different. The indwelling Spirit of Christ is God's agent in effecting this inside-out transformation, reproducing Jesus in the lives of committed Christians (see Rom 8:29; 2 Cor 3:17–18; 2 Thess 2:13). As Greathouse notes, "the transformation of believers that Jewish apocalypses

---

21. Jewett, *Romans: A Commentary*, 733.

(2 Bar. 51:5; 1 Enoch 71:11) expected only in the end of time, Paul claimed was a present possibility."[22]

Paul's description of this sacrifice shows both dissimilarity and similarity with the Old Testament sacrifices. The Christian's self-sacrifice involves, not death—as in the Old Testament—but life. The one who has been set free from the body of death (Rom 7:24f.) and is being given life through the indwelling of the Spirit of Christ (Rom 8:9–11) has the opportunity and the option of presenting that Spirit-enlivened body to God. Not only is this sacrifice to be a live one, it is to be holy—no new notion to the Jews, whose commandments regarding the sacrifices had long since established that the sacrifices were holy or most holy things (see Lev 6; 10:17; 21:22; 22:2–4, 10–14). The sacrifices of Israel were holy in that they were set apart to belong to Yahweh and to be used by his chosen priests (and their families, under certain conditions). It was established that when holy (*qadash-hagios*) was used in the passages, such as Lev 19:2, Exod 19:4–6, and Exod 22:30, with reference to people, the term basically bore a significant ethical content.

Qadash designated the character of persons whose lives are in conformity with certain Yahweh-enunciated ethical standards in their relationship with others. Both these two verses that introduce the ethical section of Romans, and the section as a whole, strongly lead us to conclude that when Paul used *holy* in 12:1 it was with an ethical significance, just as the passages cited above have done.

At this point in Romans, Paul has not referred to the readers as the holy people or sanctified ones (*hoi hēgiasmenoi*). Nevertheless as Rom 6:11, 22; 8:9–11, 15–17 indicate, they are the sanctified ones, those set apart to belong to God through union with Christ Jesus. Consequently when he exhorts them to present their bodies as a holy and living sacrifice, he is not calling them to present themselves as set apart—something that is an already accomplished fact for the believer. Paul is exhorting the set-apart ones to present to God *ethically pure* physical bodies. They can do this on the basis of their personal relational transformation that occurred when they were sanctified.

Agape Love and the Spirit of Christ

In the context of Romans, those who have "ethically pure bodies" or "bodies which are holy, living sacrifices" are those who respond positively to the commandments enunciated by Paul, particularly in chapters 12–15. The sum of his exhortation, both here and elsewhere, is that "You shall love your

22. Greathouse and Lyons, *Romans 9–16*, 135.

neighbor as yourself . . . Love is the fulfilling of the law" (Rom 13:9–10). Therefore essentially the holy person is the person who is characterized by love—as Paul would define love (*agapē*) (cf.1 Cor 13:1—14:1; Rom 5:8). To love is not to adhere to a code of ethics *per se* so much as it is to give concrete expression to the will of God, which is revealed in Christ Jesus (see Col 2:16–23) and mediated through the Spirit of Christ (see Rom 8:13f; Gal 5:16–18) to the believer in his particular moment of existence.

The Spirit may use a variety of means for this task, and Paul would have viewed his letters and such passages as Rom 12ff. as one such means (see 2 Tim 3:14–17). Persons who have "the mind of Christ" are being renewed in their inner being. They can, consequently, discern God's will. Actualizing the will of God is to live in love, which is to live in holiness. That life constitutes a sacrifice that is well-pleasing to God and is the genuine worship of God by the Christian.

Romans 15:15–16 is the only occasion when Paul used the verb form *hagiazein* ("to make holy") in his letter to the Romans. Its setting is striking in that Paul has relied so heavily on the imagery of the Old Testament cultus to describe his mission relative to the Gentiles. Through examining his use of these cultic terms, one is able to grasp something of the gulf that separated Paul from the Jewish faith in which he had been reared, and to understand better the nature of the Christian commitment and its responsibilities.

Paul uses the cultic word *leitourgos* simply translated as "minister" or "servant" to describe his apostolic mission. It was a term that was commonly used in the Hellenistic world to designate a person who held a public office and had no special significance.[23] Paul's use of the term could be understood as denoting simply that he is a minister, with Christ Jesus providing the theological significance. It may well be the case, however, that Paul, in choosing the term, was recalling the significance in the LXX of the verb from the same root: *leitourgein* ("to serve").[24]

Paul asserts that he has the authority to write to the Romans precisely because God in his grace has made Paul a minister, not so much of Yahweh, as of Christ Jesus. Although Paul doesn't serve at an altar or a temple, he nonetheless performs a valid ministry in the new priesthood.[25] Paul's min-

---

23. Cf. Barrett, *Romans*, 247.

24. Cf. Exod 29:30; 30:20; Num 3:6, 31; 4:3, 9, 12, etc.; Deut 10:8; 17:2; 1 Chr. 6:32; 15:2; Ezek 40:46; 42:14. One immediately observes that these references are from priestly sources (except the Deuteronomic passages, which nonetheless make reference to the cultus). They are all concerned with ministering to Yahweh in the context of the sacrificial system.

25. The latter expression is Peter's, not Paul's. Cf. 1 Pet 2:9 and note the role which this priesthood is to play. It is to ". . . declare the wonderful deeds of him who called you

istry requires no physical, literal temple, nor is it restricted to the Jewish folk or those who become Jewish proselytes. He ministers to the Gentiles on behalf of Christ Jesus. The priestly imagery refers not to the role Paul typically depicts himself fulfilling—as a preacher of the gospel concerned with *converting* unbelievers.[26]

The word *hieourgounta* usually translated "to serve as priest," neither occurs elsewhere in the New Testament text, nor is it used in the LXX, though it was used a number of times by the classicists, as well as Philo and Josephus. For Paul to refer to himself as one who serves as a priest is quite striking in that, for Paul, the role of priests in the Old Testament sense has been superseded as a consequence of Christ's sacrificial death. That Paul could nevertheless do it well illustrates the way in which he could expand or reapply concepts to fit the Christian church. The only occasion when Paul made reference to the *hieros* ("sacred," or "temple area") was when, for illustrative purposes, he referred to the Jerusalem Temple and the priests who serve at the altar there (1 Cor 9:13). But to serve as a priest was not the way in which Paul generally characterized his work; instead he was an *apostolos*. The sense in which he could designate himself as a priest is only with reference to the gospel of God. He was no priest of the Temple and the Mosaic Covenant. Those priests presented at the altar those offerings that were brought by the people and they ate of those gifts (1 Cor 9:13).

Paul, by contrast, proclaimed the gospel (1 Cor 9:4). The New English Bible's rendering of Rom 15:16a is precisely correct: "My priestly service is the preaching of the gospel of God." Paul's priestly ministry is one of proclaiming God's gospel to everyone—in this case, to the Gentiles. Hence Paul's priestly service is notably different from that which is usually associated with a priesthood; the gift comes from God to humanity. In Paul's presentation of the gospel, God has acted; in response, Paul proclaims what God has done.

Paul's use of offering (*prosphora*) to describe his gentile converts is significant. The word occurs twice in the LXX: Ps 40:6 [LXX: 39:7] and 1 Kgs 7:48 [LXX: v. 34]. In the former it was used correctly to translate *minhah* ("prayers offered in the afternoon"); in the latter as a paraphrase to translate *hapanim* ("the Bread of the Presence").[27] Based on Ps 40:6, it is sufficient to suggest the propriety of viewing *prosphora* ("sacrifice") as a term with sacrificial significance. Still more suggestive with respect to the Old Testament

---

out of darkness into his marvellous light." That is an excellent statement of what Paul saw as his priestly task.

26. Greathouse and Lyons, *Romans 9–16*, 244.

27. Because the "Bread of the Presence" was technically an offering to God, the translation of 1 Kgs 7:48 is a correct paraphrase.

cultus is the use of *prospherein* ("to sacrifice"). Even a cursory examination of a list of the verb's occurrences in an LXX concordance reveals its importance in Leviticus (see e.g., Lev 1, 2, 7, and 9) where it speaks of bringing and presenting offerings to Yahweh. Among the New Testament materials, Christ is depicted as one who loved us and gave himself for us—in the words of Ps 40:7—an offering to God (Eph 5:2). In similar fashion, the letter to the Hebrews depicts Jesus as the offering *prosphoras* by which atonement has been effected (see 10:10, 14, 18). In Acts 21:26 and 24:17, Paul recalls how he made preparation to present offerings at the Temple in response to the request of James and the Jerusalem elders that he do so.

In the present context, the offering of the Gentiles is nothing less than themselves (see Rom 12:1) and this is an offering, which, according to 12:1, is to be made by the worshipper. Paul, in his priestly function, is not concerned with presenting that offering, but that it be acceptable.[28] He explicitly declares that his priestly role is with respect to the gospel of God. He also explicitly declares, as just noted above, that each person bears responsibility for *presenting himself* to God. No one else has that responsibility.

Paul modifies the OT sacrificial system. In the same manner as the OT priest, he is concerned that the offering be acceptable. However, unlike the OT priest, he does not present the offering to God; he seeks to ensure that the one who makes the offering knows how that offering may be acceptable to God. To that end, he has written rather boldly (in perhaps 6:11, 19; 8:9; 11:17; 12:3; 13:3, 13; 14; 15:1[29]), exhorting those who have been sanctified to live in such a fashion that their offerings will be acceptable.

According to Lev 22:20–25, the sacrifices of the Mosaic Covenant were to be without blemish, spot, bruise, or any defilement, if they were to be acceptable. Hebrews 9:14 and 1 Peter 1:19 indicate that Christ's offering of himself to God, which offering was acceptable, was without spot or blemish (see 2 Cor 5:21). Similarly the offering of the Gentiles must be without spot or blemish if it is to be acceptable—it must be holy (see Rom 12:1). As seen in our discussion of the *qadosh-hagios* ("holy, holiness") terminology in the Old Testament, the term is used in the Old Testament to show the set-apartness to Yahweh's possession.

In Rom 15:16, *hēgiasmenē* is in apposition to *prosphora*—the offering has been sanctified and the effect of the sanctification continues. The offering to which Paul refers is most notable—it is the Gentiles. Zechariah

---

28. Cf. Greathouse and Lyons, ". . . he characterizes himself in terms of the original imagery of a sacrificial priest making *an offering* [*prosphora*; see Heb 10:5, 10, 14, 18] *acceptable to God* [*euprosdektos*; lit. *well-pleasing*; see Rom 15:31; 2 Cor 6:2; 8:12; 1 Pet 2:5]

29. So Sanday and Headlam, *Epistle to the Romans*, 404.

14:16 and Isa 60:3; 66:18 are representative of the Old Testament Jewish minds who could envision any role for the non-Jew in the redeemed community. For Paul, the Gentile, as well as the Jew who accepted Christ as Lord and Savior was thereby sanctified and incorporated into the church of Christ Jesus. The understanding of *hagiazein*, "to make holy or sanctify" as espoused by Hering and Morris in their studies of 1 Corinthians is apparent: The offering has been set apart or consecrated to God with no reference to a qualitative change. It has occurred "by the Spirit." Earlier (Romans 6) Paul established that the Christian is set apart to God's possession by means of Christ's death and resurrection (see 1 Cor 1:2 and 6:11). In 1 Cor 6:11 and here, the significance of the Holy Spirit as the one who makes the work of Christ personally relevant is emphasized, although how this occurs is not indicated.

One might ask, "If the Christian has become sanctified, is he not acceptable to God?" Evidently Paul would have said, "Not necessarily so!" When considering the Deuteronomic legislation, it was observed that the relationally holy people (Deut 7:6; 14:1, 21) had to become the ethically holy people (Deut 26:18–19; 28:9). Paul reflects a similar outlook. Those who have been separated unto God must validate their separation by living the life that has been designated by God as acceptable to him—the holy life.

Chapter 3

Holiness in 1 Corinthians

IN HIS ARTICLE "CHRISTIANITY at Corinth," C. K. Barrett succinctly comments that in Paul's letters to the Corinthians "we gain the most complete and many-sided picture of how Paul believed that his theological convictions should be expressed in the life of a Church."[1] He goes further to say that, "there is in fact no more important source for Paul's conception of the Christian way of life."[2] In several ways, the life of the twenty-first-century Church reflects that of the first-century Corinthian congregation, thus making a study like this compelling. The challenge of what it means and entails for the believer to live in a morally polluted and decadent society remains the same. It is therefore important to examine the Corinthian correspondence (in this and the next chapter) and see what constitutes holiness in Paul's thought from those letters. To do so would require an examination of words and concepts that show Paul's concern for holiness, particularly the use of the *hagios* word group that plays a prominent role.[3] Therefore, the basic approach in this chapter is to examine passages in 1 Corinthians with special focus on, but not limited to the use of, *hagios* and its cognates.[4]

---

1. Barrett, "Christianity at Corinth," 269–97.
2. Ibid., 269.
3. Of the fifty-seven occurrences of the hagios word group in the Pauline corpus, twenty are to be found in the Corinthian correspondence.
4. Cf. Hewett, *Use of the Hagios*, 192–96. Hewett's study has been invaluable. However, it needs be noted that Hewett does not consider the corporate nuance of the word group.

HAGIOS GROUP OF WORDS

If one seeks a complete view of Paul's understanding of the *hagios* word group, it is not difficult to conclude that the meaning of *hagios* ("holy") and its cognates in 1 Corinthians is representative of Paul's basic position of *hagios*, etc. in his other letters. The relational significance of this word group is quite plainly seen in 1 Cor 1:2; 6:11; and 7:14. It is also to be observed in the use of *hagios* in 3:16f., a reference to the temple of God, which is holy. An examination of several passages will demonstrate Paul's multifaceted understanding of holiness.[5]

1 Corinthians 1:2

In his survey of the use of the verb *hagiazein*, B. F. Westcott concluded that in the NT, it signifies a) "to set apart for God; to separate from 'the world'" and b) "to make conformable in character to such a dedication."[6] He is certainly right. However, one must note that "either of these two aspects may be dominant in any given instance, or both may be equally present."[7] These distinctions will be pointed out below as considered appropriate in determining the nuance of the word in any specific context.

The first of these is the most common meaning given to *hagiasmenois*, "sanctified in Christ" in 1:2. The Corinthian church is so designated because it is comprised of those who are set apart to be God's people. Here, Paul is declaring a fact that has occurred, the consequences of which continue to exist. In this dual description there is a tension between the concept of holiness as a result, which has been consummated, and as a goal that has yet to be achieved. Hence, for Paul, holiness is both something that the Corinthians have already, and something to which they are called. As believers in Christ, they have already been sanctified—they are now God's people. They belong to him. Yet they are called to be holy—they are to become that which in a sense they already are.[8] Thus, Paul urges the Corinthian Church "to become what it is, that is those 'called to be holy ones.'"[9] The participle

---

5. As suggested in Chapter 2, the basis of Israel's holiness is relationship with God. It is so with the Corinthian Christians as well. However, it is still possible to speak of ethical or required aspect of holiness in a given passage in terms of focus, that is, the use of the word group, as to be shown often emphasizes one aspect even when the other is to be assumed present.

6. Westcott, *Epistle to the Hebrews*, 346–47, Hewett, *Use of Hagios*, 193.

7. Greenlee, *What the New Testament Says*, 20.

8. Watson, *First Epistle to the Corinthians*, 3.

9. Roetzel, "Grammar of Election," 230.

expresses a relationship of having been set apart to God; the conception is of an eschatological community, established by God, which finds its life in Christ Jesus. The relational significance of the participle *hēgiasmenois* is further suggested by the fact that the believers in Corinth are subsequently rebuked for sins committed by members of their community. In this regard, the holiness of the Corinthians resembles that of the Israelites of the OT who were both exhorted to be a holy people and were called a holy people (see Exod 19:6; Lev 11:44–45; 19:2; 20:7; Deut 7:6; 14:2, 21). Yet when we read about how the people behaved through their generations, particularly in their wilderness wanderings and through the period of the judges, one wonders how such people could be called "holy."

Perhaps the answer to the puzzle lies in the understanding of holiness, primarily in terms of relationship and belongingness. They were holy inasmuch as they were people with whom God had a covenant relationship, and people whom he had set apart from other nations to serve him. They belonged to God in a special way. Thus, it is right to say that holiness was not to be reduced to morality, although it certainly includes it. Reduced to morality, holiness loses its grace character and becomes mere performance.

The relevance of this phrase "sanctified in Christ Jesus" in the context of Paul's salutation is worth considering. Perhaps an important reason for Paul's using the phrase in question was to anticipate his argument of 1:11–31. The church in Corinth was sanctified in Christ Jesus. Therefore it owed allegiance, not to Paul, Apollos, Cephas, or any other, but to Christ. A most essential point to note in this connection is the meaning of "in or by Christ Jesus" as this is the definitive element attached to "being sanctified": for Paul, sanctification occurs in Christ Jesus (see 1 Cor 1:30; 6:11).[10]

In the Old Testament, Israel was constantly reminded that it was Yahweh who sanctified them. Paul could be following this emphasis and attributing the action to Christ. On the other hand, the incorporative idea is stressed by Paul in 1 Cor 1:30. Given the OT background, both thoughts may have been present in Paul's mind and because that Greek construction allows both, one must not dogmatically exclude either.

We should further note that in addressing the group, Paul has modified the singular noun "church" by the plural participle, "those who are sanctified." This shift to the plural suggests that Paul is not thinking about the community in Corinth only as a unitary body—that is, as "the Church." He also has in mind the individual members of this body and the significance

---

10. In this formula it is difficult to decide whether to interpret the dative construction as instrumental or locative. See Fee, *First Epistle to the Corinthians*, 32n20.

for each one of their being incorporated into the church, which God has established in Christ Jesus.

Paul develops this in his use of the metaphor "body of Christ," in 1 Cor 12:12–27. As such, it is appropriate again to suggest that Paul has the "sanctification" of the Corinthians as a corporate community in mind, as well as their individual participation in that event. The starting point for Paul is the community, and the individual is seen as a constituent part of the community. It is safe to say that Paul does not maintain a dichotomy between corporate and personal holiness.

1 Corinthians 1:30

In this passage, Paul uses the noun *hagiasmos* for sanctification. This verse is the climax of Paul's argument in 1 Cor 1:26–31, where the issue of status within the Corinthian Christian community is dominant. Paul affirms his belief that human social understanding and effort can have no role in salvation. For Paul, those who had status by reason of their birth, wealth, and position do not enjoy greater or special privileges in the "church." Instead it is what people are "in Christ Jesus" that gives them status. To be in Christ Jesus is to be united to him. Being "in Christ" in the present context is a way of saying that the Corinthian believers have become related to God as covenanted people through the event of Jesus Christ. Christ has become everything to the Christians because of his incarnation, death, and resurrection.

Of this union with Christ, the apostle teaches here, first, its origin, and secondly, its effects. As to its origin, it is of God, by saying of the Corinthians, "Of him you are in Christ Jesus," "of him" being the efficient cause.

How is sanctification to be understood in this context? One problem with the understanding of sanctification (*hagiasmos*) in 1 Cor 1:30 is the presence of justification (*dikaiosyne*). Because of this, Barrett has suggested that Paul is using different metaphors not just to describe the same reality, but to mean the same thing.[11] In other words, Paul is employing sanctification in a purely forensic manner, that is, a matter of being declared to be holy or set apart without ethical signification. However, the following reasons make this view highly improbable.

First, it should be noted that this is not the only passage where Paul combines *justification* and *sanctification*. For example, Paul places *sanctification* alongside *justification* also in Rom 6:19, 22, a passage that is very

---

11. Barrett, *First Epistle to the Corinthians*, 60–61, sees righteousness here as primarily forensic, but not just as a forensic "counter," rather as "a direct product of Christ's self–offering for men, the work of redemption."

significant in Romans for the understanding of sanctification. In Romans 6:19, Paul exhorts his readers to present the members of their bodies to God "as servants to righteousness for the purpose of a *state* ("lifestyle") of holiness." Similarly in Rom 6:22, he says, "having been freed from sin and having become enslaved to God, you have your fruit unto holiness." The Roman Christians have "holiness as their fruit," that is, the result of this relationship is a *state* of holiness or sanctification.[12] It is clear from these passages that Paul uses the term sanctification in an ethical sense and does not employ it as a synonym for justification or righteousness.

Second, as Lightfoot argues, justification and sanctification are added to clarify the meaning and content of wisdom (*sophia*) because of the lack of any connecting particle between wisdom and justification.[13] If this is correct, we are to take both these terms in the same way as wisdom, that is, primarily as God's, and also one's own insofar as one is in Christ. In that case, a forensic meaning of *hagiasmos* is impossible. Our life in Christ is marked by that holiness which comes from God in the person of Jesus, a holiness in which we may participate. Because 1 Cor 1:30 refers to that righteousness, sanctification, and redemption which belong to Christ, it is appropriate to think of an ethical quality concerning those terms. After all, Paul never depicted Christ as righteous or holy in a forensic sense. He was actually holy.

The use of prepositions with *hagiasmos* is notable. Its appearance with a preposition usually is to characterize the comprehensive goal of the new conduct of those who believe: *eis hagiasmon* in Rom 6:19 (over against *eis tēn anomian*); v. 22 (over against "death as the fruit of the life lived under the power of sin"); and *en hagiasmō* in 1 Thess 4:7 (over against *epi akarthasia*).[14] Even Ridderbos, despite his insistence on the non-ethical usage of the *hagios* word group, concludes that "in the most comprehensive sense of appropriation and moral renewal it occurs in 1 Cor 1:30. Frequently *hagiasmos* also signifies the object of active sanctification by the Spirit, and thus denotes the condition of holiness as *hagiosyne*."[15]

One may conclude that it would be surprising and uncharacteristic of Paul if he speaks of sanctification in strictly forensic terms in 1 Cor 1:30. Instead we must bear in mind that Paul is setting the tone of the whole letter

---

12. There is no basic difference between sanctification and holiness. The use of *hagiasmos* basically relates to the *"state* (italics added) of being made holy more often than a process." *BAGD*, 8.

13. Cf. Lightfoot, *Notes on Epistles of St. Paul*, 167. So also Fee, 1 *Corinthians*, 86, who notes that, "the fact that he (Paul) uses nouns to describe this event, rather than verbs, is dictated by the fact that they stand in apposition to the noun 'wisdom.'"

14. Cf. Balz, "hagios," 18.

15. Cf. Ridderbos, *Paul: An Outline*, 263.

where the holiness of the community is a significant issue. Therefore the view that Paul's use of *hagiasmos* is forensic cannot be maintained in view of Paul's overall concern for the ethical holiness of the church in Corinth and its application to Christ.

1 Corinthians 3:16–17

In many ways 1 Cor 3:16–17 reveals Paul's foundational understanding of the church. In 1 Corinthians 1–4 Paul asserts that the splintered Corinthian congregation could find a basis of unity in the message of the cross (1:18–25). Next he declares that Jesus Christ is the foundation of the church (3:10–11). When Paul reaches this stage of this argument in response to the problem of cliques, jealousy, and strife (see 1:11; 3:3) among the Corinthians, he cites as one of his primary bases for rejecting such behavior the nature of the Corinthian believers as the temple of God, or more precisely, the sanctuary of God.

It is generally agreed that Paul is referring to the church, rather than the individuals, as the temple of God. The relation between the individual and the church is found throughout Paul's letters. Therefore the application of the temple metaphor to the community of believers does not deny the importance of God's relationship to individual believers, because the integrity of the church is located in the integrity of individual lives. Paul is referring to a living community, rather than an institution or single individual (see 2 Cor 6:16; Eph 2:20–22).

Having reminded the believers that they are the temple (*naos*) of God, he then more explicitly states his thought by the statement that they have the Spirit of God dwelling in them. The one Spirit of God is at the same time indwelling the various members of the Corinthian church, but uniting them functionally.

Having asserted the character of the church, Paul then makes a general affirmation regarding the temple of God and its treatment: If anyone destroys the temple, God will destroy that one because God's temple is holy. The implication of this thought is clear. Because the Corinthian church is this temple of God and its members are thus linked one to another, then in it there cannot be internal divisions without destruction. The gravity of their offense, on the one hand, lies precisely in the fact that in separating into cliques they are destructively dividing this abode of the Spirit of God. On the other hand, such dividing is to sin directly against God, who will destroy the guilty.

When Paul here affirms that the temple is holy, he has attributed to this new spiritual temple of God the attribute that appertained to the Jerusalem temple—and for the same reason. The believers, as the church, are being used by the Spirit of God for his dwelling place. Consequently, divisions in the church actually amount to desecrating the holy temple, the results of which could only be the offenders' destruction.

When Paul concludes this reminder and warning to the Corinthians with the statement "and you are the temple," he is not asserting that some of the believers are holy. He is asserting that they are the temple of God, and one cannot divide that temple without destroying it and becoming liable to one's own personal destruction from God. This is a use of sanctification, which closely approximates to justification, and does not indicate a complete moral condition in the believer. In virtue of their response to the divine call articulated by the ministers of the word, the believers have been separated from the world dominated by sin (Rom 6:22) and have been brought into the grace and fellowship of Jesus Christ (1 Cor 1:9; Gal 1:6). They have entered a community whose existential attitudes sharply distinguish it from its surrounding environment.

1 Corinthians 6:11

It is not difficult to conclude that, for Paul, as evident in his arguments in his letter to the Corinthians, the gospel issues in transformed lives, and salvation in Christ is incomplete without Christlike attitudes and behavior.

In 1 Cor 6:1–11, Paul addresses the issue of lawsuits before pagan judges. Paul is especially aggravated by the fact that, firstly, they have so little understanding of who they are in Christ (1 Cor 6:2–4), and secondly, that this way of acting so thoroughly destroys the witness of the Corinthian community before the world (1 Cor 6:6). The failure of the people involved is primarily a failure of the church to live up to her calling. Crucial to the whole argument is Paul's view of the Christian community as God's eschatological people, a view that Paul argues must determine its lifestyle in the present age.

In seeking to understand this verse, the initial statement, "and such were some of you" is significant, and, therefore, must be carefully noted. In 1 Cor 6:11, Paul has not said that the Corinthians had acted in certain ways or practiced certain behaviors, true though that might have been. Instead, he places the Corinthians in contrast to the "unrighteous" (v. 9) who Paul says shall not inherit the kingdom of heaven. Having enumerated the sins of the "unrighteous," he says, "Such persons [as just enumerated] were some of you." Paul is not viewing the Corinthians as having changed in some forms of behavior, so much as having undergone a fundamental change of being, an understanding of the Corinthians' nature which is consonant with 1 Cor 1:30; 2 Cor 5:17. The demand for a different style of life among the Corinthian congregation must be accompanied by a fresh awareness of its own character as a washed, sanctified, and justified people. The implication of the threefold reminder is clear: a transformed moral life should flow from such a transforming experience.[16]

The basis upon which Paul rests his assertion that "what you were . . . now you are not" is his belief that the members of the church have been transformed by their having been washed, having been sanctified, and having been justified.[17] The threefold use of the strong adversative *alla* ("but") coupled with the three aorist (Ancient Greek) tenses suggest a decisive break with the past life and the creation of a new state of being. The believer has entered upon a new state of existence as he now relates to the Lord Jesus Christ (see 1 Cor 1:2) and the Spirit of God.

The phrases "have been washed" rather than "have been baptized" are striking and, as Paul nowhere else uses the former, suggests that its choice might be to emphasize, not just the act of baptism but the results of the act. As Paul has spoken of Christ as the believer's "righteousness and sanctification" in 1:30, and reversed the order in 6:11, there is most likely no temporal significance to be observed in the relationship of these two terms. Paul's concern here is not to express in an orderly fashion or manner. Also, as rightly stated by Fee, "each of the verbs is thus chosen for contextual, not dogmatic reasons; and their sequence is theologically irrelevant."[18]

It is possible to understand the following clause, "you have been sanctified" either as an amplification of the preceding one, expressing one aspect or effect of the washing spoken of, viz., their holiness; or, as a reference to their relationship with God, that is, their separation and consecration. Taken in the former sense, the two clauses would then be translated, "You have not only been purified, but also set apart as a peculiar people." Though this is possible, it is improbable that this is what Paul intends to express.

Paul's use of the passive voice for expressing "to sanctify" is quite normal and in agreement with Exod 19:10, 14, and 22 where the priests were to sanctify themselves but the people were to be sanctified by Moses.

---

16. Cousar, "Theological Task," 99. See also Watson, *First Corinthians*, 57; Fee, 1 *Corinthians*, 245, sees an inherent imperative: "Therefore, live out this new life in Christ and stop being like the wicked."

17. Here Paul uses three different images for the same experiential reality, conversion to Christ. Cf. Talbert, *Reading Corinthians*, 26.

18. Fee, *1 Corinthians*, 246.

In contrast, Lev 20:7 commands: "Consecrate yourselves therefore, and be holy," in which case the people are themselves to be active agents, whose role is one of obedience to the cultic and ethical commandments.

In 2 Chronicles 29 and 30, priests, Levites, and laity alike are "to sanctify themselves"; that is, make themselves ritually acceptable to worship (29:5, 15, 31, 34; 30:15, 17). Elsewhere the OT and Paul are in agreement that the one being sanctified is at times a passive recipient. In 1 Cor 6:11, Paul's thought runs parallel to Ezek 36:25–29. The Corinthians are the people whom Ezekiel prophesied God would purify by sprinkling and so sanctify once and for all. In being sanctified, the believer was made to participate in that separation from sin and obedient commitment to God, which was characteristic of Christ Jesus. Consequently, it is possible to suggest that to be sanctified involved a relational change.[19] It is to be separated from a former life to experience a new life; as earlier noted, it is to be related to Christ in such a way that he becomes one's salvation—life.

However, such an assertion has enormous ethical overtones. When Paul here affirms that the Corinthians have been sanctified, it is in the context of complete changes having occurred in their lives from an ethical standpoint. Because they have been sanctified, they have changed from a life of idolatry to the worship of Christ; from immorality to a life governed by the principles of Christ and his Spirit.[20] As such, Paul could write:

> Do you not know that wrongdoers will not inherit the kingdom of God? Do not be deceived! Fornicators, idolaters, adulterers, male prostitutes, sodomites, thieves, the greedy, drunkards, revilers, robbers—none of these will inherit the kingdom of God. And this is what some of you used to be. But you were washed, you were sanctified, you were justified in the name of the Lord Jesus Christ and in the Spirit of our God. (1 Cor 6:9–11)

Although Paul affirms that the Corinthians have been justified and are to be contrasted with the unrighteous (*adikoi*) who will not inherit the kingdom of God (vv. 9–10), one is not thereby to assume that the Corinthians are righteous in terms of their own ethical behavior, although he expects them to be.

---

19. Cf., Barrett, *1 Corinthians*, 142; Bruce, *1 and 2 Corinthians*, 62; Morris, *First Epistle of Paul to the Corinthians*, 98; Moffatt, *First Epistle of Paul to the Corinthians*, 66; Héring, *1 Cor*, 42.

20. Cf. Parry, *First Epistle of Paul to the Corinthians*, 99: "It [the new life] is consequently wholly separate and diverse from the old heathen life and demands new principles, practices, and habits." Cf. Hewett, *Use of Hagios*, 202.

Paul's statements "you have been washed" (*apelousasthe*) and "you have been sanctified" (*hēgiasthēte*) express two aspects of the Corinthian believers' new relationship with Christ. He now employs a third aspect to denote, not that the believers are living a life in conformity to any given ethical standards, but that in their new position in Christ by faith, they now participate in his righteousness (see 2 Cor 5:21; 1 Cor 1:30).

1 Corinthians 7:12–14, 16

The meaning of the words "holy" and "sanctify" in 1 Cor 7:14 and 16 remain a subject of discussion, particularly with regards to Paul designating an unbelieving spouse and unbelieving children as holy. In order to analyze 7:14, it is crucial to understand first the importance of the term *syneudokeō*, "approve of" or "consent" used of the unbelieving wife (7:12) and the unbelieving husband (7:13). Although Paul describes both as unbelievers, it is clear that they are also actively consenting in cohabitation with the believing partner. It is their own personal choice to do so, regardless (or perhaps because) of the fact that Paul has made specific ethical and religious demands upon the believers which they are obliged, as Christians, to heed (see e.g., 1 Cor 4:15–17; 5:1–5, 11; 6:7, 9, 13, 15, 18, 20b). Consequently, it should be noted that the attitude of the non-believing spouse, although a non-Christian, is probably not one of antagonism. The spouse appears to have at least tolerated the conversion of the partner.

In the marriage relationship, the participants do not experience the defilement that accompanies an adulterous situation; the temple of God's Spirit is not desecrated. Because the non-believer wishes to maintain the marriage relationship, he (or she) is set apart from the unbelieving community to be a participant in the holy community—as it is embodied in the believing spouse. It is pertinent to note the fact that in this most unusual statement (verse 14) Paul does not explicitly relate the unbeliever to the whole Christian community in Corinth (church) or on a larger scale.[21] Instead, Paul's assertion is that the unbeliever is sanctified with reference to the believing spouse. The primary issue in this passage is the relationship of the unbelieving spouse to the believer. Should the relationship continue or not? It is amiss to suggest that the unbeliever is immediately related to the church of God. Rather the unbeliever is indirectly related to the church of God through the association with the believer who is personally one of the church and a member of Christ.

---

21. Hewett, *Use of Hagios*, 215.

Paul does not discuss the character of the unbeliever or the role that he or she has in this new association with the community of believers. But it is apparent, as already noted, from verse 12, that the unbeliever is consenting to the continuation of the marriage in terms of it being within the sphere of the Christian community. It is also apparent from Paul's question of verse 16 that the unbeliever is not a converted Christian.[22] Hence Paul did not say that the unbeliever became a participant in the believer's being a part of the temple of God's Spirit. God's Spirit indwells only the believer (see 1 Cor 6:19). Nor did Paul say that the unbelieving partner in the marriage became a "member of Christ." Such might logically follow from Paul's statements in 1 Cor 6:15 and 17b, but Paul does not—as noted above—always set forth as his thought what might appear to be logical conclusions to his reader.

Those who are members of Christ in 1 Cor 6:15-20[23] are those who have professed their belief in Christ Jesus and their commitment to him as evidenced by their baptism. The unbelieving spouse is not to be viewed as a recipient of either the blessing of salvation or the blessings that accrue from salvation (e.g., the fruit of the Spirit, as enumerated in Gal 5:22-24). Rather the unbelieving spouse is a recipient of blessings that may accrue from an association—an intimate association—with a believer.

One important question remains to be answered, which is, "Is there then any way in which holiness can be transferred from one person to another?" Or, stated differently, "Is there any way holiness can be contagious?" In this regard, one must note that implicit in Paul's argument in this passage is that people affect one another by their actions and the way they live. This was very much so in Paul's day when the family was conceived as a cohesive unit, contrary to today when our society has a more individualistic attitude. As Best notes,

> our more individualistic attitude derives in part from the Renaissance and in part from the Reformation, the latter with its emphasis on the necessity of personal belief. We thus find it difficult to view holiness as passing from a believing member of a family to the remainder of the family. However it is possible to argue that even in our much more individualized society, we ought to recognize family solidarity.[24]

---

22. In virtually all the authentically Pauline letters, *sōzō* denotes a salvific spiritual act, sometimes with an eschatological consequence. Cf. Porter, "What Does It Mean," 160–75.

23. See discussion below.

24. Best, "1 Corinthians 7:14," 165. Best is certainly correct in his observation. However, it needs be stated that family solidarity must not be pressed too far to minimize individual responsibility and personal belief as Best seems to do.

However, Paul, not unaware of the Old Testament and Jewish concept of corporate solidarity, has, in this passage, presented a two-pronged application of this notion. First, the believer has, in matters of religion, become the dominant factor in the household, so as to relate the spouse to the church. Similarly, the believer is the dominant factor in the household with respect to the children's relationship to the church.[25]

Thus, the children of such a marriage are also considered holy (v. 14b). That is to say, as members of a sanctified family, they also participate in a mediated membership in the church. Here again the idea is that the children of mixed marriages are acceptable within the church and that in both the home and church, they are surrounded with the blessings related to the believer.

Witherington's comments on this verse are worth quoting at length:

> In 1 Cor 7:14, we see a dramatic difference from Old Testament holiness. Far from the unbelieving spouse causing the believer to be impure, just the opposite is the case; sanctifying or cleansing, is what happens to the unbeliever, at least when he or she is in intimate relationship with a believer. Paul is perhaps talking only about the "making clean" of the relationship and the fact that the unbeliever does not defile the believer by marital relationships. So sanctity here does not mean "to save" but has its nonsoteriological sense of "make clean" or "consecrate." Nevertheless this is still a remarkable statement for someone with the background of Paul to make. He sees Christianity as a world–transforming, not merely a world–denying religion. This is most important because it means that Christians do not have to sever relationships with the world to be Christians, to be sanctified and acceptable to God. Indeed as 7:16 implies, Christians have the possibility of positively affecting others in the world, rather than being defiled by them. Paul here urges detachment from worldly attitudes, not withdrawal from the world.[26]

Perhaps the primary relational signification of "sanctify" (*hagiazō*) and "holy" (*hagios*) in 1 Cor 7:14, 16, as suggested earlier, can be further clarified when we consider Paul's earlier condemnation of the believer's sexual relationship with a prostitute in 1 Cor 6:15–20. In that passage Paul attributes the power to unite the participants in one body or one flesh to a man's act of intimately joining himself to a harlot (v. 16ff.). In 6:19, Paul asserts that the

---

25. Cf. Cullmann, *Baptism in the New Testament*, 53: "... The idea of family solidarity in holiness, on the basis of the marriage tie and membership of the Body of Christ, is the fundamental ground of the declaration of 1 Cor 7:14...."

26. Witherington III, *Paul's Narrative Thought World*, 321.

body of the believer, whether viewed as the group that comprises the church or as the individual person, is the temple of the Holy Spirit. It should follow, then, that as a result of the union of the believing partner, whose body is the temple of the Holy Spirit, that the unbelieving partner is now sanctified in the believer and is now a temple of the Holy Spirit. However, in the case of the believer and the prostitute, it must be noted that the relationship is that of defilement, rather than consecration, because of its temporary, immoral character. The believer is putting himself in the sphere of the immoral because the very choice itself is corrupting rather than sanctifying. Therefore, Paul says that the believer is corrupting the temple of God's Holy Spirit (see Ezek 44:7–9), rather than bringing someone into the church. Paul's argument in this passage is well summed up by Hays:

> The man who has sexual intercourse with a prostitute is not only committing infidelity to Christ but also taking something that belongs to Christ (his own body) and linking it to the sphere of the unholy. . . . The union of a member of the church with a prostitute is disastrous for the Christian community precisely because it creates a bonding with her; therefore it creates an unholy bond between the Lord's members and the sinful world. The result is both defilement and confusion.[27]

1 Corinthians 7:34

The context of verse 34 is crucial to understanding Paul's use of the word "holy." Due to little time, Paul wanted to minimize the diversions and concerns of life. The goal was "undistracted devotion to the Lord" (7:35). Paul suggests that the married remain married and the single remain single, not because of an intrinsic value in either relationship, but because of "the present necessity" (7:26) and because "the appointed time has been shortened" (7:29). The backdrop of Paul's thought here was a passing away world (7:29–31).

Throughout this letter Paul tries to instill into the Corinthian Christians what it means to live in an eschatological age. Although the nearness of the end may not be the sole driving force behind Paul's exhortation, it is difficult to conclude, as Witherington suggests, that it is "only a possibility" in Paul's mind.[28] However, he is right to note that, "Paul believes Christians

---

27. Hays, *First Corinthians*, 104–5.
28. Witherington III, *Community and Conflict in Corinth*, 179.

are already living in that age begun by Christ's death and resurrection, and so are living on borrowed time."[29]

The unmarried woman . . . the married woman. Despite some ambiguity in the text as to whether or not Paul, in referring to "the unmarried woman" and "the virgin," means the same group or two different sets of people, it is clear that he is contrasting women with different responsibilities in life. Some women are married and consequently are concerned that they please their husbands. Other women are not married and so have no responsibilities to a husband. Consequently, their concern in life may be exclusively "with things of the Lord, in order . . . that . . . they may be holy both in body and in spirit."[30]

As used here, the word "holy" can basically have one of two significances: It may denote simply a relationship of having been separated unto God as one of the *hoi hagioi* ("holy ones"), or, it may denote ethical purity.[31] In determining its use here, one must give proper weight to what Paul says has happened for the benefit of all believers at their conversion experience.

As noted previously, Paul explicitly affirms that Christ became the believer's sanctification (1 Cor 1:30) and those who are baptized into Christ are therein sanctified (1 Cor 6:11). Paul affirms that the body of the believer belongs to the Lord (1 Cor 6:13); that he who joins himself to the Lord is one spirit with the Lord (1 Cor 6:17). It is not, therefore, the case that a believer—whether married or single, with a family or without—must be concerned about being consecrated (i.e., to belong) to the Lord. In conversion that becomes an accomplished fact.

Also, it cannot be said that in conversion the believer comes to belong to the Lord only "in spirit" or "in body" and that Paul is here emphasizing—through "body and spirit"—the necessity for a more complete relational separation to God. The argument of 1 Cor 6:12–20 rests upon the assumption that the believer has already been joined—body and spirit—to the Lord (see Rom 6:22; 7:4, 6; 8:9; Gal 3:26). Hence the person whose concern is with "the things of the Lord, that she might be holy," is not concerned with establishing a relationship with the Lord. That exists.[32] It follows then that, rather than a term strictly denoting relationship with God, Paul is here using *hagia* as a term denoting ethical holiness[33]—holiness that is both demanded and results from a previously established and continued relationship with God.

29. Ibid.
30. Hewett, *Use of Hagios*, 226–27.
31. Ibid., 230.
32. Ibid., 231.
33. Although Paul says the unmarried one is concerned about how to be ethically

This is similar to what we find in the OT. There it was repeatedly affirmed that Israel was exclusively the people of Yahweh and not that of any other god.[34] The responsibility consequently fell upon Israel to heed the commandments of Yahweh, and, by fulfilling his commands, be a people who are not only holy in the sense of ethical purity, but also in not belonging to other gods (see Exod 19:6; 22:31; Deut 26:16; 28:9; Lev 19:2; 20:7, 26). The Pentateuchal writers were convinced that the privilege of being Yahweh's holy people brought with it the responsibility of obedience to his commands, and that obedience would make the people ethically holy (i.e., reflectors of the nature of their holy God). Among the prophets, Ezekiel expresses this idea when he delivers the word of Yahweh that promises the vindication of Yahweh's holiness before the nations by means of the creation of a remnant of Israel that will be cleansed from all sin, given a new heart, and caused to walk in Yahweh's statutes and observe his ordinances (Ezek 36:23–28).

Paul, in the same manner as the Pentateuchal writers and the prophets, believed that the church of God had the responsibility as his holy people (i.e., as those who belong to God) to mirror his holiness (i.e., his ethical purity) in their daily lives. In 1 Cor 7:34, Paul's use of body and spirit indicates the extent to which the believer is to be characterized as holy: she is to be holy in her entire being, her whole personality. The willing, thinking, doing self is to be included in these two terms.[35] The whole person who has been sanctified (i.e., related to God) through her commitment to Christ Jesus must now become ethically pure—it follows on the basis of the above OT pattern—through her adherence to "the things of the Lord."

Because chapters 5 through 7 are all oriented around the issue of ethical purity, one may suggest that to be anxious about the things of the Lord would entail a concern on the part of the believer to adhere to the ethical imperatives of the Lord, and, in turn, live an ethically pure life. Immorality, which Paul so strongly denounced in these chapters, is but one form that ethical impurity might take. Other forms are listed in 6:9f. Thus, it is clear that the whole life of the believer—whether married or single—is to

---

pure, whereas the married one is concerned about how to please the spouse, one is not to assume that the unmarried person has or is capable of a greater ethical purity than the married person. To the contrary, as noted earlier, Paul's concern is to spare the believers from undue anxieties (cf. verses 28b, 32a). He acknowledges that if one marries ". . . it is no sin" (verses 9, 28a, 36). But Paul was sufficiently aware of the realities of married life to know that the marriage relationship places legitimate demands upon the marriage partners so that they each have *less* time to commit to "the things of the Lord" than their unmarried fellow Christians have.

34. Cf. Exod 19:5; 23:30; Deut 6:7; 14:2; Lev 20:24, 26b.
35. Cf. Best, *One Body*, 76.

be characterized by purity and truth (see 5:8). Only by leading such a life will the believers glorify God in their bodies (see 6:20) and be properly concerned with the things of the Lord, in order that they may be ethically holy.[36]

OTHER HOLINESS-RELATED PASSAGES

In several passages in 1 Corinthians, Paul deals with what he perceives as threats to holiness among the Corinthians. Although Paul never attempts to give an exhaustive account of the material content of the Christian obligation, he does have certain recurrent motifs that are emblematic of Christian conduct and of what they are to avoid. He is content to indicate the sort of conduct the Christian ought to pursue or avoid, in view of the fact that they form the new covenant people of God.

1 Corinthians 5:1–13

In 1 Corinthians 5, Paul expresses his consternation at the unabashed tolerance by the Corinthian community of the sexual sin in its midst. It is significant to note that Paul holds not just the offender accountable but the whole community who were seemingly complacent over the sin and treated it with levity. To leave the situation as it was only left the entire body contaminated or "leavened" (1 Cor 5:7, 8). The thought of guilt by association may not be ruled out here. Paul had no difficulty in applying to the community in Corinth a provision of the Law intended to assure the sanctity of the Old Testament people of God: "You shall purge the evil from your midst" (see Deut 17:7; 1 Cor 5:13). This too shows the sharp contrast of church and world. Hence, he advises them to take appropriate steps, as he was about to suggest, to solve the problem.

This particular sin, Paul says, is not found "even among the Gentiles" (5:1). The offender should be excommunicated, Paul would urge, in line with an injunction that comes from the Holiness Code. Leviticus commands that those who commit sins discussed in chapter 18 be "cut off from their people" (18:29) and that the man who lies with his father's wife be put to death (20:11). Paul approximates this penalty when he advises the Corinthians "to hand such a man over to Satan for the destruction of his flesh in order that his spirit should be saved in the day of the Lord" (1 Cor 5:5). Although Paul is calling for the man's excommunication rather than his execution, the phrase "destruction of his flesh" is probably based on the

---

36. Hewett, *The Use of Hagios*, 233.

biblical injunction that the offender be executed. In addition, Paul instructs the Corinthians to "expel the evil one from among you" (5:13).[37]

Why does Paul urge such a ruthless punishment? Because, he says in 5:6–8, the Corinthians must scrupulously maintain the character of holy people.[38] The language he uses to illustrate this holiness comes directly from the Mosaic law.[39] Paul's use of the leaven as a symbol of evil was common in both Jewish and Greco-Roman circles. The lesson that Paul teaches (that God's people should be holy) and the basis for his metaphor (Exod 12:18–20; Num 28:16–17; Deut 16:3–4) show the large extent to which he was working within the pattern established by the Mosaic law. Just as a little leaven works its way through an entire lump of dough,[40] therefore all leaven must be purged from the home at Passover, so the Corinthians are to purge themselves from the evil within (5:6–8). As Shedd notes, "this metaphor in itself portrays more than any other Paul's conception of the solidarity of the Church. The sin of one member (in this case the incestuous man) implicates the whole community." Thus, Paul suggests that the entire community is susceptible to contamination.

Paul then goes on to draw an extremely sharp dividing line between church and society, a line that has no blurred borders (1 Cor 5:9). He makes this distinction as a matter of principle on the basis of the new reality that has begun in the midst of the world with Christ and the church. In this sense he is even prepared to distinguish between those "inside" (1 Cor 5:12) and those "outside" (1 Cor 5:12–13; 1 Thess 4:12). Paul is concerned with drawing social boundaries of the community with heavy strokes, separating insiders from outsiders. As noted by Mitchell, such distinction is not without parallel in the ancient world.[41]

In 1 Cor 5:6–7, Paul uses *ekkatharate*, to "cleanse out or away," which is related to the verb *katharizein*. The Corinthian church had harbored an incestuous man within the fellowship (1 Cor 5) and by so doing had defiled the temple of God (1 Cor 3:17). The failure to assume the responsibility of rebuking sin was a leaven that had to be removed in order that the witness

---

37. Cf. Deut 17:7; 19:19; 22:21; 24:7.

38. Thielman, *Paul and the Law*, 90.

39. For the cultural environment from which Paul's language emerges see Windisch, "ζύμη," in *TDNT*, 2:902–6, and Fee, 1 *Corinthians*, 215–16. Patrick, "Rhetoric," 434: "While the Law seeks to limit accountability, a community also rather naturally recognizes a collective dimension to violations of public order. Deuteronomy raises this inchoate awareness to the Level of theory. The recurring motive clause "you shall purge the evil from your midst" is the key to Deuteronomic thought."

40. Shedd, *Man in Community*, 177.

41. Mitchell, *Rhetoric of Reconciliation*, 228.

to Christ be unsullied. The Corinthians were then forcefully urged to "purge out," or "clean away" from among them the leaven of malice and wickedness (or a bad attitude and evil disposition of mind), so that the Lord's Supper could be eaten in sincerity and truth. The exhortation certainly has to do with the sinner himself, but it would miss the whole import of the passage to let this personal matter exhaust the meaning, or to eclipse the real matter in this passage.

Paul is charging the church itself with insubordination. *Ekkatharate*, "to cleanse out or away," means much more, here, than to punish the erring man. It is rather to purify the very heart of the church from evil irresponsibility to a mature and sanctified and responsible attitude toward truth itself. The significance of this word as it is used in this passage is directed toward a personal, moral rectitude where personal responsibility is assumed and the awareness of it sharpened. In these two cases, the active participation of the people in the church must be recognized as of vital importance. The cultic sense is seen in Rom 14:20, where Paul asserts the basic cleanness of all created things. There, Paul says that "all things are pure," or "everything is indeed clean" (*katharos*), but may become an occasion for sin when a brother or sister whose intentions are selfish uses them in a way to cause others to stumble.

Immoral behavior is not only dangerous to the individual perpetrator, but even more importantly, endangers the whole society, both in itself and in its effects it has on the harmony of that body (see 3:17). The community's relationship with God is endangered by the evil and must be restored to health by rooting out the offender.[42] Barrett aptly comments: "one corrupt member is sufficient to corrupt a whole church."[43]

In summary, it may be concluded that Paul's primary concern in this passage is the purity of the church, the body of Christ, and his anxieties center on the incestuous man as a potentially polluting agent within Christ's body; an agent whose presence threatens to pollute the *entire body*. Paul's main concern is with the health of Christ's body; the man's individual fate is secondary, at best.[44]

Paul simultaneously confronts a specific instance of immorality in the Corinthian community and defines the nature of the community itself.[45] This not only shows how the basic lines of the Old Testament continue in

---

42. Cf. Zaas, "Cast Out the Evil" 1 Cor 5:13b, 259–61.

43. Barrett, *First Corinthians*, 27.

44. Cf. Campbell, "Flesh and Spirit in 1 Cor 5:5," 331–42. Campbell perhaps goes too far by insisting that Paul is *only* concerned with the church's "flesh" and "spirit."

45. Zaas, "Cast Out," 261.

the New, but also makes definitively clear that the concept of communal holiness or sanctification of the community is the central concept with which the Bible formulates in its own language its conception of the people of God as a distinct community in the world.[46] Hence it is clear that in 1 Cor 5:1–13, Paul's concern is the need to deal with the sinner in order to safeguard the standing of the community before God.[47]

1 Corinthians 6:1–11

Something of the same dynamic is at work in chapter 6. Although the connections between the various sections of the two chapters may not be immediately obvious, what underlies and connects all the issues addressed in both chapters is Paul's concern about the boundaries of the body. In 6:1–11, Paul chides the Corinthian Christians for bringing their private legal disputes before pagan judges. Paul's desire is to develop and maintain purity in the church, and the failure to maintain even the appearance of unity, mutual respect, and care, appear to scandalize Paul when he hears that one member of the Church is suing another in the civil court of a pagan city. There were probably several aspects that caused him concern, not least the lack of faith in each other's integrity, which led them to take the dispute outside the fellowship and entrust it to the "pagan law courts."[48] Paul's concern is not just the embarrassment caused by the display of dirty linen in public, nor the corruption endemic in Corinthian civil courts. Rather, it is the fact that the Corinthian judges were "unbelievers" and representatives of the "world," which makes them inappropriate adjudicators of the affairs of believers.[49] For Paul, it is "absurd for Christians to submit to the judgment of the *unrighteous* and *unbelievers* whom they will soon themselves judge along with the rest of the 'world' (6:1–3)."[50] Conflicts of this sort affect the whole community; they must therefore be settled within the community itself. As noted by Cousar, "the congregation's root problem lies in its lack of

---

46. Cf. Rosner, "Function of Scripture," 515: "Furthermore, Paul's notion of corporate responsibility of the Christians whom he addresses with the plural pronoun throughout, and calls upon to mourn over the sin of the erring man as it were their own, is again reflected in the teaching associated with the expulsion formula in Deuteronomy."
47. Ibid.
48. Reid, "Paul: A Pattern," 65–80.
49. Winter, "Civil Litigation," 559–72.
50. Barclay, "Thessalonica and Corinth," 59.

theological depth. It shames itself by not understanding itself as an eschatological community."[51] Thielman rightly suggests that:

> Paul is appalled at this behavior for two reasons. First, it compromises the holiness of the community because it asks those outside God's people to adjudicate the very ethical conduct that constitutes the boundary between God's people and those outside (vv. 1–8). Second, Paul also condemns the kinds of behavior that produced the civil suits in the first place as incompatible with the status of God's restored people.... They are the people whom Ezekiel prophesied God would purify by sprinkling and so sanctify once and for all (Ezek 36:25–29), and Paul echoes Ezekiel's vision of the restored people of God as he registers his dismay at their behavior.[52]

Paul's language echoes Deut 1:15–16, where Moses describes the system of adjudication that he set up within Israel. For Paul, the Corinthian community has violated the character of the people of God as it is described in the Mosaic law by taking its cases before unbelieving magistrates. For Paul, the Corinthian community was supposed to be an alternative society. This is the reason why Paul highlights the distinction between those within and outside the community by calling the members "holy ones" as opposed to "the unrighteous" (6:1), "the world" (6:2), and "those who have no standing in the community" (6:4). Holiness involves separation or distinctiveness.

1 Corinthians 6:12–20

First Corinthians 6:12–20 addresses a case of fornication (*porneia*) in the Corinthian church. The Corinthians have failed to exercise sexual purity (6:12–21), once again thinking that their freedom in Christ meant a license to sin (6:12). But since they had been bought at great cost and since their bodies were the temple of the Holy Spirit, they ought not to go beyond the bounds of true grace.

This issue of license with the flesh probably also grew out of their pagan background, and, in part, Greek philosophy (for both Stoicism and Hedonism divorced the soul from the body).[53] Thus, if there is any unity in the issues raised by Chloe's people, it is found in misunderstandings of

---

51. Cf. Cousar, *Theological Task*, 98.
52. Thielman, *Paul and the Law*, 90.
53. There are a number of remarkable parallels in thought between the Stoics and the NT, although the NT writers did not share the Stoic view of the ascetic life. In Paul's Corinthian correspondence, he sounds very much like a Stoic philosopher.

the Christian life due to pagan philosophy, focusing on the twin themes of wisdom and license. In his argument, he insists that sex is not immaterial to the life of freedom in the kingdom of God. On the contrary, Paul insists, freedom is shown in doing what is advantageous to others (12a), what demonstrates the resurrection power in the life of the individual (6:14), what expresses being part of Christ's body (6:15), and what shows the believer's new identity as a "temple of the Holy Spirit."

Note how Paul conceives of freedom in this passage. In his argument here, he reinterprets the freedom of the individual by setting it firmly in the wider context of significance and obligation—"in the context of a solidarity whose members are not just earthly but heavenly as well."[54] The union of the believer with a prostitute is wrong and disorderly because it violates and contradicts the most important union of all: with the Lord and the Lord's people.[55] Dale B. Martin rightly comments that Paul is worried about the integrity of the body—the individual Christian's body and the body of Christ which will be compromised by the breach in the wall occasioned by dangerous sexual intercourse.[56]

As Kenneth Bailey has pointed out, and as we have argued above, there is a strong corporate dimension to the problem.[57] He notes the shift from the word "bodies" in v. 12 to the singular "body" in v. 20 preceded by possessive pronoun "your" which is plural. He writes, "the shift is unmistakable. Paul is not merely interested in the personal/bodily health of the individual but of the whole body of Christ . . . he is very anxious about what libertinism is doing to the health of the corporate body of Christ."[58] As Hays rightly observes, Paul's exhortation to the Corinthians to "glorify God in your body" (1 Cor 6:20) grows out of his passionate concern, expressed repeatedly in 1 Corinthians for the sanctification of the whole community as a whole.[59]

1 Corinthians 8–10

Much has been written on the Corinthian participation in idol feasts (1 Cor 8–10), the details of which do not need to detain us here. However, beyond question, the nature of Paul's remarks in these chapters indicate his

54. Barton, "Christian Community," 9.
55. Cf. Hauerwas, "What Could It Mean?" 1–21. See especially page 9.
56. Martin, *The Corinthian Body*, 212.
57. Bailey, "Paul's Theological Foundation," 34–35; see also Kempthorne, "Incest and the Body of Christ," 568–74.
58. Bailey, "1 Cor 6:9-20," 35–36.
59. Hays, *Moral Vision*, 391.

sensitivity to the strong individualistic claims made by those who eat but who disregard any consequences that such eating might have on the weaker members. In Paul's eyes, a certain individualism describes those who claim knowledge and would eat; they are basically concerned with themselves, their rights, and individual freedom—no holiness, no group concerns, no regulation of freedom colors their thinking. Paul understands these arguments, but they do not represent his viewpoint at all (8:7–13). For Paul, Christian freedom is not achieved in unbounded self-presentation and self-realization, but rather it is by nature a relational concept: it gains its true shape only in relationship to fellow Christians and to the Christian community.[60] Hence, freedom cannot be understood as an attribute of an autonomous subject; rather, it finds its limitation in the conscience of another.

When one considers 1 Cor 8–10, one fact seems certain: the whole of Paul's argument is predicated on the distinct nature of the Christian community in Corinth as "a holy people of God," whose lives stand in contrast to the society in which they lived.[61] At issue, therefore, is the nature of the community—who they are, and the consequent responsibility of living up to what they are called. Here he assumes that they stand in continuity with ancient Israel. Israel's ancestors are the Corinthians' ancestors, Israel's history their history (10:1). Because of this, Paul says, the Corinthians should not participate in meals eaten in pagan temples as part of the worship of pagan gods. Instead, they should learn from the experience of their ancestors that neither baptism nor nourishment from spiritual food will exempt God's people from judgment if they sin (10:2–10). Just like the Israelites, the Corinthians were holy inasmuch as they have been called and chosen by God. However, this was not enough. They were not only to be distinct from the community in which they lived, but must show in an ethical manner, both individually and collectively, the proof of their calling and chosenness.

Two important facts emerge from that observation. The first is the communal nature of meals. Even in the matter of meals, selfishness must be rejected. The second and more important is the symbolic nature of meals. It is a sharing of life and fellowship. Therefore, one may readily understand the issue of meals offered unto idols. To participate in such is to share life with such idols, and this is unacceptable to Paul.

It is important to note that one of the fundamental problems in that passage is the selfish attitude of the Corinthians who savored their freedom above the wellbeing of others. Paul's overall concern is not only

---

60. Schnelle, *Human Condition*, 85.

61. Cf. Fee, "Toward a Theology," 55: "God's eschatological salvation is creating a new people, who collectively must live the life of the future in the present age, as they await the consummation."

fundamental but also obvious. There is a distinctly corporate dimension to his thought. This dimension shows up when Paul shows that any act that harms an individual Christian is really an affront to Christ himself (8:12), and especially when he argues that although an act performed in isolation may be insignificant and harmless, as a social act it can become intensely meaningful (10:16–30).[62] Thus Paul argues that ethical responses to the problem of idol-food were not only to be done within a creedal but also a relational framework. They must not be determined solely on the grounds of any perceived effects or non-effects on the individual Christian himself/herself.[63] As Meeks rightly points out, the emphasis in Paul's counsel in 1 Corinthians 10 is not just about the maintenance of boundaries. Rather, Paul's stress is "upon the solidarity of the Christian community: the responsibility of members for one another, especially the strong for the weak, and the undiluted loyalty of all to the one God and one Lord."[64] Horrell also concurs that fundamental to Pauline ethics, at least in 1 Corinthians 8–10, is a Christologically patterned orientation to others. He concludes,

> Ethics is not about the actions and decisions that an individual justifies on the basis of theological principles, but is about the common good, about building up the Christian community.... Each member of the community is a brother or sister for whom Christ died; each is a member of the body of Christ, and to cause anyone to stumble is therefore to sin against Christ.... It is these concerns that should determine one's actions.[65]

COMMUNITY-ORIENTED HOLINESS

In consonance with the suggestion at the beginning of this study, an examination of various passages in 1 Corinthians reveals that Paul's view of holiness is multifaceted, that is, a complex whole that is made up of several aspects. This observation is due to the multivalent use of the *hagios* word group. Paul does not only use the *hagios* word group in a relational sense; he also uses it with an ethical significance.[66] The noun *hagiasmos* occurs in 1:30

---

62. Fisk, "Eating Meat Offered to Idols," 70.
63. Winter, "Theological and Ethical Responses," 223.
64. Meeks, "And Rose Up to Play," 78.
65. Horell, "Theological Principle" 105.
66. Hewett, *Use of Hagios*, 224 n.3, "A logical inference from Paul's argument is that the believers as the temple of God's Spirit are in fact holy; holy in the sense often encountered in the OT of being related to God and in whom God's presence resides. This inference, however, says nothing relative to their ethical character, although one may

and the verbal adjective *hagios* is found in 7:34. In practical terms, holiness involves separation from defilement and evil associations. Also, holiness, although personal, is community-oriented.

Paul explains this in his reference to the Corinthians being the temple of the Lord, the dwelling place of the Holy Spirit. As stated above, this emphasizes that the integrity of the whole is dependent upon the integrity of each individual member.

In passages such as 1:2, 1:30, and 3:16, it is apparent that Paul concludes both the relational aspect of holiness, as can be seen in the Old Testament understanding of the holiness of Israel, and the ethical imperative of a holy life.

Again, it must surely be understood that Paul's concept of holiness cannot be reduced to some form of morality, although it does involve morality. Reduction of holiness to mere morality causes holiness to lose its grace.

---

infer a great deal from the OT analogue."

Chapter 4

Holiness in 2 Corinthians

SCHOLARS GENERALLY AGREE THAT Paul's letters are, for the most part, contingent pastoral responses to specific historical situations. His letters often "reflect the interaction, and sometimes the collision, of somewhat diverse backgrounds which met in the newly formed congregations to which the letters were sent."[1] Paul's teaching on holiness in 2 Corinthians is intricately connected with both its rhetorical and historical situations. It is clear from the tenor of the letter that one of the most urgent and important needs is that of the holiness of the congregation, in terms of what it means to be and live as people of God in a pluralistic society.

This chapter explores Paul's concept of holiness by focusing on how the Corinthians wrestled with living among people whose moral values, religious convictions, and principles were opposed to theirs. At the time Paul wrote to the Corinthians, Corinth, although a Roman colony, maintained many ties with Greek religion, philosophy, and the arts. Consequently, the faith of the Corinthians was considerably influenced by a Hellenistic worldview and attitude toward moral behavior. They were the Christian community in Corinth, but it seems that in a number of things, their attitude was more determined by being Corinthians than by their Christian faith.[2] As Gorman puts it, "the Corinthian community was Paul's problem child."[3]

---

1. Cf. Keck, *Paul and His Letters*, 14.
2. Ibid.
3. Gorman, *Apostle of the Crucified Lord*, 227.

As several studies on the history of Corinth have shown, religion was as diverse as Corinth's population. As such, a serious problem in Corinth that both the Jews and the Corinthian Christians of the first century faced were those of religious pluralism and the imperial cult.[4] Winter, noting the extent of the religious pluralism that existed during the first century, concluded that it (religious pluralism) "was woven into the fabric of everyday life."[5] Obviously, such religious pluralism presented difficult challenges to the Corinthian believers. Moreover, in Corinth, as in any cosmopolitan city then and now, vice and religion prospered side by side. One serious challenge the fledgling Christian communities faced was whether to compromise, or capitulate. Therefore, Paul wanted the Corinthians to be a good witness to the society in which they lived, but at the same time was intent on protecting the believing community from slipping into familiar pagan ways or compromising faith. This meant being morally exemplary citizens, and attacking any immorality that might compromise the witness to the city as well as disrupt the harmony of the community.

Paul's goal was to persuade the Corinthians to embody the gospel of Jesus Christ which he had preached to them.[6] Paul, therefore, employs metaphors that both depict and define the character of the Corinthians as the people of God, pointedly describing the manner of living that is required.

PAUL'S DESIGNATION OF THE EKKLESIA IN 2 CORINTHIANS

Crucial to the understanding of holiness in 2 Corinthians is Paul's attempt to establish the identity of the members of the community. Because Paul's view of the believing community in 2 Corinthians is a controlling factor in his teachings on holiness, as elsewhere in his writings, it is appropriate both to identify and to examine some of Paul's designations of the believing community in 2 Corinthians.

Holy Ones

Paul begins his second letter to the Corinthians by his customary identification of his recipients (Rom 1:1; 1 Cor 1:1; 2 Cor 1:1, 2; Gal 1:1). In 2 Cor

---

4. Winter, "Responses to Religious Pluralism," 207–26; Winter, "Achean Federal Imperial Cult," 169–178.

5. Winter, "Responses to Imperial Cult," 207.

6. Gorman, *Apostle of the Crucified Lord*, 227.

1:1–2, Paul describes the recipients as the church of God in Corinth and the *hoi hagioi* ("holy ones") in Achaia. For Paul, *hoi hagioi* include all believers in Christ who, as *eklektoi tou theou* ("God's chosen ones," see Col 3:12), do not only belong to God but are also set apart by God for his service. They are therefore to be sanctified both in the sense of separation, and living in a manner that is in agreement with their calling (see Exod 19:5–6; Lev 11:44–45).

Some important observations emerge from Paul's designation of the Corinthians as "holy ones." First, Paul uses the word *hagioi* in a relational sense. Used with a relational nuance, to be holy means to belong to God as a result of a covenant relationship that is made possible through the Christ-event. The holiness of God's people is based on their relation with him. The Corinthian Christians, in the same manner as Old Testament Israel, have been brought into a special and new relationship with God "in Christ Jesus." The Corinthian Christians, like Israel, were holy because of God's gracious choice. By virtue of this special relationship to God, they were separated from the profane world around them. Their lives, however, seemed to suggest otherwise.

Second, in its ethical sense, Paul uses *hagiazein* ("to make holy") as something required of those who belong to God, thus showing that relationship to God, instead of excusing, actually demands a moral and ethical response. A holy life is one to be lived out in the marketplace, testifying to the relationship that is present between the Holy God and those who claim to belong to him. God's people must live like God.

Third, it is to be noted that Paul always uses the word in plural. He never uses the word to describe individuals. In other words, Paul's thinking on holiness is primarily communal, although each person who belongs to Jesus Christ belongs to him personally. There is nothing individualistic about this relationship. As such, it is the church, collectively, that is called unto holy living, the individual only being important as a constituent member of the community.

Fourth, the word *hagioi* in 2 Cor 1:1 stands in apposition to *ekklēsia*. To be a "member of the church" then would be equivalent to "being a holy one," in which case it might be appropriate to translate both simply as the "people of God."

The People of God

Paul's explicit designation of the Corinthians as the "people of God" in 2 Cor 6:16 dovetails his previous designation as "holy ones" with the "church of God." In the Old Testament the "people of God" is always understood as a distinct community, living as a counterculture to the surrounding nations. "People of God" is the Israel that knows itself to be chosen and called by God in its entire existence—which includes all of its social dimension.

Primary to being the people of God in the OT is that they are possessed by God. In Exod 19:3–8, Israel is summoned to a special, covenant relationship with God described by three phrases: a special possession among all peoples, a kingdom of priests, and a holy nation. Israel is to be God's own people, set apart from other nations for his own service just as priests were set apart from other men and marked by a quality of life commensurate with the holiness of their covenant God.[7] As Christopher Wright observes, "God chose Israel not at the expense of the rest, but for the sake of the rest."[8]

It is important to note that Paul transfers the concept of chosenness to the Corinthian congregation. As "people of God," the Corinthians, like the Israelites, have been brought into a covenant relationship with God. They are not merely to receive his goodness, but, just as importantly, they are to live under his rule and so be a testimony to the presence and character of God among all the nations. The question that remains is, "How are the Corinthians, as the people of God, to explicate his holiness?"

A Chaste Virgin and Bride

In addition to *hagios* ("holy") and its derivatives, *hagnos* ("pure," "chaste") and *hagnotēs* ("purity") also occur in Paul, in the sense of holy and holiness. This terminology plays a much smaller part, however, in harmony with the usage of the LXX. Balz takes note that the "relative rare appearance of the *hagnos* ("pure") word group is probably to be explained by the shift in meaning that occurred in Hellenistic language as well as Judaism, from cultic to figurative use."[9] Such a shift, he argues, made it increasingly easy to substitute other words for this group.

Although the original background of the word "pure" (*hagnos*) in many respects coincides with that of "holy" (*hagios*),[10] in Paul it simply has the significance of morally clean, pure, innocent, and chaste. The root word for "pure," "chaste" (*hagnos*) is found four times. In Phil 4:8, Paul exhorts the reader to be selective in his or her choice of thinking. Stability of character

---

7. Childs, *Book of Exodus*, 367.
8. Wright, *People of God*, 110.
9. Balz, "ἁγνός," 22.
10. Ibid.

demands a disciplined thought life. Among the other things worthy of entertainment such as the true, the just, the lovely, and the virtuous, stands "the pure," which is to be a consciously permitted and voluntarily chosen object of thought that conforms to the norm of holiness. In a famous "charge" to him, Paul's counseled Timothy to "Keep yourself pure" (1 Tim 5:22). This is obviously an exhortation to a morally disciplined life and indicates the need for a continuing maintenance of one's integrity.

The two occurrences of the word in the Corinthian correspondence are found in 2 Cor 6:6 and 2 Cor 11:2. The first instance occurs within the context of Paul's defense of his ministerial conduct. Meeks has rightly observed that it is characteristic of Paul's mode of moral argument that even as he is asserting those qualities in himself in a defensive stance, he at the same time presents them as qualities to be imitated in the community he addresses.[11] In these verses, Paul was defending the character of his ministry from the viewpoint of his conduct and experiences as an ambassador of Christ (2 Cor 5:20–21). In 2 Cor 6:6, Paul speaks of the moral character that has characterized his ministry. He continues his appeal, explaining that there is unacceptable behavior in social life which must be shunned and other features which must be praised.[12] The latter is what Paul expounds upon next.

His ministry has been characterized by sincere love and purity, and this should characterize his converts as well.[13] Apart from the hardships that Paul has constantly experienced in his ministry to the Corinthians (vv. 4–5), purity, candor, and honesty attest to his integrity and foster reconciliation between Paul and his Corinthian converts. Paul has acted *en hagnotēti*, probably to be understood as in 2 Cor 11:2, "in purity," without deception. This verse may be in anticipation of 2 Cor 6:14–7:1. If so, Witherington has suggested, we should translate the phrase in v. 6c as in "a holy spirit," which prepares for Paul's insistence in vv. 14ff. on his audience's holiness.

In 2 Cor 11:2, Paul uses the imagery of betrothal that is in conformity with Jewish customs in his appeal to the Corinthians. The goal of Paul's ministry was to present them as a pure or chaste virgin (*parthenon hagnēn*) to Christ. Paul expresses his fear that his desire for the chastity of

11. Meeks, *Origins of Christian Morality*, 160.

12. Schnabel, "How Paul Developed His Ethics," 274.

13. Witherington, *Conflict and Community*, 400. Although this is possible, it is certainly not necessary to translate it as such in order to link it with 2 Cor 6:14–7:1. Translating the phrase as "Holy Spirit" does not diminish the link with 2 Cor 6:14–7:1. As rightly observed by Bruce, *1 & 2 Cor*, 212: The mention of the Holy Spirit in a list of virtues is striking: it is by the Spirit that these virtues are fostered, and they are the evidence of his indwelling presence." This certainly agrees with the notion of the temple in 2 Cor 6:14–7:1. The mention of the temple in that passage suggests the indwelling of the Spirit.

the Corinthians may not be realized if the Corinthians are sidetracked by Paul's opponents (the super apostles) and they veer away *from the simplicity and purity that is in Christ*. To have their minds corrupted is tantamount to a relapse into the situation prior to redemption and liberation achieved through Christ.

As we recall, in the OT, Israel is frequently depicted as betrothed to Yahweh. Paul now thinks of the Christian community, specifically the Corinthian congregation, as the pure bride of Christ, Christ as the bridegroom, and of himself as one who is to present the bride to her husband. Paul uses the marriage relationship—the complete separation of a man and a woman from all others only to each other—as a picture of the relationship that is supposed to exist between God and his people. In this one picture, we see clearly the separation aspect of holiness emphasized. As the bride is separated from all others to her husband alone, so the people of God are separated from every form of defilement, and given to him.

By accepting the gospel, the Corinthians had committed themselves totally to Christ, but they would be united fully with him only at his Second Coming. In the interval it was Paul's responsibility to ensure that they lived up to their engagement implicit in their baptism. Although betrothed, according to the Jewish law, the violation of a betrothed virgin was no less serious than if the marriage had already been consummated. Neyrey is correct in his observation that the purity language in 2 Cor 11:2 shows once again that Paul seeks to heighten the Corinthians' sense of the proper boundaries of the community, for its purity has been breached by the false apostles.[14] "Paul . . . interprets the presence of rivals on his turf as pollutant which has breached the social and individual bodies' boundaries and threatens a fatal corruption."[15]

In the same way that God was jealous for the undivided loyalty of Israel, so also is Paul with the Corinthians. Given this background, Paul's exhortation to the Corinthians in 2 Cor 11:2 becomes clearer. As people incorporated into Christ, they must live as befits their status. One cannot help but notice the *corporate* notion of purity or holiness here. Plummer succinctly states, "It is the Christian community as a whole, and not any individual, that is the spouse of Christ."[16]

---

14. Neyrey, "Witchcraft Accusations," 10–170.

15. Ibid., 166.

16. Plummer, *Second Epistle to the Corinthians*, 296.

God's Temple

In 2 Cor 6:16b, Paul affirms the community as being the temple of God (16b) as well as introduces the quotation that follows on the presence of the living God. Paul uses two terms for "temple" in the correspondence, *naos* (1 Cor 3:16, 17; 6:19; 2 Cor 6:16) and *hieron* (1 Cor 9:13). *Naos* most often refers to the believing community, whereas *hieron* refers to the Jerusalem temple. Paul's selection of terms is significant since the LXX *naos* is the term of choice for the most holy parts of the temple, including the Holy of Holies, the dwelling place of God's presence. *Hieron*, on the other hand, refers most often to the entire temple complex. Paul's reference to the dwelling of God's Spirit "among" the Corinthians (*en hymin*) is a clear echo of Ezekiel's promise that in the time of restoration, God will put his Spirit "among" (*en hymin*) his people (Ezek 36:26; compare 11:19; 39:29 LXX).

Like Ezekiel, Paul moves easily from the notion of the restored people of God to the idea that the position of God's presence among his people is the temple.[17] It is no surprise then, that in 1 Cor 3:16–17, Paul warns the Corinthians against destroying God's temple. In 2 Cor 6:16b, the term is used in a collective sense, that is, as a reference to the body of believers. The idea of the metaphor is clear: the temple, that is, the Corinthian Church, belongs to God, and is indwelt by the Holy Spirit.

It is significant to note that Paul asserts that the community, not individuals or sub-groups, is the location of the indwelling Spirit. This emphasis on the primacy of the community is seen for the first time in Paul's greeting of 1 Corinthians, where Paul salutes the Corinthians as "called to be holy ones together with those who call upon the name of our Lord Jesus Christ." The temple image firmly locates the indwelling of the Spirit within the community as a whole. When he states that the Spirit "dwells in (among) you," the plural pronoun underscores the fact that the Spirit dwells within the community, rather than just within the individual.

Although it is apparent that Paul recognizes the work of the Spirit within individuals,[18] he insists that individual inspiration be understood within the context of community edification. Therefore Paul could say that if anyone destroys the temple of God, God will destroy him or her. This is a strong point. The division of the Corinthian church into numerous cliques and "factions" contradicts the unity of the one Temple in which God has chosen to dwell through the one Spirit. As God's eschatological temple,

---

17. Cf. de Lacey, "Function of a Metaphor In Paul," 401–409; Sweet, "A House Not Made with Hands," 371–88,

18. See for example 6:19, where Paul says that the Spirit dwells within individuals and 12:4–11 where he claims that the Spirit is the source of individual gifts.

the Corinthian community must keep its unity. To be divided into various factions was equivalent within the believing community to the destruction of Solomon's temple at the hands of the Babylonians. As God's judgment on the Babylonians showed, God does not take lightly those who treat his temple with contempt. As stated earlier, any who destroy this unity through their divisive influence will be removed from the picture. The declaration that the holiness of the corporate temple is destroyed by division agrees with Old Testament injunctions against local sanctuaries, which would violate the sanctity of God's designated place of worship.[19]

In 1 Cor 6:19–20, Paul applies the metaphor to the individual believer. However, the thought remains the same. Gärtner observes that "it is not easy to say how the individual Christian can be called a temple in which God dwells with his spirit."[20] As noted by Witherington, "one of the great challenges to understanding Paul's thought is the relationship between the one and the many: Paul affirms both, holding them in tension. To be a Christian is to be a member of the body of Christ, not an isolated saved individual. At the same time, Paul holds individuals responsible for their behavior, expecting the community to discipline them."[21] Thus, the Corinthians should "flee sexual immorality" (6:18), Paul says, because each believer's body, within the community, functions as the temple of God, the residence of the Holy Spirit, and therefore should be used to glorify God (6:19–20). Paul is telling the Corinthians that they are, as individuals within the believing community, the eschatological location of God's presence, the residence of his Spirit. As such, they must live in a way that is consistent with the presence of God within them. Thus, the focus remains on the community.

What Paul does not explicitly state, but that may be assumed, is that they are the eschatological fulfillment of the prophetic promise—that God's glory would one day dwell within a newly restored temple located in the midst of a people purified from idolatry and sexual immorality (Ezek 43:2, 4–9; 44:4). Ezekial 11:19 says that God will give his restored people another heart, a new spirit, and a heart of flesh, rather than their hardened heart of stone. The purpose of these gifts, says verse 20, is that Israel might live in God's commandments and keep his righteous decrees. Similarly, Ezek 36:23–26 claims that God will be sanctified among his people in the sight of the Gentiles, will sprinkle them with pure water, will cleanse them from all impurities and idolatries, and will give to them both a new heart and a new spirit. Paul's notion of the Corinthian's sanctity closely parallels these ideas.

---

19. Cf. Deut 12:13–14; Jos 2:10–34.
20. Gärtner, *The Temple and the Community*, 141.
21. Witherington, *Conflict and Community*, 133.

Thus he urges the Corinthians to avoid a sizable list of activities that are incompatible with life in the kingdom of God (6:9-10). They should avoid them, he says, because they have experienced the eschatological cleansing of God's Spirit: "You were washed, sanctified, and justified in the name of the Lord Jesus Christ and by the Spirit of our God" (6:11).

As Webb argues, the restoration of Israel is an important motif for 2 Cor 6:14–7:1.[22] Paul continues to echo Ezekiel's prophecies of an eschatologically restored temple as he had done earlier in his first epistle to the Corinthians. In 2 Cor 6:14–7:1, therefore, Paul says forcefully what he has been suggesting at various points throughout the argument so far: the Corinthians live up to their status as the temple of God by staying clear of the influence of the unbelievers, whom he likens to idols (6:16). He bolsters his arguments by quoting and alluding to various passages of Scripture that speak of Israel's eschatological restoration, of necessity for God's people to be pure and holy. It is evident that Paul sees the Corinthians as constituting the community in which scriptural promises of the restoration of God's presence among his people have been fulfilled. As this restored community, they have the presence of God in their midst, and their vocation by God demands their own obligation to be holy. In his use of the temple imagery, Paul summoned the community to function in a way similar to the way that the temple in Corinth functioned: In each case, the temple of a particular deity provided a powerful symbol of the unity that existed among the worshippers of a particular deity.[23]

Three important facts emerge regarding the designation of the Corinthians as God's temple. First is the notion of temple as a symbol of God's presence, that is, the dwelling place of God.[24] Second is the corporate nuance of the temple. Paul's starting point is the community, and the individual is seen as a constituent of that community. For Paul, the individual is secondary to his concern for the unity of the community.[25] Third, and inseparably connected with the preceding, is the sanctity of the temple. The temple must be holy. In the Old Testament, holiness precedes worship and mediates the presence of God. Individually and collectively, the people must be holy in order to appear in God's presence.

In conclusion, the temple metaphor is a vivid, unusual image that holds together a number of different concepts such as community identity, the edification of the community, and the appearance of the community

---

22. See especially Webb, *Returning Home*, 31–71.
23. Lanci, *A New Temple for Corinth*, 134.
24. Cf. Renwick, *Paul, The Temple*, 26–46.
25. Cerfaux, *Church in the Theology of Paul*, 148.

to outsiders. The Corinthians were to be a "showcase" of God whose Spirit dwells within the temple, thus becoming God's agents of reconciliation. The imperatives in vv. 14a–16a are thus grounded in the indicative of who the Corinthians were. Believers were to avoid any association or alliance with the world that would be unworthy of a community that understands itself as the temple of the living God.[26] Yet they were to "win some" by becoming "winsome" in their lives.

ASPECTS OF HOLINESS IN 2 CORINTHIANS

Holiness as Pure Motivation

In expressing his judgment regarding the behavior of Timothy and himself in 2 Cor 1:12, Paul makes some important statements. He begins by affirming the manner in which he and Timothy have lived "in holiness and sincerity before God." For classicists, "sincerity" (*eilikrineia*) was used to denote either unmixedness and purity or sincerity and uprightness.[27]

In Wisdom of Solomon 7:25, wisdom is described as "a pure effluence [*aporrosia.... eilikrines*] from the glory of the Almighty." Paul uses the term in 1 Cor 5:8: since Christ our lamb has been sacrificed, let us celebrate the Passover, "not with the old leaven, the leaven of malice and evil, but with the unleavened bread of "sincerity and truth." However, based on the entire context of 1 Cor 5:1–12, *eilikrineia* is better translated as purity.[28] In that passage, Paul is more concerned with the purity of the Corinthians rather than their sincerity.[29] Therefore, when Paul uses *eilikrineia* ("sincerity") in 2 Cor 2:17 to describe himself and Timothy, not as "peddlers of God's word; but as men of sincerity as commissioned by God, in the sight of God " (RSV), he could be describing himself in terms of sincerity, but the context can very readily accommodate the sense "ethical purity."

As those who speak from God in the presence of God in Christ (v. 17b), the character of their entire lives would have to be pure. Their lives could not be such as that of the peddler with his bag of salesman's tricks.[30]

---

26. Furnish, *II Corinthians*, 373.

27. Cf. Liddell and Scott, *A Greek-English Lexicon*.

28. Cf. Bruce, *1 & 2 Corinthians*, 57: ". . . sin must be a thing of the past, holiness the abiding quality of the present and future"; Barrett, op. cit. 129: "Christians must . . . observe suitable paschal purity, banishing leaven in its transferred, moral, sense . . . ."

29. See more discussions in Chapter 6.

30. Cf. Bauer, "*apeleuo*," 404: "Because of the tricks of small tradesmen . . . the word

Paul testifies that the lives of Timothy and himself have been of such high character before the Corinthians and before God in Christ as to bear witness that he and Timothy are speaking in the sight of God. Paul's point is that he and Timothy have lived in ethical and religious purity; their lives have been lived in holiness.[31]

The manner of Paul and Timothy's living, "in holiness and purity," derives from God, a thought that is especially emphasized by the following clause: "by the grace of God and not by worldly wisdom." It is to be observed that in grounding the holiness of his life, not in his own human achievement, but in the grace of God, Paul nullified any reproach for his boasting. Because the life of the risen Christ is now Paul's life (Gal 2:20; see 1 Cor 1:30) and because he seeks to allow the mind of Christ, which has been given him from God, to control his life so that he is an imitator of Christ (see 1 Cor 2:13-16; 10:31—11:1), he does not draw back from asserting that he and Timothy have lived in holiness. This is not a boast as to their achievement, and consequently something for which they can claim any credit. To the contrary, this is what the grace of God has worked in them.

Paul and Timothy's lives have not been lived in some isolated haven where only they themselves could have beheld what they did, and where they would have had to relate only to themselves. To the contrary, they have conducted themselves "in the world" and especially "toward you." For Paul therefore, withdrawal from society was not the key to holiness.[32] He relied upon the grace of God who worked in him, and gave him the victory he sought. Because of the enabling power of their God, Paul and Timothy behaved themselves in ethical conformity toward all, to the will of their God and Savior.

Holiness as Forgiveness and Restoration

In 2 Cor 2:5-11, Paul deals with an offender whose identity and nature of offense remain unresolved and, as such, remains a matter of debate in New Testament scholarship.[33] Two matters of great importance in the passage are worth noting. First is Paul's willingness to forgive, and how Paul's for-

---

comes to mean almost *adulterate* . . . ." Cf. Isa 1:22 (LXX).

31. Cf. Meyer, *Handbook to the Epistles*, 146. Paul speaks of moral holiness and purity and that ". . . of his *entire conduct* not *merely* of his teaching." So also Bruce, 1 & 2 *Corinthians*, 180.

32. Although Paul would urge separation as we shall see below, he never advocates isolationism.

33. Discussions on these issues can be found in major commentaries. For a special treatment see Kruse, "Offender and the Offence," 129-39.

giveness implies forgiveness by the entire congregation. Underlying Paul's readiness to forgive is his desire for reconciliation with the members of the Corinthian believing community. The second issue is Paul's anticipation of the unwillingness to forgive, and how that could lead to Satan taking an advantage, not just of the repentant offender, but the entire congregation.

What is the reason for this juxtaposition? One should look at the sequence of Paul's thoughts in the passage. The importance of this episode is that Paul expects the Corinthians to demonstrate forgiveness. The Corinthians were to keep that brother from going into despair "that he will not be overwhelmed by excessive sorrow" (2 Cor 2:7a). They were to communicate love (2 Cor 2:8).

The church was to "be obedient in everything" (2 Cor 2:9). Paul's point in this passage is clear. The forgiveness of the Corinthians would mirror the apostle's forgiveness, which would mirror Christ's forgiveness. Moreover, Paul says, forgiveness was to be, not only for the sake of the offender, but also for the benefit of the church, for your sake. Furthermore, the phrase "for your sake" (v. 10) probably implies that not only Paul but also the whole Corinthian church may have been somehow adversely affected by the offender's punishment. Hence, implicit in Paul's call for forgiveness is that a failure by the Corinthian congregation to forgive the offender would be a threat to the very basis of their existence, which was the love and forgiveness of Christ, and Christ's apostle. Satan would take advantage and exploit the situation.

Thrall has rightly suggested that although Paul does not explain to us in a precise manner how Satan would take advantage, "perhaps he has in view the promotion of dissension within the congregation, should the offender remain penalized."[34] However, one may further suggest that in view of the pastoral concern of Paul, he intends to impress it upon the Corinthians that if the church cannot be a living demonstration of forgiveness in a community, there is no compelling reason for the people in that community to want to be a part of the church. Thus, the distorted image of the church that results as a lack of forgiveness will be to Satan's advantage.

Forgiveness is a product of Christian love (holiness) and strengthens the fellowship of believers as it reconciles the repentant to fellowship. Arrington's suggestion is on target when he says, "refusal to forgive the believer who has sinned, and who is now repentant, or receiving him with coldness back into fellowship, works to Satan's advantage."[35]

---

34. Thrall, 2 *Corinthians*, 181.
35. Arrington, *Ministry of Reconciliation*, 42.

Holiness as Reconciliation

Paul's appeal for reconciliation with the disaffected Corinthians, although embedded in the earlier part of the letter, comes to the fore in 5:11—7:16, the first subsection of which is 5:11—6:2. It opens with "commend ourselves" (5:12). The thought unit is held together by an inclusion (5:11, "we persuade men"; the two appeals of 5:20b and 6:1). It is built around two components: 5:11-12 and 5:13—6:2. Once again, Paul's defense of his ministry and character come into focus. Paul's intent is to provide the Corinthians the basis for answering those who boast in external appearances, in 5:13—6:2.

First, Paul is motivated by the love of Christ, a love that he defines in terms of his death for us. "Jesus Christ is here presented the endangered benefactor who went to the outer limits of beneficence on behalf of humanity."[36] Such love compels Paul to see things differently. Paul, unlike his opponents, can no longer judge by externals—according to the flesh.

Second, Paul goes further to define his ministry in terms of reconciliation, based on the Christ-event. Reconciliation, Paul would argue, results from an inner transformation. The Christ-event is God's way of making sinners to become saints (2 Cor 5:17). The climax of Paul's argument comes in v. 21. While on the one hand Paul appeals to the Corinthians to be reconciled with him, on the other hand he appeals to the non-Christian world to be reconciled with God because, God, in the death of Christ, has already borne the cost of any debt owed him.

In 2 Cor 6:1-10, Paul continues with his apostolic defense as God's servant. Verse 1 is crucial to the understanding of holiness. Paul exhorts the Corinthians not to "receive the grace of God in vain." What exactly does it mean? In the context of the preceding section, it is right to argue that Paul is suggesting that the Corinthians will have received the grace of God in vain if they refused to be reconciled with him—Christ's ambassador; for one cannot be in proper relation with God while at the same time rejecting Christ, the ambassador through whom God makes appeal for reconciliation.

Paul uses Isa 49:8 to make his plea, and in the same manner as the Servant, calls the Corinthians to reconciliation, with himself as a proof of their salvation. This is the essence of holiness in 2 Corinthians. A right relationship with God not only demands, but also results in, a right relationship with other believers.

Paul continues to defend his call (6:4), and he does so by returning to his paradoxical understanding of ministry (see 4:7-12). Without a doubt,

---

36. Danker, *2 Corinthians*, 78.

Paul sees his apostolic work as being an integral part of God's mission. Hence, he urges them not to receive the grace of God in vain.

Holiness as Relationship

Perhaps there is no passage in 2 Corinthians that better encapsulates Paul's teaching on holiness than 2 Cor 6:14—7:1. His choice of words is quite striking. Apart from Paul's description of the Corinthian congregation as the people and temple of God, he employs terminologies such as defilement, cleansing, holiness, and perfection.

It is pertinent to note that the focus throughout this text is the believing community—the church, not the individual believer. Paul sees humanity, in general, and in this instance, the Corinthian believers as beings-in-relation. Therefore, the interpretation must be primarily seen in terms of the church rather than the individual.

Together the Corinthians are the "people" and "temple" of God. With such designations, Paul wishes to acknowledge that the Christians at Corinth are God's chosen people, and in covenant relationship, in the same way that Israel had been (Exod 19:6), separated from all that is profane and consecrated to God, the Holy One of Israel (see Isa 6:3). In designating the Corinthians as the people of God (2 Cor 6:16), Paul has attributed to the Corinthians a title that Israel considered to be an expression of its peculiar dignity.

In the Old Testament, it was the covenant relationship that made Israel a holy community (see Exod 19:5–6). Its continued existence depended on the abiding presence of the Holy One in their midst, a presence that both makes holy and demands holiness in turn. This demand was formulated in the covenant law that stipulated how the covenant relationship was to be lived out by the people, making Israel God's holy people, separated from the nations.

In the context of Leviticus 19, the rule against an "unequal yoke" may simply be an effective way of telling the Israelites as a "people" to maintain their identity, that is, to be different. They must live up to their relationship. Thus, it is clear from Leviticus 19 that holiness entails being and keeping in proper relationship with God. However, as Leviticus 19 shows, relating with God also necessitates relating properly with others, both within and without the covenant community.

There are clear echoes of this background in 2 Cor 6:14—7:1. By alluding to the Holiness Code, Isaiah and Ezekiel, Paul wishes to recall to the Corinthians their unique covenant relationship with God. By his sanctifying presence, which is denoted by his walking among them, God makes them holy and demands that they be holy (2 Cor 7:1). Paul leaves us in no doubt that when the community is unequally yoked, it violates its covenant relationship with God and ceases to exist as the people of God, even though it continues to profess to be so.

Holiness as Separation

In the dualistic antithesis in 2 Cor 6:14b–16a, we find Paul's attempt to reinforce the incongruence of the association between the Christians and "unbelievers." Here Paul makes clear the unique identity of Christians by distinguishing them from all others. This is common to Paul (Rom 6:19; 1 Thess 4:2–8; 5:5; Rom 13:12; Eph 5:8),[37] and he frequently employs dualistic terms in defining membership.[38] In this way, the new Christian life in faith is characterized against the background of a pagan past.

The purpose of the rhetorical questions in 2 Cor 6:14b–16 is to show the incongruity of such associations. For example, nothing can be more incongruous than light and darkness, whether in the literal or figurative meaning of the terms. Such incongruity is true of holiness and sin. Because Christ and Belial are discordant and opposite, how can their followers agree? Readers should note 1 Cor 10:21, where the impossibility of uniting the service of Christ and the service of Satan is presented in much the same terms as it is here. Elements so discordant can never be united into a harmonious whole. Paul is clearly thinking of associations that involve a partnership, rather than a casual or occasional working relationship.

In verses 16–18, Paul asserts the incongruity of the association between believers and unbelievers by dwelling on the metaphor of the temple. It may be further suggested that, although the contrasts focus on the relationship between the Corinthians and the "unbelievers," implicit in the synonyms is what Paul thinks should characterize the Corinthian Christians. Because the Corinthians are related together "in Christ," they cannot be related to

---

37. Such perspective was not lacking in early Christian paraenesis, for example, 1 Pet 2:4–11. It is a section of Christian paraenesis containing the combination: (a) Christians as God's house (v. 5); (b) holiness (vv. 5, 9); (c) contrast between believers and unbelievers (v. 10); (d) contrast between light and darkness (v. 9); (e) combination of flesh and soul (v. 11). Statements which draw a contrast between "once" and "now" (corresponding to what we term "us" and "them" in this place) form a pattern in parts of the New Testament. See Rom 6:19; 1 Thess 4:2–8; 5:5; Rom 13:12; Eph 5:8.

38. Dahl, "Form-critical observations on early Christian preaching," 33–34. See 1 Cor 1:20–28; 2:12; 3:19; 5:10, 12–13; 6:1, 2; 7:12–15, 31, 33; 11:32; 2 Cor 4:4; 6:14; Gal 4:3; 6:14; 1 Thess 4:12; Eph 2:2; Col 2:8, 20; 4:5.

unbelievers in the same manner. To do so is to be contaminated and to compromise their holiness.

There is a certain ambiguity suggested in the Corinthians' relationship to the outside world.[39] While, on the one hand, they must have the strong group boundaries of an eschatological sect, on the other hand, and at the same time, they must maintain an openness to evangelize the people who surround them.[40] Paul is not so much concerned that standards of the wider culture differ from those of the Christian movement as he is that the community adhere to its own principles, and live to its calling.

The promise commenced in v. 17 is continued in v. 18. God declares that he not only will receive into his favor those who regard themselves as his temple and keep themselves aloof from all contaminating associations with the wicked, but that he will be a father to them. Hence, holiness in 2 Cor 6:14—7:1 must involve separation.

Paul's desire for the Corinthians to manifest holiness in terms of separation continues in the much controversial chapters 10-13. Although these chapters deal primarily with Paul's answers to his critics, his objective nevertheless remains the same. A danger confronts the Corinthians, and things looked so bad that Paul says in 2 Cor 13:5, "Test yourselves and see if you are in the faith!" They have been influenced by liars who know how to speak smooth, logical, and clever speeches that appear wise. It is similar to Shakespeare's *Othello* where Iago, the villain of the play, gains the trust of Othello and others in order to destroy them. He is a master at disguising himself as an honest, beloved friend, all the while working skillfully at evil and poisoning the minds of those who trust him until they do Iago's wishes. In the end the hero, Othello, jealously kills his wife and himself because he believed the lies of Iago, that his wife was cheating on him. Likewise, Paul's opponents in 2 Corinthians 10-13 are undermining the truth and making those who once trusted in him turn away from him.

The issue was not loyalty either to Paul or the false apostles but to Christ and the gospel. Paul's concern was more—the spiritual progress of the Corinthians was at stake. The false teachers are not what they appear to be, and instill pride and a false sense of wisdom in those they influence, distorting the way of Christ. They are deceivers who dangerously look impressive to the Corinthians.

One thing is clear in these chapters—Paul desires that the Corinthians separate themselves from his opponents whom he describes in various

---

39. This is true of all Pauline communities. See Meeks, *First Urban Christians*, 97–103.

40. Cf. 1 Cor 5:9–13.

ways. Paul, with a God-given jealousy, was jealous for their purity in life and doctrine.

Continuing his "foolish" boasting, in 2 Cor 11:2, Paul describes the Corinthians, collectively, as a virgin awaiting the consummation of their wedding ceremonies at Christ's Second Coming. In his appeal to the Corinthians, he uses the imagery of betrothal that is in conformity with Jewish customs. In the OT, Israel is frequently depicted as betrothed to Yahweh (Isa 50:1; 54:1–6; 62:5; Hos 1–3). Although betrothed, according to the Jewish law, the violation of a betrothed virgin was no less serious than if the marriage had already been consummated.[41] Paul's usage of the Old Testament "father and daughter" image (Deut 32:19; 2 Kgs 19:21; Isa 62:5; Jer 18:13; 31:4) underscores the intimate relationship that exists between him, and subsequently, Christ, and the Corinthians. However, the point of the imagery is to show Paul's concern for the virginal purity of the Corinthians, and it was Paul's responsibility to ensure that they lived up to their engagement implicit in their baptism.[42]

Holiness as Cleansing

Katharizein ("to cleanse") is not a verb Paul uses often, but the words with the root *kathar* play a large role in the letters of Paul. In the LXX *katharizein* is frequently used with reference to making persons, things, or places ceremonially fit for participation or use within the culture.[43] In Ps 51: 2, 7, and 10 (LXX: 50), for example, the adjective and verb are both used in the prayer for ethical purity in the entire person. In its general usage the group denotes physical, religious, and moral cleanness or purity in such senses as clean, free from stains or shame, and free from adultery. Purification in the Old Testament usually has to do not simply with dedication to holy use, but with removal of ceremonial uncleanness (or ritual impurity), which occurred in several ways. Isa 52:11, a passage to which Paul alludes in 2 Cor 6:17, mentions purification in anticipation of the return from the Exile. This need for purification, along with the usual purification for holy service, was probably in mind as the priests and Levites purified themselves (Ezra 6:20) and then the people and the rebuilt city gates (Neh 12:30) after the Exile (see 12:45; 13:22).

---

41. Murphy-O'Connor, *Theology of the Second Letter*, 108.
42. Ibid.
43. See for example the Levites who had to purify themselves for service in the tabernacle (Num 8:12; 9:13; 18:11, 13; Lev 12:8; 13:13, 17, 37; 11:36; 4:12; 6:11).

Paul's presentation of the cleansing aspect of holiness comes to the front in 2 Cor 7:1: "Since we have these promises, beloved, let us cleanse ourselves from every defilement of body and of spirit, making holiness perfect in the fear of God." Paul continues to emphasize the separation aspect of holiness. The call to cleansing in 2 Cor 7:1, although applicable personally, is communal.

Paul is calling the Corinthians, who are both God's temple and people, to live up to their calling. The basis for Paul's exhortation in 7:1 lies in the fact that the believers are the recipients of the promises enumerated in 6:16b ("I will be their God and they shall be my people"), 17b ("then I will welcome you"), and 18 ("and I will be a father to you and you shall be my sons and daughters"). In response to the fulfilment of these promises, which were initially made to Israel "according to the flesh" (or to David, in the case of the last [2 Samuel 7:14]), Israel was to be obedient to the ethical and cultic demands of Yahweh.[44] Because the Corinthians, as members of the new church of God in Christ Jesus, have now become the recipients of these promises from God, they are likewise confronted with the responsibility to effect complete ethical and religious renewal in accordance with the directives of their God.

In 1 Cor 6:11, Paul had reminded the Corinthians that they had been washed (*apelousasthe*), sanctified, and justified. Here, Paul is addressing those who have experienced that initial renewal, so that in Christ they have his righteousness; they are in the light; they are believers; they are the temple of the living God (6:14–16a). They are the sanctified people of God in that they have been set apart to belong to God in Christ. They are consequently in a position to be confronted with an ethical imperative that they can be expected to fulfill.[45] Now their task is that they so cleanse themselves that they become holy in an ethical sense. They can accomplish this by the removal of every defilement of body and spirit.

Paul's demand for the cleansing of flesh and spirit is a reference both to the physical body and to the "seat of emotion and will."[46] In short, the total life of the believer is to be rendered free from anything that would make the believer objectionable to God. Paul is exhorting the Corinthians to make the outward expression of their lives conformable to that which

---

44. Cf. Lev 26:1, 11f.; Jer 32:31–41; 31:9, 23, 31–34; Ezek 11:9, 12, 17–21; 36:25–38; Isa 43:6.

45. Cf. Rom 8:6–13 and Phil 2:12–15 where Paul affirms that it is only the one who has received the Spirit of God and thereby has the power of God at work in him who can—through that power which God himself exercises in the believer's life—do that which is pleasing to God.

46. Cf. Burton, *Epistle to the Galatians*, 486–27.

their "salvation-life" actually is. Thus, there is to be no phase of the Corinthians' lives that is to be ignored in their efforts to make themselves clean. By carrying out this cleansing process, they will increasingly come to be in the likeness of Christ. Therefore, cleansing, in this passage, has to do with a proper use of the temple, the dwelling-place of the Holy Spirit, through which God is to be glorified (see 1 Cor 6:15–20).

Believers in 2 Cor 7:1 are made holy by the cleansing of every defilement, while living a life of reverence for God (i.e., submission to his Lordship). Paul prays that the Thessalonians will stand before God at the return of Christ with hearts "blameless in holiness" (1 Thess 3:13).

As Paul uses holiness (*hagiōsunē*), it expresses that essential character of God as apartness from all evil, and his just dealings in his relationship with humanity; likewise, the believer may possess holiness in greater or lesser degrees, in proportion to his conformity to the will of God. As a result of cleansing both body and spirit, it will become increasingly possible to describe the believer by the term *hagiōsunē*—"holiness." Ideally, the whole person, body and soul, is totally involved in worship.

When Paul urges the Corinthians to bring holiness to completion, he is not suggesting the possibility of a holiness as ethical purity, which is somehow not wholly pure. To the contrary, he is exhorting the believers to pursue an ethical purity that is limited, but not tainted—an ethical purity that reflects only a portion of the holiness of God, and must come to reflect ever more of God's holiness. Holiness may expand—indeed it must—as the believer comes to be more in the likeness of Christ through a greater awareness of what constitutes defilement of flesh and spirit, and subsequently cleanses himself of that defilement. As used in 2 Cor 7:1, holiness is not "merely a static condition, a holiness obtained by observance of cultic practices . . . the context is not one of resting content with an unholy life . . . but one of acting out one's status in Christ."[47] It is therefore right to suggest that holiness (*hagiōsunē*) in 2 Cor 7:1 refers to "a quality of life and character, arising from a relationship with the Holy One."[48]

In sum, the whole exhortation, including the call to cleansing, is to be seen as having ethical, relational, and corporate significance. Paul had acknowledged earlier (1 Cor 6:9–11a) that the Corinthians had been washed, a reference to their conversion-initiation experience. Therefore, cleansing in this passage has to do with a proper use of the body as it is regarded as

---

47. Porter, "Holiness, Sanctification," 400.

48. Peterson, *Possessed by God*, 78. Peterson is right only in so far as his observation on relationship with God is concerned.

a temple, a dwelling-place of the Holy Spirit through which God is to be glorified (see 1 Cor 6:15–20).

Missional Holiness

It is important to note the relational image of God as a "father" in 2 Cor 6:18. Perhaps it may be suggested that implicit in the use of that image is the need for the Corinthians, in the same way as Israel, to mirror God and model his holiness. The Corinthians must live consistently as God's sons and daughters. Their behavior must confirm his paternity and their covenantal relationship with him. Paul's call for holiness in 2 Corinthians forces us to recognize that the Christian church really has to be a contrasting society, with its own social norms and an alternative style of life.[49] However, just like Israel, the church's alternative lifestyle was to produce a missionary effect of revealing God to the idolatrous environment in which it lived. It was not to degenerate to asceticism. Simply put, God is to be made known by the Corinthians by their alternative lifestyle.

Paul gives a hint of this in the previous chapter (2 Cor 5:18–20). In Christ, God forgives the Corinthians. But with that responsibility comes a purpose. God gives to believers "the ministry of reconciliation." Believers are to be living vessels pointing to God (2 Cor 5:18–19). God has called believers to be his stand-in representatives for the rest of humankind. The believers' ministry of reconciliation is not limited to reconciling the lost to God—it also includes reconciling people to one another.

IMPLICATIONS FOR THE CHURCH TODAY

The discussion on holiness in 2 Corinthians reveals that although for Paul holiness is a complex whole, it has several aspects. Importantly, Paul's rebukes, instructions, and exhortations on holiness proceed from his understanding of the nature of the church as the people of God. The implications are as follows:

First, what is our motivation for ministry? This is a question that is as relevant today as it was for Paul. The first hint about holiness in 2 Corinthians is contained in Paul's boast about his integrity as he faces the criticism from the Corinthians about the change in his travel plans. Because of his ministry to the Corinthians, Paul can make certain claims about his personal behavior and that of Timothy. These claims are made in 2 Cor 1:12,

---

49. Lohfink, *Jesus and Community*, 136.

a passage that is not only important for its content but also for the holiness terminologies employed. The claims that Paul makes in the passage are not on the basis of any testimony given by any people whom they encounter or who know them, but on the basis of the witness of their consciences.

Second, the church's self-understanding of its identity and purpose is crucial to its relationship with God and the wider society. The church must not primarily define itself against a fallen world or the pluralistic society in which it is located, but in relation to God. In other words, the church must first answer the question of what it is called to be. As such, Pauline holiness must always be formulated in ecclesial terms. Although not excluded, for Paul, the primary sphere of holiness and moral concern is not the character of the individual, but the corporate obedience of the church.

Third, the two grounds for the church being a holy people are clear. On the one hand, there is the redemptive work of God through Christ.[50] The church's holy status is found precisely in her being the people whom God chose to be his special possession (see 7:6; 14:2) and to be his sons and daughters (14:1). The church is holy because of her call to be God's own people. The holiness of the church does not stem from its members and their moral and religious behavior. However, on the other hand, the relationship of believers with God has serious implications. Holiness is not only to be based on her relationship with God as a separate, distinct people, but also on the actualization of that holiness in the relationship with the wider society. The church's holiness demands that she really live in accordance with the social order which God has given her, a social order which stands in sharp distinction against the pluralistic society. Thus, the church's holiness is based on a dynamic, ongoing relationship with God—a relationship, which, in turn, is to govern believers' relationships with the wider society, and members of her own community.[51]

Fourth, the church's holiness is to be a responsible (or required) one. It is difficult to argue that one may be related to God without a corresponding actual holiness that involves ethical decisions.[52] For Paul, holiness is not

50. See Rom 1:1; 1 Cor 1:1, 2, 28–30; 2 Cor 1:1; 5:17–20; 1 Pet 1:16; 2:5–9.

51. See 1 Cor 5:9-13; 2 Cor 6:14—7:1; 10-13.

52. Israel's example is important in this regard. Although God had declared that Israel had been selected to become his holy people, this declaration was hardly enough to make Israel holy. Israel, in order to achieve the holiness associated with God and His acts, would have to obey God's laws and commandments. Therefore, one may say that Israel's holiness has a required aspect. Israel was to be actively and intensely committed to God in loving obedience and trust. The call of Israel was to a people with a common goal and destiny and not just individuals. Israel's holiness is to be understood as having a communal dimension. It is to be manifested in social relationships. So also is Christian holiness.

the status of the community only, and the sense of having been called to be God's people.[53] It is the character of God in which his children might participate.[54] Holiness is something the church continues to pursue because God calls the church to the task of living into and out of the full power of the Holy Spirit. The church must display the reality of sanctification framed, first and foremost, in corporate terms.

Fifth, Christians in general, like the Corinthians, are to have the distinction of being the people of God—people who are in the world but are not of it. Believers are to live in the midst of unbelievers and interact with them, hoping to reconcile the world to God through Christ. Nevertheless, the church must be watchful so that the world doesn't squeeze her into its own mold. There still remains a need for clear boundaries between believers and the secular culture where they live. For Paul, there were some things with which the Corinthians could not compromise, and apparently, some people with whom they could maintain no close ties. Such were matters of concern for them, and they ought to be for us, too. Without clear boundaries, the church will lose her "prophetic" voice and moral ascendancy. As Gorman rightly suggests, holiness for Paul means a "countercultural cruciformity in expectation of the coming day of judgment and salvation."[55] Without doubt, "Paul's understanding of holiness reflects both his communal and eschatological understanding of the church."[56]

Sixth, the claim of the church to be holy demands that the church be an effective agent of reconciliation. Such reconciliation consists of two aspects: The church must first cater to her own needs of restoring offenders. But reconciliation goes beyond that. In addition, for the church to live out her calling as the people of God, she must do so in reconciled relationship with God and one another within the church and, where possible, with other churches regardless of racial, ethnic, national, and gender identities. As Gelder rightly states, "our fragmented world needs to see that a community of diverse persons can live in reconciled relationship with one another because they live in reconciled relationship with God."[57]

Seventh, the church must take seriously what it means to be the "people of God." The division of the world along racial or ethnic lines and institutionalized into national, political units, has taken and continues to take its toll on the church. The "people of God" is to be formed around a

---

53. Conzelmann, 1 *Corinthians*, 22; cf. Barrett, 1 *Corinthians*, 32.
54. Cf. 2 Cor 1:12; Heb 12:11.
55. Gorman, *Apostle of the Crucified Lord*, 237.
56. Adewuya, *Transformed by Grace*, 85.
57. Van Gelder, *Essence of the Church*, 107.

different identity: one that transcends race, ethnicity, and nationalism. The church ought to be a detribalized community comprised of diverse, racial, ethnic, national, and political identities.

Eighth, if the church is truly holy, she will take seriously the work of God in the world, rather than becoming inwardly focused and becoming preoccupied with maintaining purity, as important as that is.

Holiness is missional. God is about the mission of reconciliation in the world. Paul states that God has given to the church the "ministry of reconciliation, that is, in Christ, God was reconciling the world to himself" (2 Cor 5:18–19). It is God's purpose to make all things new, reconciling everything to reflect creation's intent while looking forward to consummation. For those who are separated from God, this means being brought into right relationship with God and others.

Chapter 5

Holiness in Galatians

As the study of holiness in Paul's letters has so far demonstrated, it is unmistakably clear that one of Paul's overriding concerns is the moral implication of the faith of a person *in Christ*. Paul's concern for holiness is evident in his exhortations and prayers.[1] When addressing the issue of sanctification in different contexts, Paul, as part of his rhetorical strategy, employs different metaphors—cleansing, crucifixion, purification, perfection, yielding to God, etc.—both to define sanctification as well as to describe its experiential reality in believers' lives. This is due to the occasional nature of Paul's letters.

The *hagios* word group does not appear in Galatians. Nevertheless, there is a sustained discussion of holiness in the book as Paul focuses not merely on what it requires to become the people of God, but having become such, to remain such, and live in a corresponding manner. Primary attention will be focused on Paul's use of the message of the cross, particularly the crucifixion metaphor[2] and its implication for the understanding of holiness in Galatians. However, we will examine other important motifs as well, as Paul maintains a close connection between the believer's justification and sanctification.[3]

---

1. Cf. Rom 6:19–22; 12:1–2; 1 Cor 1:30; 5:1–13; Phil 1:9–11; 1 Thess 4:1–7; 5:23–24; 2 Cor 6:14—7:1.

2. It is a metaphor that, curiously, with various nuances, appears most in Paul's letter to the Galatians, occurring in Gal 2:20; 5:24 and 6:14, three important texts that will be examined in their respective contexts later below.

3. The precise nature of the relationship between justification and sanctification continues to be a subject of scholarly debate. It is not within the purview of this essay

As Vincent Taylor rightly states, "the reconciling work of God is itself a sanctifying activity, in the sense that the believer is set apart and consecrated to holy ends and purposes; but in the Christian experience, both in its personal and communal aspects, this divine separation remains and needs to be worked out in a life of ethical and spiritual progress."[4] This was Paul's main concern and what he continued to discuss through the medium of his letters, as he continued to serve as a pastor. He dealt with the problems facing real people in the mid-first century as they struggled to understand their identity as Christians. Paul also carried out his pastoral task as a theologian. He appealed to authoritative formulas of faith (see Rom 1:3–4; 1 Cor 15:3–5; Phil 2:6–11; etc.) and the Scriptures. He reflected on the implications of Jesus' death and resurrection, drawing consequences for Christians' conduct and behavior. He resolved disputes on theological principles. It is thus clear that Paul's letters are the work of a pastoral theologian.

Reading Paul's letters to various congregations, one cannot help but notice that a significant struggle most of the Pauline churches faced was that of identity. The problem is particularly acute in Galatians, where we see the Pauline churches struggled with the issue of identity in two ways. First is the problem of identity in relation to the Jews, and particularly the rite of circumcision. In this regard, the question that needs to be answered relates to the conditions a person would need to fulfill in order to become part of God's people. The issue of Gentile-Christian identity with regard to the Jewish Christianity and Judaism was among the most pressing matters that Paul treated in Galatians. Paul sought to explain to Gentiles why they did not have to take up circumcision and Torah observances to become Christians. And he tried to make clear to Jewish Christians that they should not impose their kind of Christianity upon Gentiles. He wanted both Christian groups to live in harmony and mutual respect. For Paul, the Galatians, although Gentiles by birth, have through their belief in Jesus Christ—his death by crucifixion and resurrection—become part of God's holy people. Moreover, the Spirit has been poured out. They need nothing in addition to these.

Second is the problem of how the churches were to relate to the wider Greco-Roman society in which they were situated. This essentially is the issue of lifestyle—how believers should, having become the people of God, live in a hostile society whose values and principles are often opposed to theirs. Inseparably connected to this is how the members of the believing community were to relate with one another as the holy people of God. In

---

to engage that debate or provide a detailed discussion. An interested reader may wish to see an overview of the discussion in Furnish, *Theology and Ethics in Paul*, 242–79.

4. Taylor, *Forgiveness and Reconciliation*, 144.

short, Paul has to set out the implications of the gospel for the life of the community.

In addressing these issues, one must note two important strategies that Paul consistently employs. First, when Paul addresses moral or behavioral issues both in his life and in those of his converts, he does so with reference to the legacy of his and their past. Hence, his frequent formula, "once you were . . . now you are" (See 1 Cor 6:9–11; Eph 2:1–10; Phil 3:5–10; 1 Tim 2:15), which he uses both to impress upon and remind them of their new status—who they were, whose they were—and the ethical responsibility that goes with it. Second, as part of his rhetorical strategy, Paul always *shares a testimony*. He often refers to himself not only for apologetic purposes, as one finds in many of his letters, but also as a powerful tool showing the transforming power of the Gospel that he proclaims. In doing so he also presents himself as a worthy example to be emulated. In this way, he could confidently admonish his converts to imitate him (1 Cor 11:1).

Galatians 2:19–20

Galatians 2:19–20 is one of the best-known and most significant Pauline texts. It comes at the end of the autobiographical section of the book (Gal 2:11–20), where Paul writes about the truth of justification by faith, a central gospel truth of the letter. Paul has already made it clear that one is not justified by works of the Law, but through faith in Jesus Christ (2:16). In 2:17–18, Paul shows the radical nature of the gospel that he proclaimed and that he is now defending. For Paul, any attempt to secure acceptance by God on the basis of the works of the Law puts a person in direct opposition to what God has revealed and provided for in Christ Jesus, namely justification by faith. As Ziesler rightly notes, "the real sin is not infringing the Law, but in disloyalty to Christ and the new way of acceptability in and through him."[5] Hence, as Hansen suggests, "Paul refuses to reconstruct the barrier of the Law between Jews and Gentiles because he had died to the Law in his experience of the cross of Christ."[6] As such, the theological basis of Christian ethics will have to be redefined.[7]

In order to seal his argument and further explicate the meaning of what he has just said, Paul makes a startling statement, giving a personal testimony: "For through the Law I died to the Law" (Gal 2:19). He does not only present himself as a paradigm for his converts specifically, and believers

---

5. Ziesler, *Meaning of Righteousness in Paul*, 173.
6. Hansen, "Paradigm of the Apocalypse," 148.
7. Lategan, "Is Paul Defending His Apostleship in Galatians?" 429.

in general, but also presents in a nutshell the essence of his own theology, when he talks about his own dying to the Law in a manner reminiscent of Rom 7:1–6. Although the word "I" may be taken either in a strict personal sense or as an example to follow,[8] it seems inconceivable to see the word as completely devoid of personal overtone or lacking reference to a personal concrete experience. However, one should be careful not to limit what Paul was saying to his personal experience, since what he is saying is valid for every Christian.[9] Here, "to the Law" and "for God," (see Rom 6:2, 10–11) are placed against each other to indicate to whom the believer belongs and is subject. Paul once again reveals his thought of the Law as a power that is hostile to (sinful) humans, that brings humans under its jurisdiction, and that obstructs the way to life. To this Law, Paul has now died. His death with Christ (crucifixion with Christ), which he goes on to discuss in the latter part of the verse, results in death to the Law and its slavish control.

Christ's death satisfied the demands of the Law and nullified its lordship, both over him and over those who are bound in solidarity with him—those who, like he, have died to sin. Believers, of whom Paul was representative, have been crucified with Christ, as a result of which they had become free from the bondage of the Law. They are now free to live a mode of existence that is no longer dominated by the Law. The thought here is that, as in Christ's death on the cross, the believer has died to the powers of sin, world, and law; so also in the resurrection of Christ, the believer has been set at liberty for God, in order to live for him, under his control. The demands of the Law have been fully satisfied and therefore the Law has no more hold on the believer.

The positive side of dying to the Law is indicated in the subordinate clause, "that I may live for God" (Gal 2:19). The similarity of these verses to the passage in Rom 6:3ff. is quite striking. A personal appropriation of Christ's death and identification with his crucifixion takes place at conversion-baptism. Through faith, Christ's death becomes one's own death. For Paul, freedom means transfer from one dominion to another: from law to grace (Rom 6:14), from sin to righteousness (Rom 6:18), from death to life (Rom 6:21–23), and in this place, from self to Christ. This is the very essence of the believer's relationship with God. This relationship, which could also be understood in terms of discipleship, certainly means more. The same phrase is also reminiscent of Rom 6:10 and it portrays the believer's faith-union relationship with Christ, which begins at conversion-baptism. Being raised with Christ is an aspect of being joined with him existentially.

---

8. So Longenecker, *Galatians*, 91; Tannehill, *Dying and Rising*, 55.
9. Tannehill, *Dying and Rising*, 57.

Paul's death to the Law was inseparably connected to the person and mission of the crucified Jesus. When he proclaims, "I have been crucified with Christ," what does Paul mean? Does this refer to self-crucifixion, is it to be construed as merely a reference to self-denial, or does it mean more? Probably more. It includes an existential reality by which he personally experienced the benefits of Christ's crucifixion.

When it is suggested that believers are crucified with Christ, it needs to be understood as being more than a figure of speech describing a psychological separation or deliverance from sin. The death and resurrection of Christ are not only historical events but events in which, through faith-union with him, his people have come to share. The point is that death with Christ is the only way that those enslaved by the Law can find freedom. Longenecker sums up the thought of verse 19 very well: "Crucifixion with Christ implies not only death to the jurisdiction of the Mosaic law (v. 19), but also death to the jurisdiction of one's ego . . . which is antagonistic to the Spirit's jurisdiction."[10]

What one finds in Gal 2:20 is a greater detail of what Paul has stated more generally in v. 19. The counterpart of death with Christ is always resurrection and a new life in him. Crucifixion with Christ is significant only because it made the new life possible. For Paul, the resurrection forms an integral part of God's redeeming operation. Not only may such an impression be drawn from the present context, but also such a conclusion may be drawn from passages where Paul plainly connects the resurrection with the redemption of humanity.[11]

The death and resurrection of Christ are regarded as inseparable parts of the same mighty achievement. For Paul, the cross is unintelligible apart from the resurrection. There is always an interaction between death and resurrection.[12] Here Paul interprets the death of Christ from his experience of the risen Lord. This he does by linking "dying to the Law" and "crucifixion with Christ" to living for God, which bears an unmistakable affinity to Rom 7:4, 6. The death to the Law spoken of (v. 19a) is correlative with death to sin (see Rom 7:4, 6; 6:6, 18, 22).

Therefore, since this death is described in terms of participation with Christ in his crucifixion, and this life is obviously life in the individual, existential union with Christ ("Christ in me"), the co-crucifixion and the co-resurrection must also be primarily experiential in nature. The communion

---

10. Longenecker, *Galatians*, 192.
11. Phil 3:10; Gal 1:1–4.
12. Cf. Schnelle, *Apostle Paul*, 429; Kennedy, *Theology of the Epistles*, 71.

between Christ and believers is so close that they not only participate in his death; the risen Christ indwells them, directs them, and fulfills their lives.[13]

Paul goes on to describe the result of the union with Christ as a life that is lived by faith while still "in the flesh" (*en sarki*). The reference to flesh in this verse does not carry the negative ethical connotations that one sees later in the letter. Although the emphatic personal pronoun could simply be a reflexive emphatic construction, thus suggesting the translation as: "I myself no longer live," the result of Paul's crucifixion with Christ is particularly striking if one were to translate literally the statement as: "I no longer I, but lives in me Christ." This is very significant in light of what follows. Paul is simply saying, "I do not live any longer as I once did, but in a new way—*no longer I*—now Christ lives in me. He is the Lord of my new life." Paul has surrendered his sovereignty to Christ. It is a new life, the reality of which is known and experienced by faith.[14]

Paul lives in the eschatological tension of "already, not yet." On the one hand, the life of the new age that is designated as "in Christ" has begun; on the other hand, he continues to live in the flesh, a realm dominated by evil.[15] Believers are left with an inevitable tension between the datable, historical, and unrepeatable acts of Christ's death and resurrection on the one hand, and the application and realization of those acts in the believer's life on the other.

Summarizing what has been argued thus far, it is clear that Paul's main emphasis in Gal 2:19-20 is a concern with the believer's ethical life that results from his or her relationship with Christ that begins at justification. As Lategan rightly states, "it is a life in faith and a life for God, of which the ethical 'style' is at the same time exemplified by the event of the cross ... Theology and ethics remain inseparable in Paul's thinking."[16] Paul was talking about a faith-union relationship with the crucified and risen Lord. His testimony illustrates that the gospel's call is to live a holy life that is characterized by a surrender of one's former way of life. Furthermore, Gal 2:20 holds out the prospect of God's enablement by the Holy Spirit to live a sanctified life that is received and appropriated by faith.

---

13. Ibid., 284.

14. This faith denotes a personal relationship with Christ. The relative pronoun "which" is an accusative of content and is probably to be taken as a substantial synonym for life (cf. Longenecker, *Galatians*, 93).

15. As deSilva, *Paul's Letter to the Galatians*, 133n118 rightly states, "There is an eschatological dimension to the phrase 'living to God' as well: Paul may enjoy a new life now before God, but ultimately he embraces the death and life of Christ in his mortal body as the path to sharing in Christ's resurrection, 'living to God for eternity ....'"

16. Lategan, "Argumentative Situation of Galatians," 393.

For Paul, believers now have a new mode of existence. It is not just an existence dominated by a new psychological motivation. As Cauthron succinctly states, "the motivating principle of Christian living is no longer the self-centered attempt to be worthy of God's favor. It is rather the selfless giving of gratitude and profound appreciation for all that God has done for us and in us by his grace."[17] As a result of the indwelling Christ, the believer is supplied with a new principle of activity on the ontological level of his or her very being, based on his initial conversion experience and more. It involves a dynamic, ongoing, and intimate relationship with the Lord that not only is the ground of the life of holiness, but also is grounded in a life of holiness. Whatever holds true for Paul in these verses also holds true for all believers.

Galatians 5:24

Galatians 5:24 is the climax of the first unit (Gal 5:13–24) of the exhortatory section of the letter (5:13—6:10). It is helpful to examine briefly how Paul builds up his argument to that point. In this verse, Paul basically repeats what he has already said in v. 1a: "For freedom Christ has set us free." In v. 1 he had continued: "Stand fast, therefore, and do not submit again to a yoke of slavery," that is, do not become subject to the Law (see 4:21). The continuation in v. 13, however, is different, although freedom's opposite, the theme of "slavery," is likewise repeated: "only do not use your freedom as an opportunity for the flesh, but through love become slaves to one another." Paul recognizes that freedom can be bent to justify harmful behavior. As such, the believer's liberty is seen as freedom from restraints, even of the moral law. But Paul suggests otherwise, forcefully asserting that freedom must not be used as a means of self-indulgence.

For Paul, mutual service and love of neighbor are seen as a curb on any kind of misguided freedom. In vv. 14–15, then, this love of neighbor is further taught. But how could the Galatians live that life of love? Paul provides the answer in v. 16. They must continue living by the Spirit, and the Spirit must be the ground and norm of being and action. Christians are now in the realm of life determined by the Spirit and as such, must be guided by the Spirit. Thus, Paul sets the stage for the following contrast of the two ways of living—living by the flesh and living by the Spirit. As Howard suggests, "Spirit is neither the human spirit nor the divine Spirit considered independently of each other, but the divine Spirit as he indwells the human spirit."[18] As Schnelle notes, "Paul's statements on the relation of the Spirit

17. Cauthron, "Holiness," 248.
18. Cf. Howard, *Galatians*, 93.

of God to the human spirit are intentionally open and nonspecific because this mystery eludes static conceptuality."[19] In the present context where the main issue is about community conflict and communal wholeness (holiness), Paul is speaking of the divine Spirit's indwelling the human spirit in community with one another.

As it is often in Paul's thought, one discovers the significance of a concept by first understanding its opposite. So, before giving further explanation on how living by the Spirit is to be manifested, he describes the opposite, "life in the flesh," an indication that all was not well in the Galatian church.

Without a doubt Paul uses the word *flesh* in quite a number of ways. However, two distinct meanings are present, "ethical" and "non-ethical." Hence it requires some care in determining what it means in a particular context. What is provided here is a summary.[20] Paul uses *sarx* ("flesh") in two different senses—sometimes physical and sometimes in the sense of proclivity to sin. The flesh is still the sphere of the Christian's activity but it is no longer the dominant pattern or motivating power for his or her actions.[21] For Paul, to live in the flesh is sometimes equivalent to living in sin. However, this is true when a person has made the flesh the basis of his or her existence.

When Paul thought and spoke of the human situation, he had the human predicament in mind. For Paul, our humanness is not morally neutral. Because of what sin has done to us, our human desires that were once

---

19. Schnelle, *Apostle Paul*, 489n12.

20. Cf. Howard, *Newness of Life*, 28–33. Whenever Paul uses the word, he does so in his description of humanity's actual situation. For example, having described the Corinthians as fleshly he goes on to explicate what that means by saying that they were walking like *mere humans*, or in plainly, *human* (1 Cor 3:1–5). The term flesh, with its basic meaning of "human" can be seen in three significant relationships to humans. First, it is descriptive of a person as a human being. As such, it is a person's *basis of existence*. Humans exist as flesh. This is in keeping with similar usages in the New Testament (cf. Rom 3:20; John 3:6; Rom 8:3; 1 Cor 1:29). Second, it is a human's *sphere of existence* or where a person (*inner*) lives, in which case it is synonymous with the human body (cf. 2 Cor 4:10–11). Third, the flesh represents *something that a person uses*, that is the means or basis for living, revealing *how man lives* (cf. Gal 3:3). This is often expressed by the phrase *kata sarka* ("according to the flesh"), a phrase which can also be interpreted in many ways. For instance, in 2 Cor 10:3, Paul draws a distinction between the two. There is a strong difference between the two uses, one expressing human frailty and the other a principle of life dominated by wrong moral standards. Cf. Hughes, *The Second Epistle to the Corinthians*, 348f. For further discussions on Paul's use of "flesh," the reader may consult any standard scholarly work on the theology of Paul.

21. Cf. Cranfield, *Epistle to the Romans*, 337. "They (Christians) are no longer in the flesh in the sense of having the basic direction of their lives determined and controlled by their fallen nature."

morally neutral[22] are perverted, twisted, and slanted toward evil. Thus, to live *by* the flesh results in sinful living, not because the flesh is our sinful nature, but because our *human nature* is no match for sin—so a person could be "in the Spirit" and yet live "in the flesh" (Gal 2:20). Paul does not believe in constitutional sinfulness—that is, locating sin in the physical body and leaving no room for deliverance from sin until physical death.

Paul continues in Gal 5:22 to explain what it means to live a life filled with love. It is a life by the Spirit—a life that issues in the fruit of the Spirit. In discussing the fruit of the Spirit, three important observations must be made. First, it needs to be stressed that Paul does not see the items listed as the fruit of the Spirit as human virtues that can be cultivated, watered, or fertilized as if they grew on a tree. They originate from God and their growth and development occur only as believers continue to live by the Spirit and be guided by him.

Second, as helpful as it may be to have an analysis of each item on the list of the fruit of the Spirit, such analysis fails to capture Paul's point. What is important to note is that each item is not only related to the other, but also is best understood in the context of social relationship, rather than existing or describing personal virtues that exist apart from the wellbeing of the community.

Third, we need to remember that the word "fruit" is one of those words that not only can be used both as singular and plural, but also has a collective sense. It can be argued that by using the collective sense, Paul intends all of the qualities he mentioned to exist, at least to a certain degree, in every believer—not distributed among the body of believers as are the spiritual gifts (see 1 Cor 12:4–12; Rom 14:3–5).

What makes possible Paul's imperative to live by the Spirit? The answer is provided in v. 24: "Those who belong to Christ Jesus have crucified the flesh."[23] To belong to Christ is to participate in the life of Christ.[24] Here, Paul expresses the fact of the believer's crucifixion in the active rather than in the passive voice (see Gal 2:19; Rom 6:6). In the former sense, crucifixion is what the believer does, while the latter implies what is done to the believer—namely, he or she is crucified. Believers are the agents of crucifixion.[25]

---

22. Cf. Howard, "Two Ways to Live," 201: "That they were once morally neutral is seen in the fact that every one of the works of the flesh (5:19–21) has a potential right and good fulfillment."

23. The possessive genitive leaves no question as to Paul's meaning—those who belong to Christ. However, as Witherington suggests, it probably also implies those who are in Christ Jesus. Cf. Witherington III, *Grace in Galatia*, 412.

24. Cf. Matera, *Galatians*, 204.

25. Cf. Barclay, *Obeying the Truth*, 117.

It has been sometimes suggested that Gal 5:24 is similar in thought to Gal 2:20, and it can be said that believers have crucified the flesh because of the presence of the crucified and risen Christ in them. It is this overwhelming presence of Christ, the crucified and resurrected Lord, his Spirit, the "fruit of the Spirit," that prevents the intentions of the flesh from discharging the works of the flesh. Therefore, Paul can say that the flesh has been crucified.[26] However, this interpretation is unlikely. In the immediate preceding context, Paul has presented the catalogue of vices and virtues. He described the former as the manifestation of "the works of the flesh," and the latter as the "fruit of the spirit" (see v. 22). In Gal 5:24, Paul links the crucifixion of the flesh with the belongingness to Christ, so it is understandable to think about the crucifixion of the flesh and its desires with the crucifixion of Christ.

Paul is expressing the same idea as in Rom 6:6. Our "old self" (the person we once were) has been crucified with Christ. This conveys a change that has already taken place. The death of the flesh is not, however, something that works automatically. It is an event that must be appropriated by faith. It is probably no accident, nor is it without significance, that here Paul states in the active voice what elsewhere he puts in the passive. The verb tense points to a completed action in the past and might most naturally refer to conversion.[27] Paul is speaking of an act of will on the part of those who belong to Christ. It is therefore not correct to see this just as a theological statement referring to one's position in Christ,[28] but as something that occurs in the Christian's consciousness. The believer has renounced fellowship with sin whose seat is the "flesh." Interpreted this way, both the force of the active voice, as well as the distinctive Pauline usage of the metaphor, are preserved. While on the one hand, the temptation of forcing a juridical interpretation is avoided; on the other hand, it clearly goes against the view that crucifixion in this verse is a reference to a continuous self-denial, a daily carrying of the cross, a usage that is more noticeable in the Gospels.

Paul probably has in view the free moral decision by believers who belong to Christ, and have made a conscious decision to follow the Lord. They have responded to God's saving grace in Christ. They have been regenerated, and now, they say a radical "No" to sin and thus pass judgment on the whole of their previous life. Hence Gal 5:24 refers not to the mystery of

---

26. Betz, *Galatians*, 289.

27. Longenecker is probably right in his observation that, 'the aorist verb..., since it identifies the crucifixion of the flesh in the believer's experience as being a past event but assigns that event to no specific time in the past is best translated as a perfect, "they have crucified." Cf. *Galatians*, 264.

28. So Ladd, *Theology of the New Testament*, 485.

baptism but to an ethical act on the part of Christians.²⁹ Therefore, in this present context, Paul is evidently thinking of the believers' past decision that should form the basis of present action.

Galatians 6:14

Here, Paul once again employs the language of crucifixion in his description of himself. He had previously talked about "crucifixion with Christ," and the "crucifixion of the flesh." In the present context, he talks about "crucifixion to the world." Once again, Paul employs personal language, although what he said about himself could be seen as true of believers in general.

Crucifixion for Paul is more than a mere figure of speech. It usually depicts an identification with Christ, and leads in the direction of the conversion or baptism experience. Paul, in the context, was discussing what constitutes appropriate boasting in contrast to his opponents who boasted in circumcision and the Law (see vv. 12–13).

For Paul, there was no other ground for boasting except the cross. What a great reversal! The cross that was once considered to be scandalous has not only become the center of Paul's message,³⁰ but also has become the reference point around which his entire life has been restructured.

Although the word *cosmos* ("world") is often used in a general sense, for example, as a created world (Rom 1:20), and as human living space (Rom 4:13), it usually means the human situation qualified by sin, or humanity itself. As such, "cosmos" is the world (humanity) turned away from God, rebellious and hostile toward him, and depraved humanity that is headed for judgment. However, in the context, it seems appropriate to understand the word *cosmos* ("world") to which Paul refers here not merely as a life of outbroken sin, but also including his Jewish heritage. For on such heritage (circumcision and Pharisaical righteousness), Paul had once hung all his hopes, lived, served as a slave, and even was willing to die.³¹

Further, this "world" denotes all that stands at enmity with God, the sphere of pleasure and ambition related to the flesh in which the Judaizers find their boast. It could therefore be seen as representative of everything in which a person would wish to boast. That is to say, in a religious sense, he would be able to depend, for example, on the Law and circumcision (see v. 13).³² It is not just the physical world, the world of sinful humanity

---

29. Schneider, "σταυρόω," 583–84.
30. Schnelle, *Apostle Paul*, 85.
31. Howard, *Galatians*, 122.
32. Cf. Ridderbos, *Paul*, 210; Fitzmyer, "Letter to the Galatians," 788.

alienated from God, but as Burton aptly puts it, "the mode of life which is characterized by earthly advantages, viewed as obstacles to righteousness."[33] This world was once to him a living, vast, and tremendous reality . . . he was the world's servant and slave, and the world was his absolute, imperious, and cruel lord. This service was hopeless and degrading bondage. But now, through the death of Christ upon the cross, it had utterly and forever passed away."[34]

Through the cross of Christ, the world is crucified to him and he to the world. What does this mean for Paul? Paul has died to the world through the historic event at Calvary, which is the realization of the Father's plan of salvation for humanity. However, the adoption of that event into his life is nothing short of a mystical experience, brought about by the Spirit. Certainly Paul does not wish to give the impression that identification with the cross of Christ means an end to a person's relation to the physical world or humanity. For Paul, "the world" in its self-sufficiency as well as its legalistic righteousness has received its judgment and has been done away with in the cross of Christ. Hence, Paul's relationship to the world is to be determined by his faith-union relationship to Christ.

It seems to me that the focus of Paul's preaching was on the believer's participation in the redemptive significance of Christ's work.[35] The believer can be said to have been crucified to the world in the same sense that he or she died to sin and the Law. It was both positional and provisional. The perfect indicative passive "I have been crucified" (*estaurōtai*) expresses the fact that this is an event that has enduring effects. It expresses the condition in which Paul finds himself through his share in the Christ-event by faith, of which baptism is an expression (see Rom 6:3–11). Paul discovers that the cross is precisely where his link with the world is severed, since he has come to share in that fundamental salvation-event by death to sin and baptism into Christ (Rom 6).

THE DYNAMIC RELATIONSHIP OF SANCTIFICATION

Though Paul's statements that talk about the believer's crucifixion are formulated differently, they point to the same experiential reality. Paul was describing not only what happens to the believer at the time of the new birth or conversion—the initial moment of putting one's faith in the redemptive work of Christ on the cross—but also the pursuit of a dynamic, ongoing

33. Burton, *Epistle to the Galatians*, 354.
34. Beet, *St. Paul's Epistle*, 176.
35. Longenecker, *Ministry and Message of Paul*, 90.

holy life. The Christian, crucified with Christ, has died not only to the Law (Gal 2:19) but also to self (Gal 5:24), and to its earthbound degrading tendencies (Gal 6:14).

As far as Paul is concerned, since the death and resurrection of Jesus and the outpouring of the Spirit, the new people of God are identified, not by the rite of circumcision, but by the Spirit in their midst. The key criterion for being a part of the new people of God is the presence of the Spirit—the circumcision of the heart. The sanctified life is one that is both energized and lived by the power of the Spirit. Paul presents sanctification as a new way of living, which, although dependent on the Holy Spirit, does not minimize or abolish human responsibility.[36] For Paul, there is a fundamental transformation in the believer's life, and it is based on more than just a sacred memory. It is a dynamic, life-shaping relationship, walking by the Spirit with lives controlled by the Spirit. It is a journey in which the orientation of the whole being is toward God and his purposes. Believers no longer live out of their own resources.

Sanctification comprises a dynamic relationship with God made possible through Christ's crucifixion and resurrection as well as the believer's participation with him in those events. Yet, it is a life to be lived on a daily basis in a real world. Paul does not shy away from articulating his otherworldliness as a believer. Though in the world, he is not of the world.

In the same manner as Paul, the believer's hopes and aspirations are no longer based on his or her national and religious heritage. Instead, it is his or her being "in Christ" that determines every course of action.

---

36. With regards to this, the statement of Schrage, *Ethics of the New Testament*, 178, is seemingly problematic: "The Spirit is rather the very essence of the new life, in all its apparently insignificant and mundane details."

Chapter 6

Holiness in Ephesians

THE PRIMARY MOTIVATION FOR Paul's exhortations to holiness, as expressed throughout the book of Ephesians, is his view of the believer's union with Christ. The book is preoccupied with "expounding the nature of Christian salvation with respect to the church composed of Jews and Gentiles, and then the character of the new life that flows from this."[1] Paul identifies the very existence of the church only as a function of the person and work of Christ in his death and resurrection, and in his glorification (1:19, 20). The church is not to be passive observers of the exalted Lord, but is to know and attain to participation with him (1:5). Holiness, according to Ephesians, is essential for the achievement of that participation.

Paul never distinguishes between "practicing" believers and Christians who belong only nominally to the community; being Christian and belonging to the visibly assembled community are for him evidently equivalent. Beyond this, being Christian also requires correspondence between the sanctification received in baptism and the moral life of the baptized. Paul insists that if too great a gap exists between the two, the appropriate consequences be drawn. This is seen as we consider Paul's vocabulary of holiness in the Ephesian correspondence.

As Daniel Darko notes, "The author employs the language of differentiation to distinguish them from outsiders and to mark a radical departure from their previous way of life."[2] Paul's concern for the spiritual growth of the

1. Marshall, *New Testament Theology*, 380.
2. Darko, *No Longer Living as the Gentiles*, 110–11.

Ephesians was expressed in various ways, including prayer and exhortation. To drive home his point, Paul, in addition to the use of the *hagios* word group, employs such metaphors as light, temple, and body, among others, both to describe the Ephesians as well as to motivate them to live in a manner that is congruent with their calling.

Ephesians 1:1

In his opening address, Paul refers to his addressees as "saints" or "holy ones" (*hagioi*) as well as those who believe in Christ. It is striking that in describing the predominantly Gentile believers as saints, Paul is not afraid of using, for all believers, regardless of ethnicity, a term that is prevalent in the Old Testament as a designation for the old covenant people of God (Exod 22:31 [22:30]; Dan 7:18, 21, 22, 25). They were called "holy ones" because they had been chosen by God and consecrated to him as his own people. Thus, by status, they were the people of God. *Hagios* is a descriptive expression that portrays the new covenant people of God as the redeemed eschatological community prophesied by Daniel (Dan 7:22).[3]

The plural form of the word is instructive; it precludes individualism and isolationism. God's people are holy ones (saints) in communion. However, holiness was more than mere status. It was a state of being. God called them to reflect his own purity and integrity in their lives (Lev 11:45; 19:2). As such, Abbott's observation concerning the use of the word *hagios* here suggests that "the notion of inward personal holiness becomes attached to it from the thought of the obligation laid on those who are so set apart to a 'holy' God"[4] is apropos. To be holy entails being separated from defilement and becoming devoted to reflecting the character of God.

Ephesians 1:4

In Col 1:22, Paul refers to the reconciling effect that the crucifixion of Christ had for those who had been estranged and hostile toward God. Through Christ's work, the believer may now anticipate being presented before God as holy, blameless, and irreproachable. In Eph 1:4, Paul views not Christ's death, but God's selection of "us." He is thinking of an activity that was antecedent to that discussed in Col 1:21–22. In both passages, God and Christ's

---

3. Muddiman, *Epistle to the Ephesians*, 58–59.

4. Abbott, *Ephesians and Colossians*, 2. Contra Klein, "Ephesians," 45–46, who suggests that the term holy may not have an ethical component here.

work have the same end: the presentation before God of the believers who are holy and blameless.

To understand the use of *hagios* here, one needs to note that Paul is speaking strictly of God's activity, not humans'. God *chose* us in him—in Christ. "Us" most logically would refer to Paul and those to whom he was writing. When Paul says that believers have been chosen before the foundation of the world (*pro katabolēs kosmou*), he probably had in mind God's act of selecting these believers before all creation, independent of any and all circumstances appertaining to these created persons. When pieced together, then, verse 4a asserts that God has chosen "us" proleptically in Christ before any of "us" was created.

The reason Paul and his readers were chosen, that they might be holy and blameless in God's presence, is to be understood in the same way as Col 1:22b.[5] In that these people were chosen, they were separated to God. The reason they were separated to God was in order that they be ethically pure and subject to no charge when they stand before God at the time of judgment. They were not separated in order that they be separated. As Taylor rightly states,

> Holy (*hagios*) expresses the positive experiential purpose of God's choice. More than ceremonial holiness is meant here; that is, more than a mere difference stemming from a divine separation. Holy expresses the inner, moral difference which prevails when God's grace is operative in the heart. This fact is abundantly indicated in the second word describing the result of the choice, namely blameless (*amōmos*).[6]

Hans Conzelmann suggests that "holy," "blameless," and "irreproachable" signify "perfection," which is the purpose of God's election.[7] However, he is sure to emphasize that this perfection is not something into which the believer may work himself or herself and thereby claim as a personal accomplishment. To the contrary, the believers are presented as perfect before God ("Wir werden als solche dargestellt vor Gott").[8]

Conzelmann is surely correct in stressing that the believer will be perfect when presented before God. Paul held the same high expectations as he did of any other Christians. In praying that the believers "may be filled with all the fullness of God" (3:19b); in reminding them that the gifts of Christ were given that they might "attain . . . to the measure of the stature of the

---

5. See discussion on Colossians below.
6. Taylor, "Ephesians," 147–48.
7. Conzelmann, "Der Brief an die Epheser," 141 and 60.
8. Ibid., 141.

fullness of Christ" (4:13); and in urging them to "be imitators of God" (5:12), Paul was doing nothing less than calling the Christians to seek after ethical purity and blamelessness in this life. Here again one sees the relationship between Paul's idea of the ethically holy life and *love*, as he urges their lives be so oriented (see 3:17; 4:2, 15–16; 5:2, 25, etc.). Consequently, one cannot properly speak of a completed (and in that sense, perfect) holiness because its growth knows no bounds; but one surely can speak of a Christian living and acting in love generated through the power of the Spirit of Christ.

The goal or purpose for which God chose his people in Christ is that we should *be holy and blameless* before him *in love*. Evidently, election does bring privilege while it also carries with it responsibility. As Grizzle trenchantly puts it, "far from giving a false sense of smug complacency to sin, far from encouraging moral laxity, election places an ethical demand upon the Christian."[9] God's purpose in the believer's election was not simply to repair the damage done by sin but also to fulfill God's original intention for humankind, namely, to create for himself a people perfectly conformed to the likeness of his Son (Rom 8:29–30).

Holy and blameless in his sight echoes the language of Col 1:22, where the purpose of Christ's reconciling work is the presentation of his people "holy, blameless and irreproachable in his presence." The two adjectives *holy and blameless,* which also appear in 5:27, were used to describe the unblemished animals set apart for God as Old Testament sacrifices (Exod 29:37–38; see Heb 9:14; 1 Pet 1:19). As O'Brien contends, this language was already present within the Old Testament and used to describe ethical purity.[10] He argues that both terms have lost any cultic overtones in Col 1:22 and Eph 1:4,[11] referring instead to ethical holiness and freedom from moral blemish.[12] However, one may suggest that inasmuch as a temple is cultic space, the words *holy* and *blameless* are capable of both nuances. Moreover, as Flemming notes, Paul's flexibility and ability to contextualize "allowed him to appropriate traditional language images and recontextualize them under the guidance of the Spirit."[13] This is the case here, where Paul uses the language of sanctification in the Old Testament purity code and "transposes that language, consistently applying it to the ethical character and behavior that was the responsibility of the believer."[14]

9. Grizzle, *Ephesians*, 33.
10. E.g., Ps 15 [LXX 14]:2; 18:23 [17:24].
11. See Eph 5:27; Phil 2:15; Jude 24.
12. O'Brien, *Letter to the Ephesians*, 100–1.
13. Flemming, *Contextualization in the New Testament*, 110–11.
14. Ibid., 110–11.

The term *amōmos* is used in the Old Testament to describe sacrificial animals (LXX Exod 29:37; Num 6:14; 9:2). In this usage it has an ethical connotation as it does in Col 1:22. Abbott,[15] Beet,[16] and Findlay[17] are correct in viewing Paul's statement as asserting that the ultimate end of God's choice is our sanctification—our being ethically pure and without blame.

Ephesians 1:15–23

As Samuel Chadwick says, "Paul's prayers are the best expositions of his theology."[18] If the preceding statement is true, Paul's prayer in chapter 1:15–23 is an important text for the discussion of holiness in Ephesians. The prayer comes as a result of Paul's joy in and desire toward the Ephesians. As believers who were "in Christ," these Ephesians had been selected to be holy and blameless before him in love (1:4); they had trusted in Christ (1:12); they had been sealed with the Holy Spirit of promise (1:13); and they had been made alive spiritually (2:1, 5). Here in 1:15, they had expressed faith and love to all.

Paul begins his introductory prayer by reintroducing love and holiness as cardinal values to the church, and continues that thought throughout the prayer in this passage. Verses 22 and 23a present the image of a unity between the church and Christ. In conjunction with the introduction of the letter and the opening of this prayer, God's purpose for his people is drawn into focus. Paul, by calling the church Christ's body, describes the intimacy intended between Christ and the church. Many commentators addressing these verses focus on the aspect of headship conveyed in this metaphor. It is clear, however, from the context, that there is an intimate union between Christ and the Church greater than that of just a group being led.

Ephesians 2:21

In the discussion of the reconciling work of Christ Jesus set forth in 2:11ff., Gentiles and Jews, two alienated peoples, have been reconciled to God through the death of Christ and have been made "one new man in place of the two" (v. 15b). As "one new man" in Christ Jesus, the Gentile and the Jew

---

15. Abbott, *Ephesians and the Colossians*, 7–8.
16. Beet, *St. Paul's Epistle to the Ephesians*, 275.
17. Findlay, *Epistle to the Ephesians*, 29.
18. A statement attributed to Samuel Chadwick as cited by McCumber, *Holiness in the Prayers of St. Paul*, 11.

together now belong to the household of God. Using a variety of nominal and verbal variations on the *oikos* word group in verses 19–22, Paul states that all those who are members of the household of God are growing compositely into the holy temple (*naos hagios*). This thought (v. 21) he further explains by the clause "in whom, that is to say, you are growing together into a dwelling place of God in the Spirit." The temple into which these Gentiles and Jews who have become Christians are growing is holy by virtue of its being the dwelling of God's Spirit (v. 22), and because the growth taking place is "in the Lord" (v. 21). "In the Lord" may be understood in its incorporative sense. The temple is holy because Christ, in and through whom the temple exists, is himself holy.

Ephesians 3:5

In the immediate context, Paul contrasts those persons of the first Christian generation (himself included; cf. vv. 2–3) who have received by the Spirit the revelation of "the mystery of Christ" with those of former generations who failed to receive this revelation. Those to whom the revelation has been given are called "his holy apostles and prophets." The antecedent of "his" is "Christ" (v. 4b). These apostles and prophets are holy, in part, because they comprise a portion of the foundation of the new holy temple of God (see 2:20–22).

The thought in 2:20–22 differs from 1 Cor 3:10ff.; in the latter, Paul "laid the foundation . . . which is Christ Jesus." In the present context, Paul, the other apostles and prophets, and the Jews and the Gentiles who have become Christians are all growing together with Christ Jesus, "for a dwelling place of God in the Spirit." As apostles and prophets who are commissioned to the apostolate by the will of God (see 1:1) and who serve by the grace of God (see 3:7), it is quite natural that Paul would refer to these persons as *hagioi*. It is not clear if he means to imply anything regarding their ethical status. They are holy in that they have been set apart unto the service of God the Father and Christ Jesus (see 4:11–13).

As stated earlier, Paul's reference to these apostles and prophets as holy is no surprise. It has been repeatedly maintained that Paul used *hagios* with reference to people to denote either that they were to be ethically pure or that they were set apart to belong to him. Just as *hagios* was quite commonly used as a designation of the believers (*hoi hagioi*), meaning those set apart to belong to God, so *hagios* could be used by Paul to refer to the apostles and prophets. Even if the term in this context had a qualitative significance, such a thought would not be impossible for Paul.

The context suggests a relational significance for the term. It is not because of their ethically pure lives that the apostle and prophets have been granted insight in the mystery of Christ. They have received this insight precisely because God graciously set them apart (see 3:7–8).

Ephesians 5:1–4

In this section Paul uses the vocabulary of imitation to describe the holiness that should characterize the people of God. Paul exhorts the Ephesians to become imitators of God. In other words, those who claim to be God's must portray a likeness of God. Paul's audience would have been very familiar with the word *mimeitai* ("imitators") in Eph 5:1a, since the Greeks portrayed their heroes and gods in several plays in which actors would put on masks of heroes and gods to portray them to their audience. However, Paul's usage of the word here is unique.[19] It is the only time in all of the New Testament that this expression is specifically made.

Patterning after the likeness of God is implied in many ways throughout Scripture but not in so direct a command. Although it is evident that the exact vocabulary of imitation does not occur in the Old Testament, it is not entirely correct to suggest, as Markus Barth does, that the concept is absent.[20] However, Barth correctly notes that the concept can be found among Hellenistic Jewish writes, particularly Philo,[21] who follows Plato's idea that the one who wishes to be dear to God must be like him, and those who desire to be righteous must be likened to God as far as it is humanly possible.[22]

Paul shares commands for imitation in other passages, but not of God. To the Corinthians, his exhortation was for his "children" (converts) to imitate him (1 Cor 4:16). Later, in the context of the discussion on idol food in that same letter (11:1), he encourages the Corinthians to follow his example. In writing to the Thessalonians, Paul expands his list of people to

---

19. All but one (Heb 6:12) of the six occurrences of the word are to be found in the Pauline corpus (1 Cor 4:16; 11:1; 1 Thess 1:6; 2 Thess 3:7, 9). He described his behavior before the Corinthians and the world as *hagiotēs* (2 Cor 1:12). He reminded the Thessalonians that ". . . holy (*hosiōs*) and righteous and blameless was our behavior to you believers" (1 Thess 2:10). He could likewise have used *hagios* to designate the ethical character of the apostles and prophets.

20. Barth, *Ephesians*, 556n10.

21. Philo, *De Fuga et Inventione*, 12 § 63.

22. Plato's *Republic* X, 613; *Laws*, 716cd; *Theatetus*, 176 ab. In several places in the Old Testament, God commands His people, "You shall be holy for I the Lord your God am holy" (Exod 19:6; Lev 11:44; 20:7, 26).

be imitated, which includes not only himself, but his companions as well (2 Thess 3:7, 9). In 1 Thess 1:6, he commends his readers for doing this very thing, as well as the imitation of "God's churches in Judea" (1 Thess 2:14). As Abbott notes, to be the imitators of God "is a grand idea and ennobling one," and our Lord himself sets it before us, and in the same aspect, when he says, "Ye therefore shall be perfect as your heavenly Father is perfect (Matt 5:48)."[23]

The imitation of God is predicated on belongingness—*peripatein* ("to walk")—on the believers' relationship with him. The believers in Ephesus are dearly loved children of God (Eph 5:1). As such, they should reciprocate this love by imitation. Paul goes on to show the means of achieving this imitation by giving the command to live a life of love (5:2a). The Ephesians are to walk in love. Paul uses the word as a metaphor for living or conducting one's life. Since God loves us, his love should be evident in our own lives, expressed in all that we do. It should influence us into the unmistakable image of God as we make ourselves available to love's life-changing influence. The example of this openness to God's love is found in Jesus Christ, his Son, and we should live this life of love just as Christ loved us (5:2). The ultimate expression of this love is found in Christ's sacrificial death on our behalf (see John 15:13), as Christ gave himself up for us as a fragrant offering and sacrifice to God (Eph 5:2).

Paul then describes Jesus' sacrifice with two words, viz., *prosphoran*, translated as "offering" and *thysian*, "sacrifice." The former refers more specifically to the gift that was brought to the temple for the sacrifice, while the latter refers more to the act of sacrifice itself. This twofold expression illustrates our response to God's love that will result in our imitation of his likeness. As *phosphoran* suggests, we must be willing to see ourselves as a sacrifice given totally to God for his pleasure, whereas *thysian* is related to the smoke resulting from the sacrifice, which produced an aroma. What he receives from our lives should only be that which is pleasant and well-pleasing to him. Our surrender and subsequent living should always be seen as an action before God and, thereby, tempered with a resolve to make our lives pleasing.

Having given the positive ideal of imitating God (5:3–4), Paul begins to address in details specific expressions that imitation or holiness must *not* include. It is significant to note Paul's prohibitions are both personal and corporate. This becomes clear as one examines the sins that Paul condemns in vv. 3–4. In both instances, Paul demonstrates the relational or social nature of holiness. He makes it clear that inappropriate social behaviors are

---

23. Abbott, *Epistle to the Ephesians and Colossians*, 146.

not to be tolerated within the community. This is akin to what Paul does in other letters (1 Cor 5:1–5; Gal 1:8–9; 2 Cor 2:6–8).

Ephesians 5:3 expresses this strongly by not allowing even a hint of these acts to be found within the church. Although verse 4 is more general in its prohibition, it is no less accepting, as Paul unequivocally states, "nor should there be." Thus, the community plays a major role of maintaining holiness among its members, thereby becoming a sanctifying agent.

The Ephesians are God's holy people. In keeping with his exhortation in 4:17 to "no longer live as the unbelieving Gentiles," Paul continues to prohibit any suggestion of pagan lifestyle and worship that could become confused with the Christian faith. Such actions might have been popular before Christ came into their lives, but they could no longer even be hinted at within the church.

Paul's next list of prohibitions refers mainly to verbal expressions that are not to be a part of the believer's life. The context implies that Paul is now prohibiting from the mouth the same kind of immoral actions that are expressed by the body. Obscenity, foolish talk, or coarse joking should not be exercised (5:4). Paul is not prohibiting the good-natured fun that people have with puns or exchanging jests; he is addressing the error that results when such communication takes a downward turn and uses ideas and situations that are not in keeping with the Christian lifestyle or its expression. After all, if an act or behavior is inappropriate for us to become involved in physically, it is just as inappropriate for us to enter into verbally.

The opposite behavior of these prohibitions is thanksgiving (5:4). This is not to imply that the only thing Christians can converse about is their thankfulness for God and his salvation. Instead, Paul is setting the perspective so we remember that instead of being involved in such sinful practices, we should use our tongues to express thanks for what we have received from him.

Ephesians 5:26–27

In the midst of exhortations to husbands and wives regarding their responsibilities to one another, the author recalls the love that Christ demonstrated toward the church as an example of the love husbands should have for their wives. In the course of amplifying this through, he refers to the death of Christ (v. 25b) and its purpose (vv. 26f.) The purpose of this sacrificial act was that Christ might sanctify the church and make her holy. Paul has previously (1:4) indicated that God chose the believers in Christ to be "holy and blameless before him in love." What only Yahweh could do on behalf of

Israel (Deut 7:6–8) is attributed to the work of Christ Jesus on behalf of the church. Christ sanctified—he once and for all separated unto himself—the church.

The clause "having cleansed her by the washing of water with the word" (v. 26b) is generally interpreted as a reference to the initiation baptism one must undergo if one is to become a member of the sanctified church.[24] Although it remains a matter of debate whether the first readers of Ephesians would have understood the reference of "washing of water" as baptism, Stephen Fowl is certainly right in arguing that it is the best option.[25]

Titus 3:5 and Acts 22:16 are both similar in their emphasis upon the role of baptism in the conversion process. Baptism alone is not sufficient to redeem. The church, that is, all whom God chose before the foundation of the world (see 1:4), is sanctified by Christ's death; the individual is saved by God's grace through faith without any works, including baptism (see 2:8–10). Nevertheless the washing by the water of baptism, together with the believer's personal confession, constitute the response the individual must make in order to avail himself or herself of the sanctification that Christ has antecedently wrought through his death.

Christ died that he might separate the church to himself; he separated the church to himself in order that he himself might present it to himself as a glorious church (v. 27a). As we can see, verse 27a is amplified both negatively and positively. Negatively, the glorious nature of the church will consist in its having no "spot or wrinkle or any such thing" (v. 27b). Positively, the church will be holy and blameless (v. 27c). Fowl is correct in noting that "the use of the terms, 'holy and blameless' in 5:27 to describe the end of the church indicates that holiness is the communal end toward which God calls the church as a body."[26] Again, Paul's concern is to stress that when the believers are presented before God, they are to be ethically pure and subject to no condemnation. The eschatological dimension of the passage is worth noting. The holiness of the church is in the context of the coming of Christ, for which believers must be prepared.

Abbott[27] and Ellicott[28] suggested that *hagiasē* referred not simply to "consecration," but to the "infusion of holiness and moral purity."[29] Moral purity is not always associated with being sanctified or consecrated; rather,

---

24. Cf. Abbot, *Ephesians*, 168; Beet, *Ephesians*, 360; Conzelmann, *Epheser*, 87.
25. Fowl, *Ephesians*, 189.
26. Ibid., 40.
27. Abbott, *Ephesians*, 168.
28. Ellicot, *St. Paul's Epistle to the Ephesians*, 130.
29. Ibid.

moral purity emerges in the life of the believer as that life is increasingly committed to and obedient to Christ Jesus, the head of the church (see 5:23f.).

HOLINESS IS MULTIFACETED

The examination of holiness in Ephesians reveals that although it is true that the Ephesian believers were clearly in a state of spiritual union with Christ, they had needs that were of great importance to Paul. He was concerned with their holiness and spiritual improvement.

When one compares the situation of the Ephesians with the Corinthians, it is hard to reach the conclusion that holiness is meant only for those who had various struggles like the Corinthians had. The call and experience of holiness are for those whose lives are presently pleasing to God to move up to the full potential of life "in Christ."

It is not without significance that when Paul speaks of believers being holy and blameless, it is in the context of *parousia*, the coming manifestation of Christ. Paul's teaching echoes Heb 12:14, "without holiness no one will see the Lord." For Paul, holiness is multifaceted. It is the participation in the life of Christ. Holiness is both a status and a state. Those who belong to God must live as it befits their calling. Although certainly personal, it is not individualistic. It is to manifest in social relations within the community of faith, while it ensures the separateness of the community from the moral pollution by which it is surrounded.

Chapter 7

Holiness in Philippians

As we've seen, holiness permeates the fabric of Pauline theology. Paul's letters are full of instructions, exhortations, and admonitions calling believers to holy living. Paul continues that task in his letter to the Philippians. For Paul, holiness is not a mere mental abstraction or a dogma to embrace; rather, it is a practical reality for the present, to be experienced daily in the life of the believer. It is the essence of Christian profession.

Paul's teaching of holiness in Philippians demands that one look beyond a single word. Instead, attention needs be paid to motifs, concepts, as well as allusions to the subject. For example, although the *hagios* word group does not feature prominently in Philippians,[1] the book is nevertheless filled with holiness motifs and vocabularies. Furthermore, Paul does not only present the life of Christ as the paradigm of holy living, but also presents himself as an example of the life of holiness that ought to characterize both the individual and the community.

---

1. The three occurrences of the word group are in 1:1; 4:21; and 4:22. In 1:1, Paul employs the term in the same way that he does in other places, designating his addresses who are mainly comprised of "Gentiles" and various social standings as the holy people of God. Here as well as in 4:21, Paul speaks of them as "holy in Christ" and "holy in Christ Jesus."

Philippians 1:9–11

Paul speaks of his prayers for the Philippians in verse 4. Now he reveals some of the content of his prayers:

> And this is my prayer: that your love may abound more and more in knowledge and depth of insight, so that you may be able to discern what is best in order that you may be pure and blameless until the day of Christ, filled with the fruit of righteousness that comes through Jesus Christ, for the glory and praise of God.

As one examines the prayer, it becomes evident that Paul is concerned with the holiness of the Philippians. Several aspects of the prayer attest to this view. First, in verse 9, Paul prays that the love of the Philippians for one another may grow. When Paul prays for "love" he is not praying for mere affections. As Gordon Fee notes, "As used by Paul, and following the lead of the Septuagint, 'love' first of all points to the character of God and to God's actions toward his people based on that character."[2] As he further notes, the rest of the prayer focuses on behavior and not affection.[3]

Paul's concern is with the type of love that is motivated by a person's will and is seen in one's action: the type of selfless love that Christ demonstrated through his sacrificial living and death (Phil 2:5–9). This is the type of love that Paul is praying for in Philippians. That love is to abound more and more.

His prayer for the Philippians to abound in love is tightly woven together with knowledge and depth of insight (1:9b). The love Paul is praying for is that which is according to knowledge, and for one to be able to properly act in love. Paul's requests that the church would grow in love and grow in understanding and wisdom lead directly into his request that the Philippians "may approve the things that are excellent" (v. 10a). In other words, he prays that their knowledge and insight will be used in their discernment of the good and the bad, not just to see the difference but also to choose that which is good.

Paul continues his prayer that the church will "approve the things that are excellent" so that they will be "sincere and blameless until the day of Christ" (v. 10b). Paul prays that they will be found pure when Jesus returns. For Paul, holiness is a necessary preparation for the day of Christ. His prayer for sincerity (*eilikrineis*) relates to moral purity and integrity. Paul uses this word to describe his sincere motives as a minister of Christ (2 Cor 1:12; 2:17), and signifies Christian character that is genuine, authentic, and transparent before God and others. The second term, blameless (*aproskopos*), is

---

2. Fee, *Philippians*, 98.
3. Ibid.

used in 1 Cor 10:32 with the nuance of causing others to stumble. It can also mean to be without offense in one's personal life, as it is used in Acts 24:16.

Paul's immediate concern with standing before Christ's judgment that is expressed in the prayer favors the latter meaning. Thus, in the same manner as in verse 6, Paul envisions the work of God among the Philippians in light of the "day of Christ Jesus" when they will stand before him. Paul expects the Philippians to live a holy life in the present, even as they anticipate the day of Christ. Thus, holiness is not merely a future aspiration or goal that will happen at Christ's return. Rather it is the moral character of their lives here and now that will prepare them and make them ready to stand the test of that great day, whenever it comes.[4]

Paul is praying that the people in the church at Philippi may live lives that are growing into the holiness that God has already placed upon them. God made them pure and blameless; now may their lives be a reflection of that grace. One cannot reflect holiness, though, if his or her life is filled with sinful actions, undiscerning knowledge, and a lack of love. So Paul prays that they may be found pure when Christ returns for his church. Paul's last request in this prayer is that they will be filled with the fruit of righteousness.

As believers grow in love and knowledge, as they discern and do what is right, as they are sincere and blameless for the coming of Jesus, their lives will be marked by the abundance of spiritual fruit that comes through Jesus. The fruit that is visible in a believer's life is love, joy, peace, patience, kindness, goodness, faithfulness, gentleness, and self-control (Gal 5:22–23). It will be seen in their humility toward one another (Phil 2:1–8) and in the hope they have as they await the coming of our God and Savior, Jesus Christ (Titus 2:11–14).

The necessity of holiness is seen in Philippians not only in the prayer of Paul (1:9–11) but also in his exhortations to live a life that is worthy of the gospel of Christ (1:27); live a Christlike life (2:5–9); strive for the goal (3:12–16), and think holy thoughts (4:8–9). Paul's ultimate desire for the Philippians is their perfection. Paul's prayer for holiness is rooted in his desire for the praise and glory of God (1:11). By asking that the Philippians manifest the fruit of righteousness in their lives, the ultimate goal of Paul's petitions is to bring glory to God, who redeemed them.

Philippians 1:27–30

Paul has detailed his own personal circumstances—his sufferings as a result of his faithfulness to the gospel—and more particularly his refusal to be

---

4. Flemming, *Philippians*, 57–58.

deterred by them. He now turns to the suffering of the Philippians. In spite of the intense persecution they faced, Paul responds in one long sentence, the first part (v. 27) of which demands attention here. Paul begins the exhortation with the word "only" (*monon*). Reflecting the significance of that word, Karl Barth translates it as "just one thing!"[5] He goes on to say that it is lifted like a warning finger. The Philippians needed to pay attention to what Paul had to say concerning how they were to live in light of, and regardless of, their present circumstances.

The word translated "live" is the Greek word *politeuesthe*, which literally means to "live as citizens," or "live out your citizenship," a rare political metaphor,[6] the implications of which would have been understood by the Philippians whose city, according to Acts 16:12, was a Roman colony. The residents had legal status and enjoyed the same privileges, such as exemption from poll taxes and land taxation as native-born Romans. However, such privileges came with corresponding obligations. Paul transfers this idea to the Philippians whose citizenship is now *heavenly* (3:20). So, Paul exhorts the Philippians to live in a manner that befits the gospel of Christ—to embody the message of the gospel in every aspect of their daily lives. Their common life as a community must continually reflect Jesus' self-giving love for others (2:1–11).[7] Their state must match their status. There is to be no chasm between belief and behavior. The believer's new life in Christ demands a corresponding new life in reality. It entails living in ways that are consistent with the gospel. Believers' lives should incarnate the gospel. The gospel also establishes a norm for Christian conduct that is the essence of holiness.

Two important points emerge in this text. First, Paul's call to holiness is corporate. It was a call to the entire community of which individuals form constituent members. Second, the holiness to which Paul calls his audience is to be demonstrable. It is both moral and ethical.

Philippians 2:14–16

Here we find Paul's exhortation on holiness to the Philippians—a practical outworking of their salvation. They are to live as God's holy people in a dark world that Paul describes in stark terms as crooked and perverse. He writes:

---

5. Barth, *Epistle to the Philippians*, 45.
6. Flemming, *Philippians*, 85.
7. Ibid.

> Do all things without grumbling or questioning, that you may be blameless (*amemptos*) and innocent (*akeraios*), children of God without blemish (*amōmos*) in the midst of a crooked and perverse generation, among whom shine as lights in the world, holding fast the word of life, so that in the day of Christ I may be proud that I did not run in vain.

Paul's exhortation presents holiness both in negative and positive terms. In the negative sense Paul enjoins the Philippians to shun grumbling or questioning. Paul employs three terms to describe the state of readiness in which the believers at Philippi are to keep themselves. The first of the terms, *amemptos*, "blameless," is used in the Septuagint of Abraham (Gen 17:1). God commanded Abraham to walk before him and be blameless. It is used in several places in the Book of Job where it appears in parallel to several words such as *dikaios*, "righteous" (Job 9:20; 12:4; 15:14; 22:19); and *katharos*, "pure" (Job 4:17; 11:4; 33:9). It translates as the Hebrew word *tam*, "blameless" or "guiltless" (Job 2:3; 9:20); *tahar*, "pure"; and *bar*, "pure" (Job 11:4).

The second term *akeraios*, "innocent" is found only in Matt 10:16 and Rom 16:19. It is translated as innocent and guileless, with ethical overtones. Christ's followers are to be characterized by a balance of prudence and purity.[8]

The third term is *amōmos*.[9] It occurs frequently in Exodus, Leviticus, Numbers, and Ezekiel in the context of worship where it translates as *tam*, "blameless" and is applied to animals that were meant for sacrifice. However, it was also used to describe a person's moral state. David, in writing his song of deliverance, maintained that "he had lived a life of moral integrity, he had walked in God's ways and avoided wickedness, he had lived within God's judgments and statutes and had been blameless."[10] So he writes:

> I was also blameless (*amōmos*) with him,
> And I kept myself from my iniquity.
> Therefore the Lord has recompensed me according
> to my righteousness,
> According to the cleanness of my hands in his eyes
> (Ps 18:23, 24).

The same sense of the term is evident from Psalm 15, where David asks a question about the nature and character of the person who desires to

---

8. Hahn, *Matthew*, 139.
9. See comments on this word in the previous chapter.
10. Craigie, *Psalms* 1–50, 174–175.

enter God's presence. It is a question that is as important now as it was then, both in terms of preparation for worship as well as preparing for the end of the world:

> O LORD, who may abide in Your tent? Who may dwell on Your holy hill?
> He who walks blamelessly (*amōmos*), and works righteousness, (*ergazomenos dikaiosynēn*)
> And speaks truth in his heart.

In his call to the Philippians to be blameless, innocent, and without blemish, Paul calls for a moral transformation in every aspect of the believer's life in Christ. It is a life that should be beyond reproach in every area. The Philippian Christians, and by implication all believers, are to be innocent and free from guilt if they are to present themselves as a holy and acceptable sacrifice to God. The result of the Philippians' living, as described by Paul, is that they will shine as light. The metaphor of light both accentuates the radical difference between believers and unbelievers and shows the observable nature of holiness that should characterize the Philippians.

Philippians 3:12–16

Philippians 3:12–16 is significant for the understanding of holiness in the book, particularly for the use of the term "perfection" in verses 12 and 15. Paul not only shows how holy living can be accomplished but also demonstrates that holiness involves making progress in one's relationship with God. In other words, holiness is a sign of growth.

Philippians 3:12 begins with the apostle's confession that he has not already attained and has not already been perfected (*ouk hoti ēdē elabon hē ēdē teteleiōmai*). It is notable that the verb *elabon*, translated as "attain" or "obtain," in this verse does not have an object. In this case, the implied object of *elabon* is Paul's goal mentioned in 3:8–11: to reflect in his life all the qualities of Christ while he was on the earth, as well as those he reflected after the resurrection.[11] Paul desires to know Christ now both in terms of his resurrection power and sufferings. However, such knowledge must wait until Paul participates in the end-time resurrection from the dead.[12]

What does perfection mean in this verse? The verb *teleioō*, "to make perfect," is capable of many meanings, including completion or bringing to an end, as well as making someone or something perfect, and to become

---

11. O'Brien, *Philippians*, 422; Getz, *Profile of Christian Maturity*, 148.
12. Cf. Flemming, *Philippians*, 183.

mature.[13] Because Paul mentions that this is a state he has not yet attained, one might ask in what sense the apostle has not been perfected. Some interpreters do not only see the verse as Paul's denial of perfection but also suggest that it precludes the possibility of perfection in any sense whatever (that will include holiness), for any believer, in the present time.[14] Due to this misinterpretation, it has been suggested that Paul's confession indicates that he has not attained righteousness or holiness. If that were the case, holiness would be seen not as a present reality, but as a conclusion to the life of faith, that is, perfection in terms of "present holiness" would not come to a believer until death. But this is not the case.

As John Walters notes, "the 'as many as be perfect' three verses later (v. 15) trouble some scholars to the point that they must take *teleios* to mean 'mature' rather than 'perfect,' or recognizing the influence of the verb they say Paul is parroting his opponents derisively."[15] He further notes that "it is a common expedient to translate *teleios* as 'mature in passages that might be taken to be perfectionistic."[16] He is certainly right that the perceived awkwardness of perfectionistic espousal does not in any way justify reading "mature" and "perfect" as synonyms, which they are not in English,[17] although admittedly the Greek word is capable of either meaning.

To one extent, Paul is not perfect in his knowledge and understanding of Christ.[18] This explanation helps the reader understand what Paul means in stating that he has not already obtained it. Paul has not yet come to know Christ in the power of his resurrection. That is to say, Paul does not have the perfection that comes in the resurrection, the eschatological consummation of his salvation.[19] This ought not to be confused with ethical perfection. Rather, Paul has in mind the transition to a higher level of existence.[20]

Paul continues the verse by stating that he presses on to apprehend that for which Christ apprehended him. Apprehending, *katalambanō*, refers to more than just a passive reception. Its New Testament usage indicates seizure with hostile intent, an act of overtaking.[21] This points to an aggressive

---

13. BAGD, 817. See also Doughty, "Citizens of Heaven," 114. He renders the meaning of this word as "fulfillment."
14. Beare, *Philippians*, 128–32 is representative of this view.
15. Walters, *Perfection in New Testament Theology*, 217.
16. Ibid.
17. See further discussion on verse 15 below.
18. Hawthorne, *Philippians*, 151.
19. Martin, *Philippians*, 151; O'Brien, *Philippians*, 423.
20. Hooker, *Philippians*, 533–34.
21. O'Brien, *Philippians*, 424.

takeover. Paul is in constant, intense pursuit so that he may decisively and definitively overtake that for which Christ decisively and definitively overtook him.

With verse 13, Paul begins in this passage to point to himself as an example for the believers. The apostle reiterates to the Philippian community that he does not consider himself to have apprehended full knowledge yet. Once again Paul does not indicate a direct object for his verb, but given the goal he had mentioned in the verses preceding verse 12, it is quite possible that what he is seeking after is the full knowledge of Christ or the blessedness of the resurrection.[22] In either case, Paul is clear to admit that he does not consider his present state as having "arrived" spiritually, unlike his opponents who are quick to boast of perfection.

The apostle then shifts the focus of this verse from negative action to positive action: "but one thing *I do*: forgetting what *lies* behind and reaching forward to what *lies* ahead." Paul does not offer any specifics regarding what "one thing" is.[23] Perhaps the thought of his exhortation in 1:27 is present here. However, it is clear that he has a singular purpose in mind. The singularity of purpose is very much indicative of one of the many facets of Christian holiness. With one purpose in clear view, Paul can avoid the trap of being a double-minded person. He forgets the things that are behind him and reaches forward to the things that lie ahead.

Verse 14 provides Paul's clear description of his course of action. He is pressing on toward the goal for the prize of the upward call of God in Christ Jesus. Interestingly, Paul places the goal, *skopon*, at the front of the sentence. A literal rendering would be, "toward the goal I press on." The goal is Paul's primary focus. In using the imagery of running a race, Paul emphasizes not the race but the end of the race. Running the race is important, but the focus of the runner is not on the mechanics of running—it's on reaching the goal. The finish line is his sole focus, and the prize comes as a result of his striving toward the goal. With this in mind, the prize of the upward call can possibly be seen not as the goal itself, but rather the result of pressing toward the goal.

Paul again returns to his use of *diōkō* ("pursue") to describe his act of pressing on. The repetition shows that he is in "hot pursuit"[24] of the goal, strenuously pursuing what is before him. Returning to the imagery of the runner, Paul is not running in an effort to make the team, but rather with

---

22. Martin, *Philippians*, 152.
23. Ibid., 153.
24. Silva, *Philippians*, 201.

the enthusiasm of one who has already made the team. With his identity secure, he is able to run with all his might toward the goal.

The prize Paul seeks to receive is found in the high calling of God in Christ Jesus. There are a number of possible meanings for what this high calling is. Possibly, it is a reference to the final hope for the Christian, the ultimate goal of our lives: heaven.[25] Indeed, one would be hard-pressed to conceive of a higher call or a more excellent goal to pursue. In a sense, heaven is the final goal of the believer. However, Paul may have something else in mind in this passage.

Perhaps Paul is thinking of his eschatological life with Christ. This makes achieving the goal of holiness a distinct possibility for this life, and a goal toward which one should strive. This should not be confused with the perfection mentioned in verse 12, the final state that comes with the eschatological resurrection. Rather, it should be understood as the call to holiness in daily life. It is the call that God issues to believers in his mercy, beckoning them out of rebellion and sin into fellowship with him.[26] This fellowship is possible and is to be normative for today.

Paul's argument comes to a full circle in verse 15. He starts by urging those who are perfect to have the attitude he has just finished describing. Paul uses the adjective *teleioi* to describe those who are perfect. As previously noted, this word can have several possible translations, including persons who are fully up to standard as well as those who are fully developed in a moral sense.[27]

The immediate question that confronts the interpreter is what Paul means by "perfect" in verse 15. This issue becomes even more important when it is understood that Paul includes himself in this group. So who are the perfect? Some suggest that Paul is simply referring to those who are mature.[28] As such, the word perfect is simply to be understood as a synonym for maturity.

While maturity is an accurate description of those to whom Paul referred, such a rendering does not only diminish the force of the word but entirely misses the point. Alex R. Deasley's observation on this verse is helpful. He notes that the translation *mature* is quite possible, as long as one understands what Paul means by it. He argues that "it has a moral and

---

25. See Beare, *Philippians*, 130; Griffith, *This Is Living*, 98; Johnstone, *Philippians*, 289; Silva, *Philippians*, 202. Each of these suggests either directly or indirectly that Paul's intent is the heavenly hope that lies at the end of the Christian life.

26. Martin, *Philippians*, 154.

27. *BAGD*, 817.

28. See Johnstone, *Lectures on the Book of Philippians*, 293 and O'Brien, *Epistle to the Philippians*, 436, as two examples among many.

ethical dimension, as is evident from his use of it in 1 Cor 2:6 and his elaboration of its opposite in 1 Cor 3:1–3."[29] Also, it is not to be understood to "denote simply having been in process for a long time."[30] As Morna Hooker rightly argues,

> In the present context "perfect" (*teleios*) probably has a more specific meaning than is conveyed by the English word "mature" . . . Paul has exchanged a life that was without fault according to the Law (v. 6) for the purity and blamelessness that belong to Christ and to those who live in him.[31]

Holiness is a present reality to be lived out in this life.[32] It is not the exception, but rather it is the rule. This is by no means an experience that cannot be realized in this life.[33]

Paul instructs those who are perfect to have "this" attitude or mindset. "This" refers to forgetting the past and pressing on to win the prize.[34] Clearly, the apostle asserts that true holiness involves the constant pursuit for growth in grace. It is not a static arrogance that allows people to believe they have already arrived. Rather, it is the understanding that no believer should ever be content in his or her current level of Christian experience.[35] There is always room for further growth and development, and the one who is indeed holy will be fully aware of this and pursue that growth.

The apostle closes this verse with a statement of confidence that if any in the community disagree with him, God will reveal the truth to those individuals. Paul is certain that the paradigm for Christian living he has presented should be normative and he has already called for it to be implemented. However, he is fully aware that there may be some in the community who do not see it the way he does. Rather than assert his apostolic authority and force the issue, Paul appeals to the aid of God to enlighten and correct those who do not agree with him in this matter.[36] He refuses to engage in an argument that could be divisive. Confident that he is right, Paul feels no need to force the issue. If the ones with the divergent attitudes are among the "perfect" to whom Paul referred earlier in this verse, they are

---

29. Deasley, "Philippians," 218.
30. Ibid.
31. Wilson et al., *Galatians, Philippians, Colossians*, 219.
32. Johnstone, *Philippians*, 286.
33. Popkes, "New Testament Principles of Wholeness," 322.
34. O'Brien, *Philippians*, 437.
35. Getz, *Profile of Christian Maturity*, 151.
36. Martin, *Philippians*, 156.

more likely to be in a position to receive any illumination that God would give on any given matter. Furthermore, by trusting in God to clear up areas of disagreement, Paul is able to maintain a sense of unity and peace within the community.

In verse 16, Paul admonishes the Philippians to keep living by the same standard to which they had already attained. In this brief verse, the urge to move forward in unity is quite apparent.[37] The call to unity is made more evident upon observance of the verb *stoichein*. This word brings military imagery with it, meaning "to stand in line" or "to march in line." There is a marked progression from attitude to practice,[38] and Paul is calling for the Philippian believers to "get in line" with what he has been teaching. Not only do they need to be united in their attitude, but they also need to be united in the practice of what they have been taught.

Unity is not the only concern found in this verse. There is also a sense of maintaining one's position. Paul recognizes that there may very well be different levels of apprehension within the community. With that in mind, he calls for each to live by the highest that he or she has been able to grasp, all the while not falling back from that point. There are some within the body who for some reason or another do not grasp the truth as quickly or as readily as others. Some simply do not grow in grace at the same rate as other believers. The call is for those who do not grow as quickly to continue to live up to the level of truth they already know, because they can easily be discouraged when observing unhindered growth of others. Paul charges them though to keep living to what they have already attained and not go back. They may not have grasped the highest amount of truth available, but they have grasped some truth, and they should continue to live by that standard while pursuing further growth in grace.

A CONSTANT PURSUIT OF GROWTH

The study of holiness in Philippians not only confirms the multifaceted nature of holiness, but also contributes in new ways due to the Philippian-specific terminologies that Paul employs. Several important facts emerge from the study in this chapter.

First, Paul's call for holiness is greatly influenced by his eschatological outlook. His motivation for holiness is derived from his expectation of the Parousia. Paul lived eschatologically and so should we. Throughout his letters, the constant awareness that Christ is returning permeates his instructions.

37. O'Brien, *Philippians*, 442.
38. Ibid.

In a world then and now, when it is so easy to live without any thought of Jesus' return, it is good to be reminded that we are to be constantly growing in holiness because one day (only God knows when) Christ will return. God's people should be ready to meet their Savior by being "sincere and blameless."

Second, the holiness to which Paul calls the church is both corporate and personal. The church must embody the gospel of Christ.

Third, the examination of the term "perfection" in this place demands that we be cognizant of, and maintain, the tension that exists in the words *teleioō*, "make perfect" (verb) and *teleios*, "perfect" (adjective). On the one hand, perfection is already present and, on the other hand, it is yet to be completed. The ultimate perfection in the end has not been realized yet, and cannot be realized in this life. Therefore, the need to grow in the grace and knowledge of the Lord is always present. In this regard it is clear that Paul, while admitting of holy living in the present, maintains a tension with its not-yet aspect.

Fourth, as shown by Paul, holiness leads to growth that needs to be pursued constantly. A vigorous pursuit of holiness should not be interpreted as a frantic attempt at works-righteousness. Rather, it is an attitude in which the believer refuses to be content in his or her current spiritual state. Until we reach heaven, there is always a higher level of the Christian life to be experienced. Because of this reality, each believer should strive daily to grow further in holiness.

Fifth, Paul described his striving for the goal as "one thing." He also enjoins the Philippians to do "one thing," which is to live in a way that befits the gospel. Believers should focus just on one thing—the pursuit of the high calling of God, holiness, without which no one will see the Lord (see Heb 12:14).

Finally, as Paul shows in his exhortation to the Philippians, who were going through severe persecution, we should strive to live holy lives and not allow circumstances to determine how we live for God. Regardless of what other believers may do, we have a mandate to live according to the standard we have already reached. The lack of growth in others is no excuse for our regression. We have not been called to conform to what is around us, but rather we have been called to transform what is around us. This is holiness. This is what God has called us to. We must live by the standard we have already attained.

Chapter 8

Holiness in Colossians and Philemon

PAUL DEDICATES A GREAT amount of his letter to the Colossians about how Christians are to live, from the inner life in Christ to the outer life in Christ. In this letter, Paul's exhortations to holy living are intricately connected with the present situation in the church, particularly as it pertains to true spirituality. Although the specific nature of the philosophy that was creeping into the Colossian church and its propagandists remains a matter of debate, it is commonly agreed that a heresy downgraded the uniqueness of Christ's work and imposed false asceticism upon believers.

Paul argues in the letter for the sufficiency of Christ's sacrifice and their participation in Christ as the only prerequisites for their salvation. He speaks of the forgiveness they have experienced as well as their being risen with Christ. He goes on to exhort the Colossians that their new life in Christ must come to expression in the way they conduct themselves. Their lives, as believers in Christ, must reflect the life of Jesus Christ, possible only by the power of the Holy Spirit. Paul calls his readers to embrace and manifest a lifestyle that corresponded with their profession of faith as well as their identity in Christ—"saints" or holy people of God.

Now we continue an exploration of holiness in the Pauline corpus by examining some related words and motifs.

Colossians 1:2

The first occurrence of the word *hagios* is in verse 2, where Paul addresses the Colossians as "the holy ones" or "saints." As mentioned earlier, the word suggests separateness or belongingness, yet it has a moral and ethical content. It must also be noted that there is an unmistakable corporate emphasis in the verse as denoted by the phrase "in Christ."

The Colossian believers are in Christ not only as individuals but also as a people. They were both in Christ and in Colossae. As such, they were to live as befit the people of God in their given location. By stressing "in Christ," it is clear that the decisive factor in determining the identity of God's people and the corresponding behavior is no longer based on ethnic kinship or loyalty, but oneness in Christ.

Paul's approach to holiness in Colossians follows the same basic pattern of appeal and instructions. In the former case, Paul uses various metaphors and vocabularies that accentuate the need for holy living, while in the latter, he shows the indispensability of holiness that is based on the status of the believers as the people of God. As such, one could see the multivalent approach of Paul with regards to the discussion of holiness in Colossians.

Colossians 1:21–23

Paul's greeting in verses 1–2 is followed by a thanksgiving and prayer section (vv. 3–14), which is immediately followed by a discussion on the supremacy of Christ, an argument that is predicated on Christ's role in both creation and redemption. In verses 15–20, Paul juxtaposes Christ's role in creation and his role in redemption. The last part of verse 20 simply summarizes what has already been said about reconciliation of everything, made somewhat more explicit by the final phrase *both on earth and in heaven*, but as in verse 16, it may be necessary to indicate "all those things on earth and all those things in heaven."[1]

On the basis of what he has said about the person and work of Christ, Paul now shows the effect of that on his readers in one long sweeping statement that goes to the end of verse 23. He states their previous condition before knowing Christ (verse 21), followed by the main verb "he has reconciled" (verse 22), which describes God's saving act and its purpose ("in order to"), whose fulfillment is conditioned by the constancy and faithfulness of the Colossians in adhering to the gospel preached by Paul to them (verse 23).

---

1. Bratcher and Nida, *Paul's Letters to the Colossians and to Philemon*, 29.

In Col 1:21–23, Paul refers to the readers' former state of alienation and hostility; their reconciliation, its basis and result; and the necessity of their positive and continued response to the gospel they have heard. With Col 1:21, the tone changes significantly from the noble beauty of the Christological hymn to the specific application of Jesus' work to the Colossians. In Col 1:21, Paul describes their former state; in verse 22, their present state; and in verse 23, the condition of remaining in this present state.[2]

Paul describes the Colossians' former condition in three ways. First, he says that they were once "alienated" from God. The phrase, only used with Gentiles and never with Jews, is reminiscent of Isa 57:19. The prophet Isaiah speaks of a time to come when even the Gentiles, those "far off," will hear and receive a message of peace from God.

Paul expands upon this point in Eph 2:12. Here he affirms that the estrangement of Gentiles not only is from Christ, but also is from Israel, from the covenant, and from any hope. That this alienation has been removed through Jesus Christ, Paul calls the "mystery" (Eph 3:6; Col 1:26, 27) that was revealed to the apostles and Jewish believers first of all (Eph 1:9ff.). Until Jesus came, the Gentiles were in a continual state of alienation from God.

Second, Paul describes these Gentiles—before Jesus "reconciled" them—as "enemies in your minds" (Col 1:21). In Eph 4:18, he says that Gentiles "are darkened in their understanding." And in Romans, he describes these ones as having "thinking [that] became futile" (Rom 1:21) and a "depraved mind" (Rom 1:28). Paul likely believes that people who live without the knowledge of God cannot have their thinking in harmony with the world about them.

The third description of the Gentiles without Jesus is that they also demonstrate "evil behavior" (Col 1:21). Evil behavior results from the hostile mind,[3] since actions follow thoughts. The relationship of actions-thoughts is well known, both on a personal level as well as a corporate one.[4]

In verse 22, Paul speaks of the reconciling effect that Christ's crucifixion had for those who had been estranged and hostile toward God. The "*but now*" of Col 1:22 is rhetorically striking. Paul draws a sharp contrast to their

---

2. This section is reminiscent of Eph 2:1–13. In Ephesians 1, Paul described the privilege of being a part of Israel, God's chosen people, the original "saints." In Ephesians 2, he turned to the condition of the Gentiles in Ephesus, describing them as "dead in your transgressions and sins." Then, in Eph 2:13, he said, "But now in Christ...." The same pattern is found here in Colossians.

3. The causal relationship is not exactly as the New International Version translation "enemies in your minds *because* of your evil behavior" suggests.

4. See Schaffer, *Escape From Reason* for a discussion of the thoughts-actions relationship as demonstrated in the history of Western Europe and the United States.

present condition in Jesus Christ. This great and cosmic reconciling work of Jesus is also personal and comes about through the death of his physical body. The Christian faith is not merely a system of religion or a collection of dogma, but rather a relationship with Jesus who died and arose. Paul's use of the language of reconciliation highlights a change in relationship. Paul's readers who had previously no relationship with God are now related to him through the death of Christ.[5] The purpose of this reconciliation is "to present you holy . . . without blemish and free from accusation" (Col 1:22). The word *holy* here is the same word translated "saints" in Col 1:2. Because of Jesus' death, the Gentiles can now become the "people of God," consecrated and dedicated to a particular service.

At first sight, one might be tempted to interpret *hagios* in the same manner as in verse 2, that is, merely in terms of belongingness. However, it is much more. As Martin notes, "reconciliation touches human lives and produces the effect of a changed human character and conduct."[6] The consequence of Christ having established a new relationship between the believer and God is that when believers are presented they will be characterized as holy, blameless, and irreproachable. Without doubt, here holiness means more than a mere separation. It connotes ethical purity.

The Colossians of whom Paul speaks and to whom he writes have been separated to God in the act of reconciliation. It is therefore quite absurd to either interpret or understand Paul's statement as saying that believers have been separated in order that they may be presented before God separated. Those who have been reconciled (Col 2:12) are those who have been raised with Christ, whose life is Christ (Col 3:1–2), and who have put off the old self and put on the new. How then are believers to live while they await their final presentation before God?

Paul spells out the ethical implications of the risen life in 3:1–14. They involve "putting to death" sins with a physical basis—"those things that belong to your members which are upon the earth; fornication, uncleanness, inordinate affection, evil concupiscence, and covetousness, which is idolatry" as well as the "putting off" of the attitudinal sins: "such as anger, wrath, malice, blasphemy, filthy communication out of your mouth" (vv. 5, 8). One cannot but notice that the verbs that Paul used for "putting to death"

---

5. Sumney, *Colossians*, 85: "The relational metaphor of reconciliation points primarily to the establishment of good relations between parties. Where enmity and hostility have characterized humanity's attitude toward God, now God has acted in a manner that changes the people's outlook. Through Christ, God has shown love, goodness, and a willingness to forgive to such an extent that it overcomes the hostility that existed in the minds and actions of the readers."

6. Martin, *Reconciliation*, 123.

and "putting off" suggest a decisive and crucial act. On the basis of the transforming events that the Colossians had experienced, both expressed by indicatives and in a manner reminiscent of Romans 6, Paul exhorts them to put on virtues that match their new status (vv. 5, 12).

The outcome of Christ's death for the Christian is not simply that they be presented in God's presence—all shall stand before God's judgment seat (Rom 14:10). The consequence of Christ having established a new relationship between the believer and God is that when the believers are presented they will be characterized as holy, blameless, and irreproachable. It has been suggested that Paul, thinking sacrificially, here views God as the "*momoskopos* ('examiner') who examines the victims"[7] during the course of their lives. This is plausible. However, the form of the verb "to present" (*parastēsai*) suggests a single presentation, rather than a continually repeated presentation for the purpose of scrutinizing the believers. Whereas "to present," "holy," and "blameless" may occur in sacrificial contexts, they also occur in non-sacrificial contexts. One may justifiably interpret Paul in this context as viewing God as the judge at the end time, rather than as an "inspector for blemishes."

The three adjectives—*holy*, *pure*, and *faultless*—describe the moral and spiritual state of the believer. They are used for effect, to denote complete and total purity, the effect of Christ's redemptive death in purifying his people from their sins, blemishes, and faults. They denote respectively the positive and negative sides of the new character of the believer, and the consequences of this new character.[8] *Hagios*, per se in this context, does not denote "separated unto God"; rather it describes the believer as ethically pure. The persons of whom Paul speaks have already been separated to God in the act of reconciliation. It is therefore quite lazy to interpret Paul's statement as saying that the believer has been separated in order that he may be presented before God separated. No, the believer has been separated in order that he may be presented before God as ethically pure. As those who have put off the old self and put on the new self (3:9–10) they—in contrast to unbelievers—can anticipate being brought into God's presence with a character that is no less than holy. This expectation is based upon the sacrificial death of Christ.

Such a statement occasions the question: what will be the character of the believers in the meantime, while awaiting the presentation before God? It is a pertinent question, but not one that this text answers. For Paul's answer, one might consider Col 1:9–10 and 3:1—4:5 in the present letter

---

7. See for example, Lightfoot, *Colossians and Philemon*, 162.
8. Bratcher and Nida, *Paul's Letters to the Colossians and to Philemon*, 32–33.

and in other places such as 1 Thess 3:11–13; 4:3–8; 1 Cor 7:32–34; Rom 6:19–22; 12:1. These passages strongly indicate that Paul expected the believers to begin manifesting holiness—ethical purity—in their present lives in an ever-increasing degree of conformity to the likeness of Christ in their life. "Blameless" denotes the absence of those unacceptable qualities which characterize the person who lives apart from Christ—the person who is not reconciled.

Amōmos was used by the Septuagint to signify "without blemish" (i.e., physically whole) in sacrificial contexts (e.g., Lev 1:3, 10; 3:1, 6, 9, etc.), where the animal's freedom from any defect is consistent with the pure, holy character of God.[9] It was also used in non-sacrificial contexts, especially by the Psalmists. The term described the person who separated himself from evil by abstaining from that which was displeasing to God. The *amōmos* person did that which was right by God's standards towards those with whom he came in contact (see Ps 15:2ff. [LXX: 14:2ff.]). The person who would enter God's presence must have a life characterized not only by active goodness, but also by the absence of evil.[10] He lived by the statutes of Yahweh; he avoided wickedness and lived a life of moral integrity, walked in God's ways, and kept himself from guilt (Ps 18:23 [LXX: 17:24]). Psalm 19:13 (LXX: 18:14) well illustrates the significance of *amomos:*

> Keep back thy servant also from presumptuous sins;
> Let them not have dominion over me!
> Then I shall be blameless (*tote amomos esomai*),
> And innocent of great transgression.

Clearly there is no necessity for understanding *amōmos* in Col 1:22 as having a sacrificial significance. As it is used to describe those who have been reconciled to God and are to be presented in his presence, there is very sound reason to understand the term as denoting ethical purity, in the sense of the absence of anything that might estrange the believer from God.

Anenklētos, a word that means "beyond reproach," is used by Paul here with the same nuance as in 1 Cor 1:8 to describe Paul's audience, namely believers in Christ. In both contexts the time reference is not the present, but the future. The Corinthians, Paul says, will be sustained "to the end, guiltless in the day of our Lord Jesus Christ" (RSV). The Colossians will be irreproachable in his presence. Because they are presented holy and blameless, there is no basis for reproaching those who have been reconciled. On

---

9. Hartley, *Leviticus*, 19.
10. Craigie, *Psalms 1–50*, 151.

the basis of the justification effected by the death and resurrection of Christ, Christians are spotless and irreproachable before God.[11]

The *but now* of Col 1:22 is rhetorically striking. Paul draws a sharp contrast to their present condition in Jesus Christ. This great and cosmic reconciling work of Jesus is also personal and comes about through the death of his physical body. The Christian faith is not merely a system of religion or a collection of dogma, but rather a relationship with the Jesus who died and arose. The emphasis here upon the physical body is surely to underscore the error of the false teachers in Colosse of denying the importance of the physical. The purpose of this reconciliation is "to present you holy . . . without blemish and free from accusation" (Col 1:22). The word *holy* here is the same word translated "saints or holy ones" in Phil 1:1. Because of Jesus' death, the Gentiles can now become "saints," that is to say, consecrated and dedicated to a particular service.

The descriptions here of the reconciled ones do not refer to personal conduct, but rather their position in Jesus Christ. It is only "in Christ" that one may appear before God as described here, and no accusation can be brought against them. This will be disclosed at the last judgment. In this declaration we have a clear expression of the power of grace creating a wholly new situation. The meaning of *anenklētos* is made perfectly plain by the question of Rom 8:33–34.[12] No reproach or charge can be made against Christians.

Paul concludes this section with a condition. The Colossians can employ Jesus' reconciling work only so long as they "continue in [their] faith" and are "not moved from the hope held out in the gospel" (Col 1:23). As in the thanksgiving section, faith and hope are here linked. The language here is the same used to describe the foundation of a house. If the Colossian Christians are to withstand the threats of the false teachers, they must have this sure foundation of faith and hope. Paul affirms that the gospel is proclaimed to "every creature under heaven" (Col 1:23). Unlike the gospel of the false teachers, which was for a select few, the gospel of Jesus, which Paul preached, is for everyone. (See Col 1:28–29.)[13]

In Col 1:28 and 29, Paul uses three words to describe his ministry, as well as that of his colleagues (he has switched to the pronoun "we" here). First, he says that they "proclaim" Jesus. The word is almost exclusively used in the New Testament to refer to missionary preaching (i.e., preaching to non-believers). That which is said to be "proclaimed" includes the following:

---

11. Kittel et al., *Theological Dictionary*, 357.
12. Ibid.
13. Weedman, *Philippians–Thessalonians*, 107–9.

the Word of God (Acts 13:5; 17:13), the resurrection (Acts 4:2), forgiveness of sins (Acts 13:38), the mystery (Col 4:3), the testimony about God (1 Cor 2:1), the gospel (1 Cor 9:14), and Jesus (Phil 1:17, 18; and here, Col 1:28). He expands upon this process by the use of two other terms to describe his ministry to them. He says that he "admonishes" and "teaches" them. The gospel message is not complete in the announcement of it alone to others. There is need for a more thorough application of it to the lives of people.

Colossians 1:28

Paul states the goal of his mission: to present every person perfect in Christ. The translation of *teleios* is "complete." This activity is done to "everyone," a word that Paul repeats three times in Col 1:28 (two times in NIV). In contrast to the exclusiveness of the false teachers in Colosse, the Christian gospel is for everyone. All have access to "all wisdom," not just the elite.[14]

Paul states the goal of his ministry as a desire to present every one perfect in Christ Jesus. But, what does it mean to Paul for a person to be perfect? The word *teleios* has a wide range of uses[15] in the first century as well as in Paul's letters. It could mean "mature," "fully developed," or "perfect." In the LXX, "perfect" (*teleios*) can describe those whose hearts are wholly devoted to God (2 Kgs 8:61; 11:4; 15:3, 14; 20:3) and so are blameless before him (Gen 6:9; Deut 18:13). Used in apposition to "righteous" (*dikaios*), Noah was described as "perfect" (Hebrew, *tamim*; LXX, *teleios*) among the people and he walked faithfully with God (Gen 6:9). "Perfect," in this sense is synonymous with blamelessness. As such, it means that Noah was blameless and without reproach among the people with whom he lived.

Both qualities of blamelessness and walking faithfully describe the nature of Noah's righteousness. Understood this way, Noah's perfection cannot be equated with maturity. Rather, it is a quality of life that derives from his faithful walk with the Lord. The equivalent terms in the Dead Sea Scrolls have the senses "without defect," "unblemished," "entire," and "undivided."[16] It has a moral and ethical dimension.[17]

---

14. Ibid., 113.

15. See Flemming, *Philippians*, 192: "We see this, for example, in 1 Cor 2:6, where Paul contrasts spiritual "adults" (*teleioi*) with "infants in Christ" who are caught up in jealousy and quarrelling (3:1–3; see also 14:20). In Ephesians and Colossians, to be perfect means to be spiritually "whole" or "complete," "attaining to the whole measure of the fullness of Christ" (Eph 4:13; see Col 1:28; 4:12; compare Matt 5:8; 19:21; Jas. 1:4).

16. Kittel et al., *Theological Dictionary*, 1164.

17. Deasley, "Philippians," 217.

In Gen 17:1, God calls Abraham to walk before him and be perfect—walk as Noah! Dwight Swanson's observations about the word *teleios* are very insightful and helpful. As such, they are worth quoting at length. He writes,

> Some contemporary Bibles translate here, "Be blameless," which helps us a little, providing that we understand that blamelessness is a term of sacrificial imagery. The Hebrew word, *tamim*, includes the sense of completeness and wholeness in much the way as the Greek term "perfect" (*teleios*). This is not an absolute perfection, but a description of that which fulfills its intended function completely—a sacrificial lamb may not be a prize-winner at an agricultural show, but it will be free from disease or injury. From this sacrificial sphere, in which an animal which is offered is to be without physical blemish, the biblical writers extend the imagery to the ethical sphere as that which maintains moral integrity before God. This is seen by the terms with which "perfect/blameless" appears: the Lord's works are perfect, and his ways are just (Deut 32:4)—a term further described as "faithful, upright, without injustice"; David pleads he is perfect with the Lord, keeping himself from iniquity, just as God is supremely faithful to his covenant love, showing himself perfect to the perfect (2 Sam 22); Job argues that he is perfect and righteous in spite of the laughter of scorn from those around him. (Job 12:4)

In light of these examples, then, the command to Abraham is a call to a lifestyle of integrity, faithfulness, and justice. It is, in simple terms, a life that is in keeping with God's actions (as 2 Sam 22) because when one walks with God, one does the things God does.[18]

How then does one understand Paul's view of perfection in the present context? First, it must be stated that Paul's use of perfection language is not uniform. Basically, as Paul Johaness Du Plessis notes, perfection (*teleios*) embodies the notion of totality, which Paul uses in various contexts with greater and lesser meaning. It is the "totality of the redemptive state" (see 1 Cor 2:6; Phil 3:15; Col 1:28; 4:12).[19] Second, Paul's use of perfection is never in absolute terms. Instead, it is always relative, that is, related to the person or to the object being perfected. In other words, the meaning of perfection is totally dependent upon the nature of the goal or object being perfected.[20]

---

18. Swanson, "Re-Minting Christian Holiness," 4–6.
19. Du Plessis, *Teleios*, 204.
20. Cf. Howard, *Newness of Life*, 215.

Margaret MacDonald is correct that although Paul may have the presentation of the Colossians in the final judgment in view, present perfection is an even greater priority.[21] In light of verse 22, perfection in this verse applies to the whole person, not simply in knowledge. It refers to holiness and entails undivided obedience that knows no graduated steps.[22]

Colossians 3:12–17

As mentioned at the beginning of this chapter, Paul's concern for the Colossians is that they exhibited the character and conduct that become Christians, both as individuals and corporately. This is the thrust of Paul's exhortation in the large section, 3:1—4:6. First, Paul provides the basis of his exhortation—the status of the Colossians as people who have been raised with Christ (3:1) and who have put off the old self and put on the new (3:9–11; see Rom 6:3–11; 2 Cor 5:17). As such they ought to manifest holiness in all dimensions of life. Jerry Sumney sums it up well when he writes, "This new life has moral implications; indeed, participation in it provides the ground for ethics. For Colossians, ethics is not built only on seeing Jesus as a model or example. Rather, believers live as they do because they participate in the resurrection life with Christ."[23] Such life, Paul contends, is based on the supremacy of Christ's person and work. On the basis of these transforming events (*oun*, v. 12) Paul exhorts the readers to clothe themselves with those virtues that are consonant with their new self. He addresses these readers, using three terms that had a long previous history with reference to Israel according to the flesh.

Next Paul refers to the Colossians as the "chosen people of God" (*ekletoi*), a language that was originally used of Israel in the Old Testament.[24] The believers have been chosen (see Eph 1:4) to receive the blessings of the new covenant established by God. As those chosen, the believers are set apart so as to belong to God; they are his people. Likewise, because they are chosen to be the recipients of the new covenant, they are the beloved. As those chosen, set apart, and loved by God, the Colossians were duty-bound to exemplify in their lives that character that had been the essence of the life of Christ their Lord—Love (see 3:14).

---

21. MacDonald, *Colossians and Ephesians*, 83.
22. Barth and Blanke, *Colossians*, 268.
23. Sumney, *Colossians*, 175.
24. As Marshall, *New Testament Theology*, 333n40, rightly states, ". . . in Pauline usage the term *elect* (Rom 8:33; 11:7; 16:13; Col 3:12) is not applied to potential believers but only to actual believers who have obtained salvation."

Because Paul uses two aorist imperatives (*nekrōsate*, "put to death" in verse 5 and *endysasthe*, "put on" in verse 12) with numerous objects, one may conclude that the Colossians had a lot to put to death and a lot to put on and accomplish. Paul's use of these words is a radical way of calling the Colossians to make a clean break with the old life. Consequently his use of *hagioi* is best understood in the relational sense. The Colossians were holy inasmuch as they belonged to God. The use of *hagios* here has no ethical or moral connotation. The main idea of the term is *consecration*. However, as noted by Lightfoot, though it does not assert moral qualifications as a fact in the persons so designated, it implies them as a duty.[25] They were to be morally holy.

It is important to note the communal or social nature of the virtues that Paul expects the Colossians to exhibit. Every one of the graces listed has to do with personal relationships between the believers within the community. The holiness of the Colossians is to be demonstrated or manifested in the wellbeing of the community.[26]

PHILEMON

Paul's letter to Philemon has been, until recent times, passed over without notice, probably due not only to its shortness of length but also due to its supposed "lack of theological content in comparison to Paul's other letters."[27] Scholarly attention always and primarily revolves around the difficult and complex issue of slavery.[28] However, the letter's main focus is not on slavery as an institution. Instead, it is "carefully crafted" and "a masterpiece of suggestion"[29] that captures a glimpse of how Paul applied his theology to ethical situations. It offers a unique insight into how Paul related to other believers, and also how the issues of identity, subsequent to transformation, have a direct bearing on maintaining right relationships. Although not all the details of the story are given or are clear, it is evident that a narrative underlies the letter to Philemon. Therefore, any reconstruction of the sequence of events referred to and implied in Philemon requires some interpretive decisions and imagination.

Along with being an example of efforts to influence behavior, Philemon opens windows into the character of Paul. An often-neglected letter in

25. Lightfoot, *Saint Paul's Epistle to the Philippians*, 81.
26. Thurston, *Reading Colossians*, 53.
27. Petersen, *Rediscovering Paul*, 200.
28. Saarinen, *Pastoral Epistles with Philemon and Jude*, 199.
29. Johnson, *Writings of the New Testament*, 354.

terms of its theological relevance among Paul's letters, Philemon not only reflects the social norms of the first century Greco-Roman culture, but also has often been used in discussions concerning Paul's attitude to slavery. Such a focus, however, misses the profundity of Paul's request to Philemon to receive Onesimus back, no longer as slave but as brother in the Lord. This short letter looks like a drama, with a multiplicity of implied and explicit relationships, various actors who play prominent roles, and a community that lurks in the background.

Based on grammar alone, there is not much in Philemon that lends itself to the theme of holiness. The only occurrence of *hagios* is in verse 7 where it is used as a substitute for God's holy people. However, as argued earlier, the absence of a particular word does not suggest the absence of a particular theme, concept, or motif. This is the case with the study of holiness in Philemon, because it is bound with the dynamics of relationships.

Paul's rhetorical strategy is primarily relational, centering on the understanding of the identities of all the major players in the book, how they relate, and the moral-ethical obligations that the relationship demands. Paul's self-description "as a prisoner of Christ Jesus" (v. 1) underlines his own status as a person under legal bondage. The repetition of *desmios* and *desmoi* ("chains") in Philemon 1, 9, 10, and 13 strengthens the impression of bondage and evokes sympathy in the reader. Paul's legal bondage does not diminish his position in Christ.[30] The description fits with that of Onesimus; though he remains a slave, he is now also a brother in Christ.

Second, the references in the book to brother (vv. 1, 7, 16, 20) and sister (2), to God as Father (3), and to a house church (2), were not merely stylistic. Rather, they are among many references and allusions in the NT to the church as a family or household, an imagery that fits with Paul's understanding of the interconnectedness of the people of God and on relationships of nurture, sharing, and love that follow.

Third is Paul's appeal to Philemon's character. He begins by designating Philemon as a "beloved brother and fellow worker" (v. 2). He knew that the Spirit had produced in him both love for others and faith in Christ (v. 5), and that this Holy Spirit-induced character change could form the basis for his appeals. When Paul began his appeal with "therefore" (v. 8), he based his appeal on what he knew of Philemon's character in vv. 4–7.[31] Later in v. 21, Paul again drew on his knowledge of Philemon's character, stating his confidence that Philemon would do even more than what he asked.

---

30. Saarinen, *Pastoral Epistles*, 203.

31. Carson, *Epistles of Paul to the Colossians and Philemon*, 107. So also Walls, *Colossians & Philemon*.

Fourth is the mention of the "church in your house," a language that accentuates the communal dimension of the demands of Paul, even if the letter is addressed to a single person. Respecting the persons of Onesimus and Philemon, we know little or nothing except what we learn from this brief letter itself.

The multiple layers of relationships that connect the three men are constantly in tension; a tension that arises between the social and cultural norms of the day and the evolving transformation that arises from Paul's understanding of what being a "new creation" in Christ really means. In exploring these points of tension, one can gain an understanding of what is actually being birthed through the relationships. Perhaps there is no other book that best captures the concept of holiness in a "restored relationship" as Philemon does.

The letter reflects Paul's personal characteristics, such as tact, sense of honor, willingness to use peer pressure and irony; generosity, self-sacrifice, and politeness, so well-known to us elsewhere. He must assert the new ideas of Christian equality in the face of a system that hardly recognized the humanity of the enslaved. Paul could have made his request on the grounds of his own personal rights. However, he waived such rights that he might have claimed in order to secure an act of spontaneous kindness from Philemon. His success was a triumph of love, demanding nothing for the sake of the justice which could have claimed everything. He limits his request to a forgiveness of the alleged wrong, and a restoration to favor and the enjoyment of future sympathy and affection. Even in so doing he guarded his words as to leave room for all the generosity that Philemon's benevolence might prompt towards Onesimus, whose condition admitted of so much alleviation. Such is the nature of holiness.

Philemon 1:17–20

In verses 17–20, one finds the three requests that form the climax of Paul's letter to Philemon. Scholarly focus has been on whether Paul was asking the owner to free his slave. Such arguments appear to miss the point of the letter—restored relationships and reconciliation. Although Onesimus is now a believer with a right relationship both with God and Paul, there remains a broken relationship between Onesimus, Philemon, and the Christian community of which he was formerly part. In Christian parlance, Onesimus has repented and has been forgiven by God. As such, making restitution and getting reconciled with his former master and the household church will constitute as holiness. Paul's plea for Onesimus as well as the promise to pay whatever debt Onesimus might owe Philemon underscores the need for right relationships within the community—a right relationship with God demands a right relationship with fellow believers. Although one cannot be so sure of what the reaction of Philemon and the household church would be, it is clear what the demands are on them. They must be willing to forgive and receive Onesimus without resentment and prejudice, and it is difficult to miss an echo of Paul's plea for the offender in 2 Cor 2:5-11.[32]

A careful reading shows that various aspects of holiness in the previous chapters are indirectly reflected in the letter. In discussing Paul's instruction for the forgiveness of the offender in 2 Cor 2:5-12, the significance of holiness as "reconciliation-restoration" has been highlighted. Arguably, it can be said that the primary thrust of this letter was for reconciliation between two people. It called for forgiveness when wrong had been done. It called for the acceptance of another person as a Christian brother, even though he was from a different class distinction.[33] To accentuate the role of the community in the process of reconciliation, Paul called on several individuals as witnesses to his advocacy for Onesimus, including Apphia, Archippus, Epaphras, and the local church at Colosse. He probably did so to foster accountability, with the hope that it will encourage Philemon to do the right thing. As Petersen notes, Paul puts social pressure on the entire community in order to remind them of the "terms of their communal existence and its responsibilities."[34] This strategy was in keeping with his teaching in Eph 5:11-21—Christians are to expose sins.

In Col 3:11-12, Paul admonished the Colossians to show kindness and love when he praised Philemon for his ministry to the church, and he appealed to these as the basis for his petition to Philemon. Paul always links holiness with love. When love operates and prevails in the truest sense, it does not only become a motivating factor, but actually becomes primary in facilitating a true relational change. Such love mirrors 1 Cor 13:5, 7: "It (love) does not insist on its own way . . . it believes all things, hopes all things . . . ." Paul demonstrates this love as he appealed to Philemon's love and expected him to take action concerning his petition for Onesimus based on the same love.

---

32. See Chapter 4.
33. Staton, *Timothy-Philemon*, 200.
34. Petersen, *Rediscovering Paul*, 99-100.

CALLED TO MIRROR THE LORD

Paul's view of holiness in Colossians does not differ significantly from the other letters already examined, particularly the use of *hagios*. Paul uses the term as a designation for believers. Used in this way, holiness simply implies the status of those who belong to God. In the same way as in Philippians, the language of perfection is pronounced. To walk in holiness implies an intimate relationship with God as well as walking in integrity and justice. Paul conceives of the holiness of the Colossians in moral and ethical terms. Third, although holiness is to be manifested in personal life, it is, nonetheless, social or communal.

Once again, as in several places in his other letters, Paul makes use of the dialectical relationship between the indicatives (these refer to what actually is) and the imperatives (a call to actualize in life and make real what is an already accomplished reality). In other words, the imperative calls and challenges the believer to bring to reality, live out, and actualize the believer's identification with Christ. As those who have been chosen and called by the Lord, they are to mirror their Lord.

Chapter 9

Holiness in 1 and 2 Thessalonians

SOME OF THE GREAT biblical texts on holiness are to be found in the Thessalonian Epistles. Without doubt, holiness is a major motif in the Thessalonian correspondence and these texts of Scripture deserve a more serious hearing if Paul's understanding of holiness is to be complete.

It has been previously noted that there is a strong connection between Paul's prayer and theology. One of the striking features of holiness in the 1 and 2 Thessalonians is that, with the exception of 1 Thess 4:7, the rest of the texts to be examined are in the form of prayer. They are 1 Thess 3:11–13; 5:23–24; and 2 Thess 2:13. These prayers express Paul's earnest desire and wish before God for his young converts. Paul's exhortation to the community in Thessalonica makes a great contribution to his teaching on holiness in particular, and to that of the New Testament in general. The believer must live life in light or in view of the coming of the day of the Lord.

1 THESSALONIANS

The examination of holiness in 1 Thessalonians reveals the significance of the *hagios* word group. *Hagiosynē* (3:13), *hagiasmos* (4:3, 4, and 7), and *hagiazein* (5:23) are the members of the *hagios* word group that Paul uses here. Structurally, the prayer of thanksgiving (3:11–13) appears to be not so much a conclusion to what might have been a complete letter, as an introduction to the remaining section of exhortation and instruction (4:1—5:22). Chapters 4 and 5 actually are statements that provide some practical explanations of what Paul meant in his prayer of 3:12-13 and how holy living is to be manifested. In 3:12, Paul prays for an increase in love, and its outward expression is enumerated in 4:9-12. His desire for their hearts to be established and be blameless in holiness (3:13a) is explained in practical terms in 4:1-8.

Appearing in the presence of the Lord, a major motivation for holy living (3:13b), is further explained in 4:13-18, and its manner of occurrence is detailed 5:1-11. Paul then returns in 5:12-22 to an even more detailed exposition of that most important concern: the expressions of *agapē* within the Christian community. He concludes the section with an all-encompassing summary of love to God—negatively expressed—as shunning all evil (5:22). In 5:23-24, the section is brought to a conclusion with a slightly modified restatement of the prayer in 3:12-13. Thereby, he has opened and closed the entire section with a prayer summary-type statement of those desires he explicated in 4:1—5:22. Finally, 1 Thess 5:25-28 constitute final personal notes and the benediction to the letter.

1 Thessalonians 3:12-13

In 1 Thess 3:9-11, Paul expresses both his thanksgiving to the Thessalonians for the good report concerning them, their faith, and love, and also his desire to be able to further minister to them if the Lord wills. He then moves on to pray specifically that they may "increase and abound in love for one another" (v. 12), in order that their hearts might be "without blame in holiness before our God and Father at the coming of our Lord Jesus with all his saints" (v. 13).

Paul's reference to the believers' hearts in 3:13 refers to the volitional or intellectual aspects of humanity. However, Paul believed that as a person was in the heart, so was he or she in the whole person (see 2 Cor 3:2f.; 6:11-13). Consequently, a prayer that the believers may be established with respect to their hearts refers essentially to the whole person. Paul shows the centrality of love (*agapē*) to his idea of a holy life in 3:12. For Paul, without doubt, growth in the *agapē*-love of God leads unto holiness.

Paul looks to holiness as a principal objective of the Christian life and experience. Therefore, he prays for the maturation of his converts, to the end that God may establish their hearts to be unblamable in holiness before his presence. Note that Paul does not ask precisely that their hearts may be established blameless in holiness (*hagiosynē*). Rather he asks that they may increase and abound in love to one another and to all persons. That petition is then followed by the final clause *eis to stērixai*, "so that he may establish . . . ." The result or purpose for increasing love is the establishment of the believers, blameless in holiness. It is not therefore appropriate to speak of the Christian being ethically holy in a completed sense prior to the moment of presentation before God the Father at the Parousia. As love never ends, so love also never reaches a boundary in this life at which point it is complete. Love must increase. It must not be adulterated; it must be blameless.

In his prayer, Paul directs the attention of the Thessalonians to the limitless potentiality for growth and love to one another and to everyone. In other words, the growing love must not only be extended to everyone among the believing community, but also to outsiders, across ethnic, economic, political, and social boundaries.

One must ask whether on the basis of this prayer Paul truly expects a present realization of holiness in life or if it is meant for the future. Several reasons suggest that it is possible now. Paul provides a nudge for his petition by adding the phrase "just as ours does for you," referring to the overflowing of his love and that of his fellow workers for the Thessalonians. Second, the affinity of the prayer with that of 1 Thess 5:23, 24 suggests that Paul expected the former. Third, Paul's own testimony concerning his conduct in 1 Thess 2:10–12: "you are witnesses, and God also, how holy and righteous and blameless was our behavior to you believers" confirms the possibility of a life of holiness in the present.

1 Thessalonians 4:3, 4, and 7

As he frequently does, Paul reminds his audience of his previous instruction to them. Although the Thessalonians are walking in a manner that pleases God, he urges them to do more (vv. 1–2). Paul's discussion of concrete ways in which the Christians may walk pleasing to God leads first to a summary statement: "this is the will of God, your sanctification" (4:3; see Rom 6:19, 22 and 1 Cor 7:32–34). His choice of the verbal noun *hagiasmos* suggests that he was thinking of the process involved in the Christian becoming ethically holy, as opposed to the final state which will come into being at the Parousia (see 3:13).[1] Thus, by implication, there is a progressive aspect of sanctification. Furthermore, rather than a general declaration of God's will,

---

1. Wanamaker, *Epistles to the Thessalonians*, 150, observes that the word *hagiasmos* as used here "may denote either the process whereby the Thessalonians would become sanctified or consecrated to God through their separation from immorality (cf. v. 7) or the outcome of that process." He continues that, "Given that Paul is spelling out one aspect of the process of sanctification in his discussion of Christian sexuality, the former sense may be more appropriate." This is the position here.

he provides, in verses 4–8, a precise statement of the area(s) with which God's will is here concerned. The absence of the definite article with "will" (*thelēma*) suggests that Paul does not refer to holiness as the total will of God for the believer. Rather, it is part of what God desires in his people. It is quite significant that Paul does not outline a system of ethics to which Christians are to adhere for the sake of their common good, or because of some other humane consideration. The Christian is commanded to adhere to certain given ethical practices precisely because they are grounded in the will of God to whom the Christian must be obedient.

The will of God, as here set forth, consists in the following: a) that you abstain[2] from immorality (4:3b); b) that each take his "vessel" in holiness (*hagiasmō*) and honor (4:4); and c) that no man transgress and take advantage of his brother "in this matter" (4:6). To reinforce his appeal, he then reminds the readers that God is an avenger toward those who transgress (4:7) and, somewhat summarily, he adds in 4:7, "For God has not called us for uncleanness, but in holiness" (*en hagiasmō*).

Verse 3b is quite clear. It expresses one of Paul's recurring themes; namely, that believers must keep themselves from immorality (see 1 Cor 5:1–13; 6:13–18; 7:2; 2 Cor 12:21; Gal 5:19; Eph 5:3). It is a reminder that there is a negative side to holiness. The members of the believing community are exhorted, to "abstain from" immorality, passion, lust, transgression of a brother, and uncleanness. In the same manner as Paul would later say in 1 Thess 5:22, we are called to separate ourselves from all evil. We are expected to exercise self-control over all the faculties of our personality. And we are to conduct ourselves in all things with a view to holiness and honor, as is pleasing to God.

The exhortation to abstain from fornication (*porneia*), in this context, implicates the idea of devotion to God, and God alone. The term "fornication," of course, includes all sorts of uncleanness—in particular, sexual impurities. Paul knew that in the Thessalonian context (as in ours), one of the most difficult hurdles that any pagan convert had to clear was the area of sex. The culture of the day was saturated with polygamy, adultery, homoerotic acts, and promiscuity. But Paul exhorts the Christian community in clear words (as reflected by Phillips' paraphrase): "God's plan is to make you holy, and that entails first of all a clean cut with sexual immorality."

Verse 4 is not so readily understood, largely because of Paul's use of *skeuos*, a word that can be translated either as "body" or "wife."[3] We opt

---

2. Paul uses the strong verb *apechesthai*, which literally means to hold at a distance. Believers are not to touch immorality with the proverbial "ten-foot pole."

3. For recent and detailed discussion on the meaning of *skeuos*, see Witherington, *1 and 2 Thessalonians*, 113–16; and Bohlen, *Sanctorum Communio*, 119–23, who both

for the former translation. By rendering the phrase *skeuos ktasthai* as "to keep (one's own) body," one has the advantage of translating the terms with meanings elsewhere established and, most importantly, one thereby makes very good sense of the Greek construction.

When one translates verses 4–5 as "that each of you know how to keep his own body in holiness and honor, not in lustful passion—as do the Gentiles who do not know God," then one has a statement that deals with man on a more basic level than the interpretation endorsed by Best. If man controls himself as Paul here suggests, then if he takes a wife or remains unmarried; if he conducts a business or works for another; in whatever relationships he enters, they will be characterized—at least from the standpoint of that believer—by holiness and honor. Immorality, lust, avarice, and any other vices one might list will be excluded because the believer is controlling his body in holiness and honor (see 1 Cor 6:19–20; Rom 12:1). In this context, *hagiasmos* ("holiness" or "sanctification") is understood denoting the personal "ethical purity" of the believer.

The contrast between "in sanctification" and "in lustful passion," as well as the larger context, demands such an interpretation. The clause expresses the manner in which each person is to relate to his world. This interpretation is reinforced by the summary statement of verse 7: "God called us, not to (*epi*) uncleanness, but in (*en*) holiness." It was not within the purview of God's call that the believer's life should be characterized by ethical uncleanness of any sort, but rather that it should be characterized by ethical purity.

The final appeal is important for its direct correlation between the work of sanctification in the life of the believer, and the role of the Holy Spirit in that process. For Paul, whoever despises, sets aside, and thus disregards the divine call and injunction to holiness, disregards God in his ministry to us through the presence of his Spirit. Paul constantly links the Holy Spirit with the believer's walk in holiness (see Rom 8:3–7; Gal 5:16–24).

Impurity is more than simply a failure to keep some manmade rule or adhere to some church or denominational creed. It violates the living, indwelling presence of the Holy Spirit. Paul does not simply express the will of God for these people in these concrete terms and then assert that they themselves are solely responsible for complying with the will of God. This obedience is their responsibility, but the possibility of success exists because God has given his spirit to these believers (verse 8).

Paul then quotes Ezek 37:14 (LXX): "I will give you my Spirit" (*kai dōsō to pneuma mou is hymas*); he adds *to hagion* "holy" as a modifier of

---

argue for the understanding of *skeuos* as "wife."

"the Spirit," thereby deliberately and emphatically drawing attention to the Spirit's personal holy nature. Because the believer has received the Spirit who is holy, he may contemplate obediently fulfilling the will of God that Paul has just set forth. Paul does not explicitly designate the Spirit in verse 8 as the agent of God who empowers the believer to live in holiness. However, the verse could have been completed with *alla ton theon* ("but God"), adding a warning that to disregard Paul's instructions is to disregard God. The added restrictive attributive clause "God who gives his Holy Spirit to you" strongly suggests the above inferences.

God accomplishes his purpose of sanctification in our lives as we cooperate with him and respond in obedience. What God calls us to be or do, his Spirit enables. The Holy Spirit is God's empowering presence.[4] God not only calls but also enables us to live the life of holiness.[5] When the ministry of the Holy Spirit is embraced, he enables the holiness of a person's entire life.

1 Thessalonians 5:23–24

As noted at the beginning of the chapter, 1 Thess 5:23–24 is in the context of prayer. In 5:23, Paul even more explicitly refers to the whole person as the object of his prayer. The first "and" (*kai*) could be understood as epexegetic: that is, verse 23b could be an elaboration of verse 23a.[6] Thus "you" (*hymas*) of 23a is explained by spirit, soul, and body (*pneuma*, *psychē*, and *sōma*). Paul, in his concern that the entire person be affected,[7] expresses himself first with a general reference to the readers: "you" (*hymas*). He then elaborates with the trichotomous reference to "the spirit and the soul and the body of you (all)." From his use of these three terms, one can speculate at length regarding Paul's anthropological and psychological views of man. But as to the primary significance of this verse, the trichotomous reference of verse 23b should be interpreted in terms of "you" in verse 23a, which means that he is concerned to say, "may the readers in their entirety . . . ." It is Paul's way of stating that no aspect of a person is to be left untouched by

---

4. A play on the title of Fee's book, *God's Empowering Presence*.
5. Best, *First and Second Epistles to the Thessalonians*, 169.
6. Frame, *Epistles of Saint Paul to the Thessalonians*, 211.
7. Cf. Best, *Thessalonians*, 243–44 for a discussion of the various divisions of v. 26 and interpretations of *pneuma*, *psychē*, and *sōma* that have been proposed. However, the contention here is that Paul is referring to the whole person. He explains the term *hymas* by employing several terms he uses to refer to a human being and various human faculties.

holiness: it encompasses the whole being. The whole person, and not some part only, is to be entirely set apart to God.

Paul's first petition is that the God of peace himself may sanctify the Thessalonians.[8] Paul reflects the OT idea that it is God himself who sanctifies (Exod 31:13; Lev 20:8; 21:8; 22:9). The verb *hagiasai* does not appear to have a relational significance in this context nearly so much as it has an ethical import. Paul is addressing Christians who had entered into a new relationship of belonging to God in Christ through their salvation experience. For these persons it is not necessary to be sanctified more fully in a relational sense. The new relationship that is established between the Christian and God in Christ involves in its act of initiation a transformation of the total person and transferral of ownership of the entire person (2 Cor 5:17; Col 1:13–14). Therefore there is no need for Paul to pray for a fuller relationship change.

However, the believer who belongs to Christ needs to reflect in life the character of the new master in an ever-increasing degree. Therefore Paul quite logically prays that God will make holy the believers—every one of them. It may be suggested that in his correspondence, not only to the Thessalonians, but to other churches as well, Paul oscillates between an individualistic and a corporate view of the members of the churches, which views are not clearly set forth or separated.[9] For example, in verse 23b, Paul's prayer "to keep you, that is, the Thessalonians, blameless" (*tērētheiē amemptōs*) suggests that the believers are blameless and that he is praying for the continuation of this situation.

Because the members of the group are Christians and therefore acceptably related to God in Christ, Paul could call them presently blameless. But that is relational. Might he also assert—even by implication—that they are ethically blameless? A review of the letter suggests that this is the actual case. Of the Thessalonian congregation, he recalls that they became imitators of the Lord (1:6); they are living pleasing to God (4:1); and they love all the brethren throughout Macedonia (4:10). They are an example of what Christians should be. Therefore he can pray that they be kept as they are; namely, blameless, until the Lord returns. Such is Paul's view of the Thessalonian congregation, which means that his recollection of and his information about a significant number of the members of the community was positive, from an ethical standpoint.

8. The verb *hagiasai* ("to make holy") is an aorist optative expressing an attainable wish.

9. See for example the use of the temple imagery in 1 Cor 3:16–17. In verse 16, Paul depicts the Corinthians as the temple in a corporate sense, while he calls them individual temples in v. 17.

There is another side to the coin. Verse 4:3–7 suggests there were some members with sexual-marital problems; and that some were busybodies, others idlers (4:11). Because of these individuals Paul might pray, "May God make you (plural) entirely holy." In so doing, he is praying that the few individuals of the group may become like the majority—ethically pure in their associations with the community.

In summary, 5:23 is a prayer in which Paul's desire is twofold: 1) that the entire group may have no members who are not ethically holy (v. 23a); 2) that those who are blameless may remain so in this life and when they encounter the returning Lord Jesus Christ (v. 23b). Verse 24 is an expression of confidence in God's faithfulness in accomplishing holiness and preservation. Once again, we are reminded of 1 Thess 4:7–8, which speaks of God as the One who has called us in holiness, and then proceeds to speak of the indwelling ministry of his Holy Spirit. Holiness is "from start to finish a work of grace.[10]

The thought of 2 Thess 2:13–14[11] may also be in mind here. There, Paul speaks of sanctification in relationship to God's purpose for our salvation. It is the fulfillment or consummation of his design and calling upon our lives. Our assurance of sanctification, therefore, is based upon the character of God. Holiness, rather than something to be desired and deferred till the "sweet by and by" in the future, is something that is possible at the present. It is an experience to be enjoyed in the present and in which state the believer is to remain until the Parousia.

2 THESSALONIANS

This book deals with eschatological events in light of how the Thessalonian believers were to conduct themselves. Paul prays God would count the believers worthy of their calling, and that he would fulfill every good purpose and act that results from their faith (1:11). The goal of Paul's prayer is that God may be glorified in the Thessalonians, and they, in turn, would be glorified in him.

2 Thessalonians 2:13–14

Starting from the first verse in chapter 2, Paul delves into a lengthy discussion of the Parousia that extends through verse 12. The next section that

---

10. McCown, "God's Will," 236.
11. See below.

deals with the life of holiness in the believer consists of verses 13 though 17 of chapter 2. Paul has just given instruction as to what will occur at the Day of the Lord, and thus seeks to encourage the believers of Thessalonica as they wait for that day. In 2:13, Paul turns away abruptly from the bleak picture that he painted in the preceding verses and starts encouraging the Thessalonians again. In contrast to the godless age just described, the believers were called to a life of sanctification. Verse 10 talks of those who will not be saved, "them that perish" whereas verse 13 speaks of those who are chosen for salvation through sanctification by the Spirit and truth.

For our purposes, the question of the textual variants *ap archēs* (from the beginning) and *aparchēn* (firstfruit) need not be considered; Paul's use of *hagiasmos* may be understood apart from this issue. He reminds the readers that, "God chose them ... for the purpose of salvation through sanctification by the Spirit." The purpose of God's call is that the Thessalonians may have salvation. In this context, the salvation of which he speaks is most likely not just that salvation that is to be experienced at the Parousia (although that would be included) (see 1:7), but more importantly one that is presently experienced. The believers are standing firm and holding to the instruction they received from Paul (see 2:15 with its present imperatives) in contrast to those upon whom God is sending "a deluding influence" (2:11). For the believer, however, God has a totally different destiny.

Paul's use of the phrase *en hagiasmō* (in or unto holiness) is to be compared with 1 Thess 4:4 and 7. As in those passages, the phrase may be called a dative of manner or a descriptive dative. It denotes the ethical purity that characterizes the salvation unto which the believer is called. In contrast to those who are under the sway of the "deluding influence," the believer is under the rule of the Spirit (see 1 Thess 4:8).

"Spirit" (*pneumatos*) in verse 13 is better understood as a reference to the Holy Spirit, not to one's personal spirit. As observed earlier (see 1 Thess 5:23), Paul saw not just one's spirit, but the whole person as the object of God's salvation and sanctifying activity. Consequently, one should not interpret Paul as saying the believer is called to a salvation characterized by a holiness of spirit. True though the thought might be, it is not the statement of 2:13. As James E. Frame sums it up, "Sanctification by the Spirit designates total consecration of the individual, soul and body to God, a consecration which is inspired by the indwelling Holy Spirit, and which is not only religious but ethical."[12]

Gary Steven Shogren is correct in his conclusion that "the general tenor of Paul's language in these letters is that the *Spirit makes people holy.*

---

12. Frame, *Epistles of Saint Paul to the Thessalonians*, 278.

Because of 'the Spirit,' we may identify this verse as one of those passages that contains an implicit reference to what eventually came to be called the Trinity: the Lord (Jesus) loves them, God chooses them, the Spirit sanctifies them."[13] Elsewhere Paul (using the same preposition, *en*) portrayed sanctification as the work of God's Holy Spirit (see Rom 15:16; 1 Cor 6:11), and he probably intended the same here.

Paul is likely rejoicing because God chose these persons to be recipients of a salvation characterized by ethical purity. In continuing the sentence under examination, he asserts that God called the Thessalonians "that you might share in the glory of our lord Jesus" (2:14 RSV). "Glory" (*doxa*) is used on occasion by Paul to describe the present nature of the risen Christ (see Phil 3:21; 2 Cor 3:18; 4:6; Eph 1:6). The believer cannot participate in the person of God, but he can participate in the character of God or Christ. This is the reason for Paul's rejoicing. Unlike the recalcitrant ones who persecute the believers (see 1:4–6, 8), these believers are participating in the character of Christ in that they are growing in love (see 1:3), Paul's key word for development in the likeness of Christ Jesus or growth in holiness (*en hagiasmos*).

AN ATMOSPHERE OF HOLINESS

As in the letters of Paul previously examined, holiness in the lives of his converts was one of his chief concerns in the Thessalonian correspondence. He directs their attention to sanctification, and prays to God for the realization of holiness in their lives.

Based on the examination of various texts, some aspects of holiness are discernible in the letters. First, for Paul, holiness is very practical. This is clear as Paul often moves from general statements or principles to concrete and specific applications in the affairs of life.

Second, every aspect of the believer's life is to be characterized by holiness. This is essentially the thrust of 1 Thess 4:1–8. For example, holiness is communal in its nature.

Third, sanctification is the work of God. He is the one who sanctifies (see 3:13; 5:23).

Fourth, there must be a response to God's work of sanctification resulting in a practical life of holiness that is in contradistinction to their surroundings.

---

13. Shogren, 1 & 2 *Thessalonians*, 303.

Fifth, we live in a society that is so individualistic; the utmost desire is always to please oneself. Self-enjoyment and self-pleasing become the motivation for making choices, including where to worship. However, Paul argues for the opposite. Our main aim in life is to walk with and please God. Pleasing God is not optional.

Sixth, holiness is practical. Paul teaches that sanctification also embraces the sexual realm of human experience. The believer's conduct in these regards is to be characterized by holiness. This is true of all of life. The pagan world displayed its decadence in various forms of sexual aberrations (see Rom 1:24–32). But the apostle asserted that the Christian is to have nothing to do with such evil practices. They are incompatible with God's will: Christian sanctification. And sanctification is what God requires of us in every part of life.

On the interpretation of some, in verse 6, Paul himself extends the application to include other relationships in life as well. They were not called to a salvation that dug trenches and hid out waiting for the Day of the Lord, but a salvation that called them to action, a salvation that propagated the preached word even as they had received it. They were called to live lives of holiness contrary to the situation around them, as a witness to and against the society where they were.

Seventh, as Paul demonstrates in the Thessalonian correspondence, the teaching of holiness is intimately and inextricably connected with election and eschatology. God, who is holy, calls believers to lives of holiness as the essential preparation for the Parousia, and for life in eternity with him.

Lastly, holiness requires growth. In this sense it can be termed as progressive. Thrice, Paul speaks of abounding more and more (3:12; 4:1, 10). This emphasizes the progressive aspect of sanctification. Paul seeks not only to affirm the Thessalonian church in its perseverance, but also to call the church to press on in its walk with Christ. The church is not called to live in passive anticipation of God's deliverance, but must press on in striving toward holy living. Sanctification is not merely a goal set before us by reason of God's call, but a process to be implemented and realized now in our present lives in fulfillment of that call. Holiness is to be, as it were, the very atmosphere in which we live and breathe.

Chapter 10

Holiness in the Pastoral Epistles

It has been long recognized that although the letter addressed to Titus and the two addressed to Timothy (commonly referred to as the Pastoral Epistles) are individual compositions, they belong together by virtue of their common style and theological character.[1] Scholarly debates continue on the authorship of the Pastoral Epistles. However, with regard to holiness, it is clear that the pattern of holiness that is present in Paul's other letters is also present in the Pastorals. One of the unambiguous emphases in the Pastoral Epistles is that salvation involves a commitment to obedience to God. The believer is called to a belonging that involves the ethical transformation of his or her being. Those who are saved are both saved and called "to" a holy life, one in which there is no place for sin. This will be seen as we examine the varied holiness vocabulary and motifs in the Pastorals.

Due to the commonness of the style as noted above, the examination of the holiness vocabularies and motifs in the Pastorals will be done primarily in a parallel manner. However, any relevant language or motif holiness that is unique to any of the three letters will be treated on its own merit.

---

1. Marshall, *New Testament Theology*, 397.

HAGIOS AND ITS COGNATES

There are three occurrences of the noun form *hagios* in the Pastorals—1 Tim 5:10; 2 Tim 1:9, 14; and Titus 3:5. In the midst of the warning to widows and the qualification to be admitted as a widow, Paul lists as one of the qualifications the washing of the saints' (*hagioi*) feet. The use of *hagioi* in this text simply refers to believers or God's holy people. In 2 Tim 1:9, it is a reminder of the believer's holy calling,[2] attributed to God in the same way as in Paul's other letters.[3]

There is also a close connection between salvation and calling. It is God who has saved and called with a holy calling. By holy calling, Paul describes the Christian life. Christians are saved not only from a life of sin but to a life of holiness (see 1 Thess 4:7). In other words, the consequence of salvation is holiness. Because God is holy, he has called believers to a life of holiness. God's call to believers is holy not only because it proceeds from him; it also is a call to live a holy life.[4] Philip Towner sums it up well: "Salvation, the fact of rescue, is to find practical expression among God's people (us) in the form of *a holy life* . . . a lifestyle that is visibly different. It is a life lived in close relationship with God."[5]

Paul's last use of *hagios* in the Pastorals is Titus 3:5, where it qualifies the spirit. It comes in the midst of Paul's discussion of the moral transformation that takes place in the lives of those who profess to be believers. Here Paul says that God saved us "by the washing of regeneration and renewal in the Holy Spirit which he poured out upon us richly through Jesus Christ our Savior." Because the believer's new life is a recreation and a making new, only divine power can affect it. The Holy Spirit is the agent of this divine work. Thus the role of the Spirit in sanctification is accentuated in a manner reminiscent of Romans 8. The Holy Spirit affects the cleansing from defilement and renewing of the inner person. The metaphor of renewal is an echo of Rom 12:2. Knight's observation on this verse is helpful. He writes,

> Therefore, in Titus 3:5, Paul considers this inner transformation from two different perspectives in a manner analogous to Ezek 36:25–27 and 1 Cor 6:11. He arranges the four genitive nouns chiastically with the most distinguishable terms first and last and with the terms for the result, the transformation, in the center. The first pair of genitives focuses on the need for cleansing

---

2. Here Paul uses the adjective *hagios*.
3. See 1 Cor 1:9; Gal 1:6.
4. Zehr, *1 & 2 Timothy, Titus*, 161.
5. Towner, *1–2 Timothy & Titus*, 163.

from past sin: "washing" and a word that speaks of that washing as an inner transformation, a "new beginning." . . . The second pair focuses on the new life received and to be lived: The "Holy Spirit," the giver and sustainer of the new life, must do his work *within* Christians and so is joined to a word that speaks of such a new life as an inner transformation, "renewal."[6]

The verbal form *hagiazein*, "to sanctify" occurs only in 1 Tim 4:5 and 2 Tim 2:21. In writing to Timothy, Paul speaks of sanctifying (*hagiazetai*) food, which at once reminds us of the many inanimate objects sanctified in the Old Testament. This expression is found in a passage where the Apostle is warning Timothy regarding those departing from the faith who, among other things, command others "to abstain from meats." Paul immediately states that God had created meat to be received with thanksgiving and that "every creature of God is good." We discover from our context that food is to be "received with thanksgiving of them which believe and know the truth" (v. 3), and verse 5 reveals God's method of expressing such thanksgiving which is the sanctification of the food "by the Word of God and prayer."

What happened to the food that was sanctified by the Word of God and prayer? It was not purified, for it was already clean. It was not made holy in an ethical sense, because it is inanimate. What took place was this: it acquired "a holy quality by its consecration to God; by being acknowledged as God's gift, and partaken of as nourishing the life for God's service." This meaning is in accord with Old Testament usage where inanimate objects were consecrated or set apart unto the service of Jehovah. We translate then: It is consecrated, set apart unto the Lord, by the Word of God and prayer. Thus, the use of *hagiazō* here relates to consecration, without any ethical connotation.

In 2 Tim 2:21, the verb *hagiazō* is applied to the believer. In the close of verse 19, after a series of practical exhortations, Paul writes: "Everyone who names the name of the Lord is to abstain from wickedness (NASB)." For Paul, there must be consistency between one's profession of faith in the Lord's name and one's conduct. There is no room for duplicity. In verses 20 and 21, Paul expands the statement made in verse 19 with the use of the metaphor of the church as a "great house." In the large house there are not only gold and silver vessels, but also vessels of wood and of earthenware, and some to honor and some to dishonor. Paul goes on to say that those who cleanse or purge themselves will become vessels that are "sanctified (*hēgiasmenon*), suitable for the master's use, and prepared unto every good work (v. 21)." However, v. 21 raises some questions. First, of what does Paul

---

6. Knight, *Pastoral Epistles*, 419.

expect Timothy or the believers to purge themselves? Second, what does sanctification entail in this context?

With regards to the former, it is first important to establish the meaning of the indefinite subject "this," from which believers are to cleanse or purge themselves. The ambiguity has led to the suggestion that Paul is suggesting that Timothy separates himself from false teachers.[7] Marshall is probably right in concluding that, "the reference must accordingly be tied somewhat loosely to the activities of the opponents, including their false teaching and the associated evil way of life."[8] Such conclusion may suggest that the injunctions that followed were not only directed at Timothy but all Christians.

With regards to the second question, *hēgiasmenon* (perfect passive participle) is used here in the sense of "sanctified" or "made holy" by having been cleansed from the defilement of sin and thus becoming one, set apart for God and his service. The passive voice is in line with the usage of the word elsewhere in Paul to indicate that God is effecting sanctification (except 1 Cor 7:14). As we see, 1 Thess 4:3–4, which uses *hagiasmos*, "sanctification," is parallel in thought. Timothy cleanses himself, and in response God cleanses Timothy; the human and divine actions are intertwined.[9] It thus reiterates the aspect of cleansing but in more personal spiritual terms.[10] Here Paul speaks of a definite sanctification for the believers. As such, the main thrust of sanctification is not merely separation without reference to any subjective experience or ethical implications.

The noun form *hagiasmos*, "sanctification," occurs in 1 Tim 2:15. This verse is problematic for interpreters, especially with regards to the meaning of salvation. However, the broader questions of salvation do not have any impact on the importance and meaning of the word *hagiasmos* in this context. Its use here is essentially the same as in other letters of Paul (Rom 6:19; 1 Cor 1:30; 1 Thess 4:3, 4, 7; 2 Thess 2:13) where it refers to sanctification, an antithesis to sin and uncleanness, as well as God's will for his people.[11]

---

7. For an exhaustive discussion on various possibilities, see Marshall, *Pastoral Epistles*, 761–62.
8. Ibid.
9. Mounce, *Pastoral Epistles*, 532.
10. Knight, *Pastoral Epistles*, 418–19.
11. Marshall, *Pastoral Epistles*, 471.

KATHAROS AND ITS COGNATES[12]

One of the vocabularies of holiness in the Pastorals is *katharos* (pure). Its use in the Pastorals is very instructive as Paul frequently links it with heart and conscience. In the first occurrence of *katharos* in the letter, Paul makes a crucial statement that the goal of right instruction "is love from a pure (*katharas*) heart, a good conscience, and sincere faith" (1 Tim 1:5). Without offering any specifics about the content of right instruction, Paul sees a pure heart and good conscience[13] as its integral outcome. It makes a clean conscience the object of the exhortation to everyone, with Timothy as a model.

A pure conscience contrasts with the defiled conscience of the unbeliever (Titus 1:15). It indicates moral integrity. A good conscience is a moral predicate that designates the right conduct of the well-instructed Christian.[14] "The phrase corresponds to the 'pure heart' as a description of the good Christian existence."[15] Although "the heart is the origin of desires, the conscience functions to direct, evaluate, and control behavior along lines set by given norms."[16]

---

12. The verb "to cleanse," or make clean or purge (*katharizō*) is found thirty-one times in the NT [in addition to ekkathairo, the verb here, which is found twice]. The references fall into two main categories, objective and subjective. That the word has both moral and cultic nuances is evident in the various contexts where it is found. Paul's usage is consistent with other writings in the New Testament where *katharos* refers to moral qualities or separation, e.g., to moral qualities, in which sense it is found three times (Acts 18:6; 20:26; and Luke 11:41). Each of these passages speaks of an obligation fully met or a declaration of innocence in relation to a crime, and, to separation from the common, in which sense Jesus used the word twice. It is a curious thing that this word should be used in connection with recovery of the leper's health in contrast to healing or wholeness when other forms of sickness were reported. A blind or crippled person is healed, but the leper is cleansed. It was ceremonial cleanness to which the angel referred when Peter was reluctant to eat certain animals forbidden to the Jew: "Call that not unclean which God has cleansed," the voice said. Ceremonial cleansing is indicated by *katharotēs* and speaks of expiation or the benefits of Christ's atonement (Heb 9:12–13).

James exhorts sinners to cleanse their hands and the double-minded to purify their hearts (4:8). Both terms obviously refer to acts and motives which were not honest and which needed to be brought into integrity. Again, this cleansing is decisive and is to be done by the person. The hands are made clean by *katharizete*, but the heart is made pure by *hagnizate* that signifies a more inner and spiritual concept—innocence, blamelessness—which has to do with sincerity. Here, again, is a tacit definition of and commentary on the term "cleansing."

13. Saarinen, *Pastoral Epistles with Philemon and Jude*, 35.

14. A good conscience is more than one which is merely free from the guilt of sin. It is one that is transformed by the power and character of Christ. This is holiness.

15. Fiore, *Pastorals*, 135.

16. Marshall, *Pastoral Epistles*, 370.

The deacon should hold the faith in a "pure conscience" (2 Tim 3:9). Paul's "pure conscience" commends him to Timothy (2 Tim 1:3); and his exhortation to young Timothy is that he, too, "follow righteousness, faith, charity [love], peace, with them that call on the Lord out of a pure heart" (2 Tim 2:22). We learn that 2 Tim 2:22 is significant for two reasons. First is the connection of the language of justification (righteousness) with that of sanctification (purity). Second is the use of the word *katharos*. The meaning supplied by the context is clearly an open, sincere, honest motivation in God's sight.

Although good works do not save, the evidence of grace is a changed heart that brings forth good works (see Titus 2:11–14). Titus 2:14 gives a further definition of cleanness, in the midst of a block of ethical teaching that Paul gave to Titus. Paul introduces Christ the Savior, as he so often does. He is the one "who gave himself for us, that he might redeem us . . . and purify [both aorist subjunctive] unto himself a . . . people, zealous of good works." The phrase "purify unto himself a people" echoes the language of Exod 19:5–6 and Ezek 37:23. In the former, Israel, the people of God redeemed from Egypt are God's possession and are commanded to be holy. In Ezek 37:23b, speaking of the restoration of Israel, God says, "I will deliver them from all their dwelling places in which they have sinned, and will cleanse them. And they will be My people, and I will be their God."

Because of Christ's redemption, Christians become God's own people. The phrase *laos periousios* "people that belongs to him as his special possession," defines the church in terms of new election and possession by God. Purity here stresses a separation from iniquity and a devotedness to good works which, if we deny "ungodliness" and "live soberly, righteously, and godly in this present world," would make us his own possession. To be and to remain as Christ's possession is to live in purity, and that purity includes "good works." Without a doubt there is an ethical connotation to purity or cleansing.

With regards to its ethical import, Spross contends that even when the word purity is semantically ceremonial, "it is informed by the normative ethical understanding and entails moral renewal."[17] Christians are set free and released from sin and its control through the death of Christ; they're set apart as God's own possession, as well as made holy to the degree that they are now God's treasure. Paul's argument in the section comes full circle in verse 15. He concludes with an emphasis on moral behavior, which is the result of purification. Those who have been thus cleansed are also zealous for good deeds (Titus 2:14c). Thus, the grace that appeared in the incarnation of

---

17. Spross, "Holiness in the Pastorals," 314.

Christ and trains us to live a godly life in the present brings transformation and enables believers to walk in holiness in the present time.

THE *HAGNOS* WORD GROUP

In addition to *hagios* and its derivatives, *hagnos* and *hagneia* also occur in the Pastorals, in the sense of holy and holiness. This terminology plays a much smaller part, however, in harmony with the usage of the LXX. Balz takes note that the "The relatively rare appearance of the *hagnos* word group is probably to be explained by the shift in meaning, which occurred in Hellenistic language as well as Judaism, from cultic to figurative use, which made it increasingly easy to substitute other words for this group."[18] Although the original background of *hagnos* in many respects coincides with that of *hagios*,[19] in Paul it simply has the significance of morally clean, pure, innocent, and chaste. The root word for "pure" and "chaste" (*hagnos*) is found four times. In Phil 4:8, Paul exhorts the reader to be selective in his or her choice of thinking. Stability of character demands a disciplined thought life. Among the other things worthy of entertainment such as the true, the just, the lovely, and the virtuous, stands "the pure," which is to be a consciously permitted and voluntarily chosen object of thought that conforms to the norm of holiness.

Speaking of the ordination of elders, Paul writes to Timothy, "Do not lay hands on anyone quickly or share in the sins of others; keep yourself pure" (1 Tim 5:22). Paul does not think that Timothy will start committing the same sins as the opponents; rather he is concerned that by commissioning a sinner to leadership, Timothy may to some degree be responsible for their ministry and the sins they may commit, possibly because Timothy may appear to condone their sin and because a failure to punish sin may encourage others to sin.[20] To this warning Paul adds that Timothy must keep himself "pure," (*hagnos*) above reproach, and free from sin (see 2 Cor 7:11: "guiltless" (*hagnous*). The word is an echo of Paul's previous warnings to Timothy about sexual purity in 1 Tim 4:2 and 5:2.[21]

Although it is important not to equate purity with asceticism, as some of the false teachers were advocating, purity definitely requires and involves separation from immorality and also single-mindedness of purpose. He was to take every precaution to appoint only good individuals to labor together

---

18. Balz and Schneider, *Exegetical Dictionary*, 22.
19. Ibid.
20. Mounce, *Pastoral Epistles*, 317.
21. Towner, *Letters to Timothy and Titus*, 375.

with him. His impartial character as a leader must not be compromised. Without doubt, this verse demands high moral standards from Christians, particularly those in positions of leadership.[22] Paul's concern for Timothy's purity led him to give other personal advice to Timothy in verse 23.[23] Paul's charge to Timothy is obviously an exhortation to a morally disciplined life and indicates the need for a continuing maintenance of one's integrity.

The word *hagneia* ("purity") occurs only in 1 Tim 4:12 and 5:2. In the former, it was part of the exhortation to Timothy to be a model both in belief and behavior. As an example of holy living, Timothy's outward life is to exemplify Christian behavior in speech and conduct. In other words, Timothy is to model Christian character through daily conversation and conduct and through teaching in the congregation. It is only in so doing that Timothy's message will have credibility, integrity, and authority.

Next, 1 Tim 5:2 continues the exhortation that started in the previous verse on interpersonal relationships—in this case, how to deal with the younger women. In adding "all" or "complete" to purity, Paul underscores the importance of chastity as the safeguard for dealing with each other, particularly the opposite sex. Timothy is to avoid any situation in which his propriety is called into question.

EUSEBIA (GODLINESS)–HOLINESS TERMINOLOGY

The link between godliness and holiness in the Pastorals is evident in the use of the word *eusebia*, "godliness." It portrays the manner of life that is expected of those who profess to be the people of God. "Godliness" translates the word *eusebia*, which derives from a Greek stem *seb-*, which meant originally "to step back from someone or something, to maintain a distance," then "to have awe at something, especially something lofty and sublime."[24] This stem is combined with *eu-* ("abundance, fullness of") to form *eusebeia*, which means in classical Greek, "awe, respect for the divine, for the social order."

In the New Testament, the word is used in the sense of, "awesome respect accorded to God, devoutness, piety, godliness."[25] The word group appears as a verb, an adjective, and an adverb.[26] One also finds a contrast be-

22. Saarinen, *Pastoral Epistles with Philemon and Jude*, 96.
23. Lea and Griffin, *1, 2 Timothy, Titus*, 157–158.
24. Forester, "Sebomai," 168–96, especially 169.
25. Bauer and Danker, "*Eusebeia*," 413.
26. The verb is *eusebeō*, "be reverent, respectful, devout," in the New Testament "to show uncommon reverence or respect, show profound respect for someone" (BDAG,

tween the word *eusebeia*, "godliness," and its opposite *asebeia*, "godless, ungodliness, impiety."[27] Both words occur frequently in the Pastoral Epistles.[28]

Our respect for God shows by how we live—godly people live in such a way as to please God. On the one hand, ungodly (that is impious or godless) people do not really care what God thinks about their way of life. On the other hand, hypocrites lead double lives—one for others to see, alongside a secret life that is unseen—except by God. The presence and spread of false teachings at Ephesus are producing ungodliness, ungodly behavior, and unrighteousness. So, Paul is very concerned that the Christians in the church at Ephesus are practicing godliness in their everyday living.

For Paul, theology must have practical bearing on life. Hence, he forcefully demonstrates that there is a correlation between healthy teaching and holy living, adamantly maintaining that healthy doctrine produces healthy behavior.[29] Unhealthy teaching produces a kind of lifestyle that is only a "*form* of godliness," a kind of outward religion and religious belief, but one that lacks its real essence and power (2 Tim 3:5).

In 1 Tim 4:7–8, Paul repeats the word *eusebeia* ("godliness") to alert the reader to its importance for Paul as the hallmark of Christian existence. As Robert Wall rightly suggests, its broad expanse of meaning allows for its inclusion of inward affections and practices. He further states that, "its use here makes clear that the holy life is not something God imputes as though the believer's godly character is the irrepressible effect of God's grace alone."[30] Holiness demands the believer's active participation. It defines the Christian community as a contrast society, distinct from the Roman society in which it lived. Genuine godliness refers both to the content of truth and its visible expression in proper behavior.[31]

---

413). The adjective is *eusebēs*, "pertaining to being profoundly reverent or respectful, devout, godly, pious, reverent" (BDAG, 413). The adverb is *eusebōs*, "in a godly manner" (BDAG, 413).

27. The noun *asebeia* is used "vertically as a lack of reverence for deity and hallowed institutions as displayed in sacrilegious words and deeds: impiety." The verb *asebeō* means "to violate the norms of a proper or professed relation to deity, act impiously." The adjective *asebēs* means, "pertaining to violating norms for a proper relation to deity, irreverent, impious, ungodly" (BDAG, 141).

28. *Eusebeia* and related words are used elsewhere in the New Testament at Acts 3:12; 10:2, 7; 2 Pet 1:3, 6–7, 9.

29. See below.

30. Wall, 1 & 2 Timothy and Titus, 191.

31. Fee, 1 and 2 Timothy, Titus, 103.

Hosios

In Titus 1:5–9, Paul lists the qualifications of those who are to be appointed as elders and overseers. In verse 8, Paul specifically says that the overseer must be "hospitable, loving what is good, sensible, just, holy, and self-controlled." The word translated holy in this passage is *hosios*. In the LXX, it refers primarily to the "godly" and for the most part translates Hebrew *ḥāsîd* (in the majority of the passages in the plural for the congregation of the godly that lives in covenant relation with God; see Ps 29:5; 36:28; 49:5; in the absolute, Ps 11:2; 17:26; 85:2).[32] Its usage in this context is notable particularly for its combination with the word translated "just" (*dikaios*), which literally means "righteous." In the present context, "just" or "righteous" is used in its ethical sense of just behavior.[33] As such, *hosios* and *dikaios* combined describe the conduct appropriate toward people and God, respectively.

The two ideas are paired elsewhere with this same duality (Luke 1:75; Eph 4:24; 1 Thess 2:10).[34] In 1 Tim 1:9, they are used in contrast to the sinner whose conduct and character are described not only in their relationship to God but also in ethical terms. This is the same sense in 2 Tim 2:22, where Paul exhorts Timothy to pursue righteousness. Obviously, righteousness in this context refers to the ethical demands placed upon a believer who is already justified or made righteous.

THE HOLINESS AS INTEGRITY

Some conclusions can be drawn from the study of the holiness vocabulary in the Pastorals. First, the concerns for holiness that permeate the so-called undisputed letters of Paul are abundantly present in the Pastorals. Although sometimes expressed with unique terms, it is nevertheless clear that Paul continues to maintain the link between salvation and sanctification. The former is sometimes used in a comprehensive manner as it is in Titus 2:11–14. The concept of the sanctified life usually expressed in phrases such as "walking in love," "walking worthy of one's calling," and "walking in newness of life" is absent in the Pastorals. Nevertheless, it is clear that there exists a close relationship between sanctification as a way of life and the ethical exhortations in the Pastorals.

---

32. Balz and Schneider, *Exegetical Dictionary*, 536.

33. Ziesler, *Meaning of Righteousness in Paul*, 55, comments that every instance of the occurrence of noun *dikaiosyne* in the Pastorals has a mention of human conduct or ethics, all of which are taken in reference to God.

34. Mounce, *Pastoral Epistles*, 391.

Second, the multivalent use of holiness terms such as that of *hagios* that one finds in Paul's other letters is in the Pastorals. All God's people are set apart as God's holy people, yet they are to turn away from sin and be cleansed. The Gospel should produce a life of holiness: there is no separation between belief and behavior. Those who say they are Christians but do not show any evidence by their lifestyle or behavior should reexamine whether they are actually followers of Jesus.

Third, in the same way as in Paul's other letters, there is a connection between holy living and the Parousia. This is evident in Titus 2:11–14, where one finds an unmistakable and intricate connection between holy living in the present time and the coming of Christ in glory.

Fourth, a major contribution of the Pastorals to Paul's understanding of holiness is its importance for Church leadership. Holiness is inseparable from integrity. It is crucially important to have leaders in the church who have integrity. Furthermore, for Paul, healthy teaching and healthy living are inseparable. If a teacher's lifestyle is not consistent with the Gospel, one should not pay attention to his or her teaching.

Chapter 11

Putting It All Together

And let those who are not found living as He taught, be understood to be no Christians even though they profess with the lips the precepts of Christ.

—JUSTIN MARTYR[1]

This book was borne out of the desire to fill a perceived void in Pauline studies; a focus on holiness as a distinct category of Paul's theology. This demanded that questions about methodology, the motivation for Paul's focus on holiness in his writings, what holiness meant, and what it might mean today, be addressed. This final chapter offers a summary and draws some important conclusions.

As explained in the introduction, it is quite evident that the discussion of holiness must originate with the holiness of God. In this regard, one must remember that holiness is more than a mere attribute of God. God's holiness is not to be limited to his "otherness." Instead it is known in his interactions with people. In this regard, the eighth-century prophets added a new dimension to the understanding of God's holiness as they linked it to his justice. Thus, God's holiness has an ethical component. It was God's defining characteristic and desired purpose for Israel as God's covenant people. Israel was to be a contrast society in relation to the wider environment in which it lived. Israel's holiness demonstrates that holiness is not just a quality or power that is connected with God, but a quality of life that is enacted in, by,

---

1. Martyr, *Ante-Nicene Fathers I*, 168.

and through the life of the community. After all, God redeemed Israel and called them to be his holy people (Exod 19:5, 6; Lev 11:44; 19:2; 20:7).

As the people of God, Israel was holy by virtue of their belonging to God. Nevertheless, Israel was to demonstrate in everyday life what they were called to be. As such, Israel's call to holiness was a call to ethical purity. Furthermore, Israel's call to holiness was a corporate call. Although individual Israelites had personal responsibility to God and were to live out the covenant blessings of God, it was as constituent members of the whole. Hence, although the holiness of the Israelites was certainly personal, it was not individualistic. Holiness is the boundary marker that separates God's people from the surrounding nations, and as such, Israel's call to holiness was a call to separation. As those called as royal priests, Israel's holiness was missional. Israel was to reveal God to the other nations. In sum, the Old Testament reveals the multifaceted nature of holiness to which God's people were called.

Paul takes his cue on holiness from the Old Testament. His vocabulary of holiness derives from the same that was used by God in the Old Testament. This is particularly true of his use of the *hagios* word group.

For Paul, holiness is a necessity, one that is dictated by his view of God, the church, the world, and the Parousia. God calls the church (personally and corporately) to the task of living into and out of the full power of the Holy Spirit. The significance of holiness for Paul is accentuated by its equation with the will of God (1 Thess 4:3). His prayers for holiness demonstrate that a holy God calls believers to lives of holiness as the essential preparation for life in eternity with him.

Without doubt, Paul's persistent emphasis on holiness shows an important truth about the theological perspective from which he views believers. His designation of the Church as the people of God (eschatologically restored) in the same manner as the Israelites in the Old Testament (1 Cor 1:28–30) and as God's eschatological temple (1 Cor 3:16; 2 Cor 6:16; Eph 2:22), is an important motivation for his holiness teaching.

For Paul, the Church's identity and purpose are crucial to its relationship with God and the wider society. This is clear from the many metaphors, such as bride and virgin, that he uses to describe the church. Holiness is not only to be based on the church's relationship with God as a separate, distinct people, but also on the actualization of that holiness in relationship with the wider society. The church's holiness demands that it really lives in accordance with the social order which God has given it, a social order that stands in sharp distinction with the pluralistic society. As such, the church's holiness is based on a dynamic, ongoing relationship with God—a relationship, which, in turn, is to govern believers' relationships with the wider society, as well as those within their own community.

Holiness is the attribute by which the church, as the people of God in the same manner as Israel, is to be distinguished from the wider society. Without clear boundaries, the church loses her "prophetic" voice and moral ascendancy. The church must display the reality of sanctification that is framed, first and foremost, in corporate terms.

Holiness has a moral content. It is a false choice to make a demand between consecration and sanctification, and between holiness as either forensic, that is, as righteousness that is merely imputed, or imparted righteousness that ensues in ethical living. Although there is a past dimension in salvation, there are present ethical implications that should characterize the life of those who have been, are being, and will be saved.

In sum, Paul presents a multifaceted view of holiness like what is seen in the Old Testament, in his writings. Hence it is possible for one to delineate and speak of different aspects of holiness such as separational, ethical, communal, and missional. However, none of these aspects, in itself, constitutes the core of holiness. Paul's teaching of holiness must be understood as a complex whole.

With regards to what it means when applied to Christians, holiness or sanctification is in the first place an ethical concept, although it is based on belonging to God. This is in agreement with the view of the eighth-century prophets, with whom the transformation of the concept of sanctification into ethical holiness began. Moreover, it is clear that there is a close connection between love and holiness, both describing two ways of looking at the Christian life (Gal 5:22; 1 Thess 3:11–13). Holiness is preeminently expressed in love; and love is the essential means by which holiness is maintained. To love others is to refuse to use them for selfish ends or to take advantage of them.

On the contrary, holiness involves a commitment to live responsibly in relation to believers and unbelievers. Those who know they are unconditionally loved by God and who have committed their lives completely to him no longer live for themselves alone or according to the values of this pagan world (Gal 2:20). The hallmarks of the life of holiness are growth, maturing, and progress in the Christian life, particularly in "love." Blamelessness before God is closely linked with living in love, because love influences thinking, desires, motivation, and behavior.

God's sanctifying activity affects the Christian's entire being, an activity that involves a "complete" cleansing of every dimension of life (2 Cor 7:1; 1 Thess 5:23). Hence sanctification goes beyond inner motives. Rather, it expresses itself in tangible outward behavior. It would seem to renovate both the character and conduct of believers. It begins in our hearts, but it must eventually emerge in what we do with our hands. It is not restricted to the religious aspects of human life; Paul emphasizes its counter-cultural transformation of the most secular realm of the ethical life—the sexual behavior of believers (1 Thess 4:7). Thus, sanctification has to do primarily with ethical behavior. Entire sanctification calls for the complete expression of what it means to be God's holy people.

STRIVING TO GROW IN HOLINESS

What are the implications of this study? First it must be realized that holiness and holy living are not in any way tangential to Paul's theology. Instead they occupy a central place and, as such, deserve more attention than they have been given. This must follow from the realization that holiness is God's purpose and desire—something God longs to do in the lives of his people, both in the Old and New Testaments. He calls his people to live holy lives and, therefore, can be trusted to provide the ability and means to fulfill what his call requires. This he does through his gift of the Holy Spirit (see Rom 8:1–17; 1 Thess 4:7). He is both the Source and Enabler of holiness. It is not enough that sinners be converted and simply become believers. God wants believers to be sanctified—to live a quality of life reflecting God's character and will. He wants them to turn from their old lives to demonstrate their new allegiance to him. Holiness in the present is an essential prerequisite for the glorious future God has planned for his holy people.

Second, holiness demands a divine-human partnership. It is not automatic, as the prayers and the Pauline indicatives and imperatives indicate. God is willing to sanctify, but believers must take on the responsibility of self-control and walk in a manner that befits their calling and pleases God. To reject God's call to holiness is to put oneself in line for divine punishment. Although conversion is a transformation and genuinely sanctifying divine work, as initial sanctification, Paul's letters show that it is only the beginning. Without subsequent experience to conversion, that is, if holiness were the inevitable result of Christian conversion, Paul's demands for holiness and exhortations would be superfluous. God expects moral integrity of his people, because he has given his Holy Spirit to enable them to live exemplary, Christlike lives in this world as they prepare for the world to come.

Third, believers, who, like Paul, anticipate the Parousia, must not only desire but also pray that holiness becomes a reality in their lives, cognizant of the fact that holiness is a matter of practice, not merely a status that one attains upon justification. When Paul speaks of being preserved blameless "at the coming of our Lord Jesus Christ," he does not suggest that sanctification comes as a result of Christ's second coming, or only in the article of death. Instead, he prays that believers should be "kept blameless" in preparation for the end, not "made blameless" because of it. Paul prays that the Thessalonians may be "preserved blameless" in 5:23. In the earlier part of the chapter (vv. 1–11), Paul calls for "sober and godly lives," because "the day of the Lord" is near. In verse 23, Paul prays that God will make that possible. Paul expects his prayer to be answered prior to the Second Coming. If sanctification is the prerequisite for glorification, not its equivalent, Paul must expect it in this world and not the world to come.

Finally, for Paul, holiness is not static. It requires growth and it needs to be pursued constantly. The Church's quest for, and pursuit of, holiness should not be interpreted as a frantic attempt at works-righteousness. Rather, it is an attitude in which the believer refuses to be content in his or her current spiritual state.

Until we reach heaven, there is always a higher level of the Christian life to be experienced. Because of this reality, each believer should strive daily to grow further in holiness.

Bibliography

Abbott, T. K. *The Epistle to the Ephesians and the Colossians*. ICC. Edinburgh: T. & T. Clark, 1991.
Ackroyd, Peter R. *Exile and Restoration*. London: SCM, 1968.
Adewuya, J. Ayodeji. *Holiness and Community in 2 Cor 6:14–7:1: Paul's View of Communal Holiness in the Corinthian Correspondence*. New York: Peter Lang, 2003.
———. "Holiness in 2 Corinthians: The People of God in A Pluralistic Society." In *Holiness and Ecclesiology in the New Testament*, edited by Kent Brower and Andy Johnson, 201–18. Grand Rapids: Eerdmans, 2007.
———. "Paul, Crucifixion and Sanctification in Galatians." In *Passover, Pentecost, & Parousia: Studies in Celebration of the Life and Ministry of R. Hollis Gause*, edited by Steven J Land, Rick Dale Moore, and John Christopher Thomas, 90–105. Blanford: Deo, 2010.
———. *Transformed by Grace: Paul's View of Holiness in Romans 6–8*. Eugene, OR: Cascade, 2004.
Arden, E. "How Moses Failed God." *JBL* 76 (1957) 50–52.
Arrington, French L. *The Ministry of Reconciliation: A Study of 2 Corinthians*. Cleveland, TN: Pathway, 1998.
Bailey, Kenneth. "Paul's Theological Foundation for Human Sexuality: 1 Cor. 6:9–20 in the Light of Rhetorical Criticism." *Theol. Rev. III/1* (1980) 27–41.
Balz, H. "Ἅγιος." In *Exegetical Dictionary of the New Testament*, edited by H. Balz and Gerhard Schneider, 1:16–20. Grand Rapids: Eerdmans, 1990.
Barclay, John M. G. *Obeying the Truth*. Edinburgh: T. & T. Clark, 1988.
———. "Thessalonica and Corinth: Social Contrasts in Pauline Christianity." *JSNT* 47 (1992) 59.
Barclay, William. *Flesh and Spirit*. Grand Rapids: Baker, 1976.
Barrett, C. K. "Christianity at Corinth." *Bulletin of John Rylands Library* 46/2 (1964) 269–97.
———. *A Commentary on the Epistle to the Romans*. HNTC. San Francisco: Harper & Row, 1957.
———. *The First Epistle to the Corinthians*. BNTC. 2nd ed. London: A & C Black, 1971.
Barth, Karl. *Epistle to the Philippians*. 40th Anniversary ed. Translated by James W. Leitch. Louisville, KY: Westminster John Knox, 2002.

Barth, Markus. *Ephesians: Translation and Commentary on Chapters 4–6*. Anchor Bible 34A. Garden City, NY: Doubleday, 1974.

Barth, Markus, and Helmut Blanke. *Colossians*. Anchor Bible. New York: Doubleday, 1994.

Barton, Stephen C. "Christian Community in the Light of 1 Corinthians." *Studies in Christian Ethics* 10.1 (1997) 1–15.

Bassler, Jouette M. "The Enigmatic Sign: 2 Thessalonians 1:5." *The Catholic Biblical Quarterly* 46.3 (1984) 507.

Bauer, Walter, et al. *Greek-English Lexicon of the New Testament and Other Early Christian Literature*. 3rd ed. Chicago: University of Chicago Press, 2000.

Beare, F. W. *A Commentary on the Epistle to the Philippians*. 2nd ed. London: A & C Black, 1969.

Beet, Joseph Agar. *A Commentary of St. Paul's Epistle to the Ephesians, Philippians, Colossians, and to Philemon*. London: Hodder and Stoughton, 1890.

———. *A Commentary on St. Paul's Epistle to the Galatians*. London: Hodder & Stoughton, 1885.

Bertil, Gärtner. *The Temple and the Community in Qumran and the New Testament*. Cambridge: Cambridge University Press, 1965.

Best, Ernest. "1 Corinthians 7:14 and Children in the Church." *Irish Biblical Studies* 12 (1990) 165.

———. *A Commentary on the First and Second Epistles to the Thessalonians*. BNTC. London: Black, 1977.

Betz, Hans Dieter. *Galatians*. Hermeneia Commentary Series. Philadelphia: Fortress, 1979.

Blass, F. and A. Debrunner. *A Greek Grammar of the New Testament and Other Early Christian Literature*. Translated by Robert W. Funk. Chicago: University of Chicago Press, 1961.

Bohlen, Maren. *Sanctorum Communio: Die Christen als "Heilige" bei Paulus*. BZW. Berlin: Walter de Gruyter, 2011.

Bowen, Roger. *A Guide to Romans*. Quezon City, Philippines: New Day, 1997.

Bratcher, Robert G., and Eugene Albert Nida. *A Handbook on Paul's Letters to the Colossians and to Philemon*. UBS Handbook Series. New York: United Bible Societies, 1993.

Brower, Kent. *Holiness in the Gospels*. Kansas City: Beacon Hill, 2005.

Bruce, F. F. *1 & 2 Corinthians*. NCB. Eerdmans: Grand Rapids, 1971.

———. *1 and 2 Thessalonians*. WBC. Waco, TX: Word, 1982.

Bultmann, Rudolph. *Theology of the New Testament*. Translated by Kendrick Grobel. Vol. 1. New York: Charles Scribner, 1955.

Burton, E. de W. *A Critical and Exegetical Commentary on the Epistle to the Galatians*. ICC. Edinburgh: T. & T. Clark, 1921.

Campbell, Barth. "Flesh and Spirit in 1 Cor. 5:5: An Exercise in Rhetorical Criticism of the NT." *JETS* 36 (1993) 331–42.

Carson, Herbert M. *The Epistles of Paul to the Colossians and Philemon*. TNTC. Grand Rapids: Eerdmans, 1960.

Cauthron, Hal A. "Holiness—a Matter of Dying." In *Biblical Resources for Holiness Preaching: From Text to Sermon*, edited by H. Ray Dunning and Neil B. Wiseman, 239–52. Kansas City, MO: Beacon Hill, 1990.

Cerfaux, L. *The Church in the Theology of Paul*. New York: Herder, 1959.

Childs, Brevard S. *Biblical Theology of the Old and New Testament.* Minneapolis: Fortress, 1992.

———. *The Book of Exodus.* OTL. Philadelphia: Fortress, 1974.

Clarke, Adam. "Romans." *Clarke's Commentary: Matthew-Revelation.* Nashville: Abingdon, n.d, 93.

Clements, R. E. *God's Chosen People.* London: SCM, 1968.

Clines, D. J. A. *The Theme of the Pentateuch.* Sheffield: JSOT, 1978.

Cole, R. Dennis. *Numbers: An Exegetical and Theological Exposition of Holy Scripture.* NAC 3B. Nashville: Broadman and Holman, 2000.

Conzelmann, Hans. *1 Corinthians.* Hermeneia. Philadelphia: Fortress, 1976.

———. "Der Brief an die Epheser." In *Die Briefe an die Galater, Epheser; Philipper; Colosser, Thessalonicher und Philemon,* edited by J. Becker, H. Conzelmann, and G. Friedrich, 8:141–60. NTD. Gottingen: Vandehoeck & Ruprecht, 1981.

Cousar, Charles B. "The Theological Task of 1 Corinthians." In *Pauline Theology, II. 1 and 2 Corinthians,* edited by D. M. Hay, 90–102. Minneapolis: Fortress, 1993.

Craigie, Peter C. *Psalms 1–50.* Vol. 19. Word Biblical Commentary. Dallas: Word, 1998.

Cranfield, C. E. B. *A Critical and Exegetical Commentary on the Epistle to the Romans.* The International Critical Commentary. Edinburgh: T. & T. Clark, 1979.

Cullmann, Oscar. *Baptism in the New Testament: Study in Bible Theology.* London: SCM, 1961.

Dahl, N.A. "Form-Critical Observations on Early Christian Preaching." In *Jesus in the Memory of the Early Church.* Minneapolis: Fortress, 1976.

Danker, Frederick W. *2 Corinthians.* ACNT. Minneapolis: Augsburg, 1989.

Darko, Daniel K. *No Longer Living as the Gentiles.* LNTS 75. Edinburgh: T. & T. Clark, 2008.

Dayton, Wilbur T. "Holiness Truth in the Roman Epistle." *Further Insights into Holiness.* Compiled by Kenneth Geiger. Ohio: Schmul, 1990.

De Lacey, D. R. "οἵτινές ἐστε ὑμεῖς: The Function of a Metaphor In Paul." In *Templum Amicitiae,* edited by William Horbury, 401–9. JSNTS 48. Sheffield: Sheffield Academic, 1991.

De Vaux, R. *Ancient Israel: Its Life and Institutions.* London: Darton, Longman & Todd, 1961.

Deasley, Alex R. G. "Philippians" in *Galatians, Philippians, Colossians: A Commentary for Bible Students.* Indianapolis, IN: Wesleyan, 2007.

Denney, James. "St. Paul's Epistle to the Romans." In *The Expositor's Greek New Testament,* edited by W. Robertson Nicoll, 2:555–725. Reprint, 1904. Grand Rapids: Eerdmans, 1970.

deSilva, David. *A Sri Lankan Commentary on Paul's Letter to the Galatians.* Global Readings. Eugene, OR: Cascade, 2011.

Dodd, C. H. *The Epistle of Paul to the Romans.* MNTC. New York: Harper, 1932.

Donfried, Karl P. and I. Howard Marshall. *The Theology of the Shorter Pauline Letters.* New York: Cambridge University Press, 1993.

Doughty, Darrell J. "Citizens of Heaven: Philippians 3:2–21 as a Deutero-Pauline Passage." *NTS* 41 (1995) 102–22.

Du Plessis, Paul Johaness. *Teleios: The Idea of Perfection in the New Testament.* Kampen: J. H. Kok, 1959.

Eichrodt, W. *Theology of the Old Testament,* vol. 1. London: SCM, 1961.

Eilberg-Schwartz, Howard. *The Savage in Judaism: An Anthropology of Israelite Religion and Ancient Judaism*. Bloomington: Indiana University Press, 1990.

Ellicot, Charles J. *St Paul's Epistle to the Ephesians: with a Critical and Grammatical Commentary and Revised Translation*. London: Longmans, Green, 1884.

Fee, Gordon D. *1 and 2 Timothy, Titus*. New International Bible Commentary. Peabody, MA: Hendrickson, 1988.

———. *First Epistle to the Corinthians*. NICNT. Grand Rapids: Eerdmans, 1987.

———. *God's Empowering Presence: The Holy Spirit in the Letters of Paul*. Peabody, MA: Hendrickson, 1994.

———. *Paul's Letter to the Philippians*. NICNT. Grand Rapids: Eerdmans, 1995.

———. "Toward a Theology of 1 Corinthians." In *Pauline Theology*, edited by David. M. Hay, 2:37–58. Minneapolis: Fortress, 1993.

Findlay, G. G. *The Epistle to the Ephesians*. The Expositors Bible. Edited by W. Robertson Nicoll. London: Hodder and Stoughton, 1892.

Fiore, Benjamin. *The Pastorals: First Timothy, Second Timothy, Titus*. Sacra Pagina. Collegeville, MN: Liturgical, 2007.

Fisk, Bruce N. "Eating Meat Offered to Idols: Corinthian Behaviour and Pauline Response in 1 Corinthians 8–10." *Trinity Journal* 10 (1989) 49–70.

Fitzmyer, Joseph A. "The Letter to the Galatians." In *The New Jerome Biblical Commentary*, edited by Raymond E Brown, Joseph A. Fitzmyer, and Roland E. Murphy, 780–90. Englewood Cliffs: Prentice Hall, 1990.

Flemming, Dean E. *Contextualization in the New Testament: Patterns of Theology and Mission*. Downers Grove, IL: InterVarsity, 2005.

———. *Philippians: A Commentary in the Wesleyan Tradition*. New Beacon Bible Commentary. Kansas City: Beacon Hill, 2009.

Forester, Werner. "Sebomai, etc." In *Theological Dictionary of the New Testament*, edited by Gerhard Kittel, Gerhard Friedrich, Geoffrey W. Bromiley, 7:168–72. TDNT. Grand Rapids: Eerdmans, 1964–1976.

Fowl, Stephen E. *Ephesians*. New Testament Library. Louisville, KY: Westminster John Knox, 2012.

Frame, James Everett. *The Epistles of Saint Paul to the Thessalonians*. ICC. Edinburgh: T. & T. Clark, 1912.

Furnish, Victor Paul. *2 Corinthians*. AB. Garden City, NY: Doubleday, 1984.

———. *Theology and Ethics in Paul*. Nashville: Abingdon, 1988.

Gammie, John G. *Holiness in Israel*. Minneapolis: Fortress, 1989.

Gärtner, B. *The Temple and the Community in Qumran and the New Testament*. Cambridge: Cambridge University Press, 1965.

Gaventa, Beverly Roberts. *Interpretation: First and Second Thessalonians*. Louisville, KY: Westminster John Knox, 1998.

Gehman, Henry S. "Hagios in the Septuagint, and Its Relation to the Hebrew Original." *Vetus Testamentum* 4 (1954) 337–48.

Gelder, Craig Van. *The Essence of the Church: A Community Created by the Spirit*. Grand Rapids: Baker, 2004.

Getz, Gene. *A Profile of Christian Maturity*. Grand Rapids: Zondervan, 1976.

Gingrich, F. Wilbur. *Shorter Lexicon of the Greek New Testament*. Chicago: Chicago University Press, 1957.

Godet, Frederick. *Commentary on St. Paul's Epistle to the Romans*. Grand Rapids: Zondervan, 1969.

———. *St. Paul's Epistle to the Romans*. Translated by A. Cusin. New York: Funk and Wagnalls, 1883.

Gorman, Michael J. *Apostle of the Crucified Lord*. Grand Rapids: Eerdmans, 2003.

Greathouse, William M., and George Lyons. *Romans 1–8: A Commentary in the Wesleyan Tradition*. New Beacon Bible Commentary. Kansas City: Beacon Hill, 2008.

———. *Romans 9–16: A Commentary in the Wesleyan Tradition*. New Beacon Bible Commentary. Kansas City: Beacon Hill, 2008.

Greathouse, William M. *Wholeness in Christ: Toward a Biblical Theology of Holiness*. Kansas City: Beacon Hill, 1998.

Greenlee, Harold. *What the New Testament Says About Holiness*. Salem, OH: Schmul, 1994.

Grenz, Stanley J. *Theology for the Community of God*. Grand Rapids: Eerdmans, 1994.

Griffith, Leonard. *This is Living: Paul's Letter to the Philippians*. Lutterworth: Lutterworth, 1966.

Grizzle, Trevor. *Ephesians*. Pentecostal Commentary Series. Dorset, UK: Deo, 2013.

Grogan, Geoffrey W. *Isaiah*. The Expositor's Bible Commentary 6. Edited by Tremper Longman III and David E. Garland. Grand Rapids: Zondervan, 2008.

Hahn, Roger L. *Matthew: A Commentary for Bible Students*. Indianapolis: Wesleyan, 2007.

Hansen, G. Walter. "A Paradigm of the Apocalypse: The Gospel in the Light of Epistolary Analysis." In *The Galatians Debate*, edited by Mark Nanos, 143–54. Peabody, MA: Hendrikson, 2002.

Harrington, Hannah K. *Holiness: Rabbinic Judaism and the Graeco-Roman World*. New York: Routledge, 2001.

Hartley, John E. *Leviticus*. Word Biblical Commentary 4. Waco, TX: Word, 1998.

Hauerwas, Stanley. "What Could it Mean for the Church to Be Christ's Body?" *SJT* 48 (1995) 1–21.

Hawthorne, Gerald F. *Philippians*. Word Biblical Commentary 43. Edited by David A. Hubbard, Glenn W. Baker, John D.W. Watts, and Ralph P. Martin. Waco, TX: Word, 1983.

Hays, Richard. *Echoes of Scripture in the Letters of Paul*. New Haven, CT: Yale University Press, 1989.

———. *First Corinthians*. Interpretation. Louisville, KY: John Knox, 1997.

———. *The Moral Vision of the New Testament*. San Francisco: Harper Collins, 1996.

Héring, J. *The First Epistle of Saint Paul to the Corinthians*. Translated by A. W. Heathcote and P. J. Allcock. London: Epworth, 1962.

Hewett, J. A. "The Use of the Hagios Group of Words for "Holiness" in the Pauline Corpus." Ph.D diss., University of Manchester, 1973.

Hogan, Maurice P. *The Biblical Vision of the Human Person*. EUS 23. Frankfurt: Peter Lang, 1994.

Hooker, Morna D. *The Letter to the Philippians*. The New Interpreter's Bible 9. Nashville: Abingdon, 2000.

Horrell, David. "Theological Principle or Christological Praxis: Pauline Ethics in 1 Corinthians 8:1–11:1." *JSNT* 67 (1997) 83–114.

Houston, Walter. *Purity and Monotheism: Clean and Unclean Animals in Biblical Law*. Sheffield: JSOT, 1993.

Howard, Richard E. *Galatians*. Beacon Bible Commentary. Kansas City: Beacon Hill, 1965.
———. *Newness of Life: A Study in the Thought of Paul.* Grand Rapids: Baker, 1975.
———. "Two Ways to Live." In *Biblical Resources for Holiness Preaching: From Text to Sermon.* Edited by Ray Dunning, Vol. 2. Kansas City: Beacon Hill, 1990.
Hrobon, Bohdan. *Ethical Dimension of the Cult, in the Book of Isaiah.* BZAW 418. Berlin: de Gruyter, 2010.
Hughes, P. E. *Paul's Second Epistle to the Corinthians.* NICNT. Grand Rapids: Eerdmans, 1962.
Hunter, A. M. *Interpreting Paul's Gospel.* London: SCM, 1954.
Jacob, E. *Theology of the Old Testament.* Translated by A.W. Heathcote and P. J. Allcock. New York: Harper & Brothers, 1958.
Jensen, Joseph. *Ethical Dimensions of the Prophets.* Collegeville, MN: Liturgical, 2006.
Jenson, Philip Peter. *Graded Holiness: A Key to the Priestly Conception of the World.* JSOTS 106. Sheffield: Sheffield Academic, 1992.
Jewett, Robert. *Romans: A Commentary.* Hermeneia. Minneapolis: Fortress, 2007.
Johnson, Luke T. *The Writings of the New Testament: An Introduction.* Philadelphia: Fortress, 1986.
Johnstone, Robert. *Lectures on the Book of Philippians.* Minneapolis, MN: Klock & Klock, 1977.
Jospe, Raphael. "The Concept of the Chosen People." *Judaism* 43 (1994) 139.
Kaylor, R. David. *Paul's Covenant Community: Jew & Gentile in Romans.* Atlanta: John Knox, 1988.
Keck, Leander E. *Paul and His Letters.* Philadelphia: Fortress, 1979.
Kempthorne, R. "Incest and the Body of Christ: A Study of 1 Cor. 6:12–20." *NTS* (1968) 568–74.
Kennedy, H. A. A. *The Theology of the Epistles.* Edinburgh: Edinburgh University Press, 1919.
Kittel, Gerhard, et al., eds. *Theological Dictionary of the New Testament.* Grand Rapids: Eerdmans, 1985.
Klein, William W. "Ephesians." In *The Expositor's Bible Commentary: Ephesians-Philemon,* edited by Tremper Longman III and David E. Garland, 12:45–46. Grand Rapids: Zondervan, 2006.
Knight, George W. *The Pastoral Epistles: A Commentary on the Greek Text.* New International Greek Testament Commentary. Grand Rapids: Eerdmans, 1992.
Kruse, Colin G. "The Offender and the Offence in 2 Corinthians 2:5 and 7:12." *EQ* 86.2 (1988) 129–39.
———. *Paul's Letter to the Romans.* Edited by D. A. Carson. The Pillar New Testament Commentary. Cambridge: Eerdmans, 2012.
Ladd, G. E. *A Theology of the New Testament.* Grand Rapids: Eerdmans, 1974.
Lanci, John R. *A New Temple for Corinth: Rhetorical and Archaeological Approaches to Pauline Imagery.* Studies in Biblical Literature 1. New York: Peter Lang, 1997.
Lategan, B. C. "The Argumentative Situation of Galatians." In *The Galatians Debate: Contemporary Issues in Rhetorical and Historical Interpretation,* edited by Mark Nanos, 383–95. Peabody, MA: Hendrickson, 2002.
———. "Is Paul Defending His Apostleship in Galatians? The Function of Galatians 1:11–12 and 2:19–20 in the Development of Paul's Argument." *New Testament Studies* 34 (1988) 411–30.

Lea, Thomas D., and Hayne P. Griffin. *1, 2 Timothy, Titus*. The New American Commentary 34. Nashville: Broadman & Holman, 1992.
Lee, J. A. L. *LXX, A Lexical Study of the Septuagint Version of the Pentateuch*. Chico, CA: Scholars, 1983.
Levine, Baruch A. *Leviticus*. JPS Torah Commentary. New York: JPS, 1989.
Liddell, H. G., and R. Scott. *A Greek-English Lexicon*. Revised by H. S. Jones. Oxford: Clarendon, 1940.
Lightfoot, Joseph Barber. *Colossians and Philemon*. Crossway Classic Commentaries. Wheaton, IL: Crossway, 1997.
———. *Notes on Epistles of St. Paul*. Reprint, 1895. Grand Rapids: Baker, 1980.
———. *Saint Paul's Epistle to the Philippians*. Classic Commentaries on the Greek New Testament. London: Macmillan, 1913.
Lipka, Hilary. "Profaning the Body: ⊠⊠ and the Conception of Loss of Holiness in H." In *Bodies, Embodiment and Theology of the Hebrew Bible*. LHBOTS 465. New York: T. & T. Clark, 2010.
Lohfink, G. *Jesus and Community: The Social Dimension of Christian Faith*. Philadelphia: Fortress, 1984.
Longenecker, Richard N. *Galatians*. WBC. Dallas: Word, 1990.
———. *The Ministry and Message of Paul*. Grand Rapids: Baker, 1971.
MacDonald, Margaret Y. *Colossians and Ephesians*. Sacra Pagina. Collegeville, MN: Liturgical, 2000.
Malherbe, Abraham. *The Letters to the Thessalonians*. New York: Doubleday, 2000.
Marsh, J. "Numbers: Exegesis." In *Interpreters Bible*, edited by George Arthur Buttrick, 2:216–40. Nashville: Abingdon, 1953.
Marshall, I. Howard. *New Testament Theology: Many Witnesses, One Gospel*. Downers Grove, IL: InterVarsity, 2004.
———. *The Pastoral Epistles*. ICC. Edinburgh: T. & T. Clark, 1999.
Martin, D. Michael. *1, 2 Thessalonians*. The New American Commentary 33. Nashville: Broadman & Holman, 1995.
Martin, Dale B. *The Corinthian Body*. New Haven: Yale University Press, 1995.
Martin, Ralph P. *The Epistle of Paul to the Philippians*. Tyndale New Testament Commentaries. Grand Rapids: Eerdmans, 1969.
———. *Reconciliation: A Study of Paul's Thought*. Grand Rapids: Zondervan, 1989.
Martyr, Justin. "The First Apology of Justin." In *The Apostolic Fathers with Justin Martyr and Irenaeus*, edited by Alexander Roberts, James Donaldson, and A. Cleveland Coxe, 163–87. The Ante-Nicene Fathers 1. Buffalo, NY: Christian Literature, 1885.
Matera, Frank J. *Galatians*. Sacra Pagina 9. Collegeville, MN: Liturgical, 1992.
McCown, Wayne. "God's Will for You: Sanctification in the Thessalonian Epistles." *Wesleyan Theological Journal* 12 (1977) 26–33.
McCumber, William E. *Holiness in the Prayers of St. Paul*. Kansas City: Beacon Hill, 1955.
Meeks, Wayne A. *The First Urban Christians: The Social World of the Apostle Paul*. New Haven: Yale University Press, 1983.
———. *The Origins of Christian Morality*. New Haven: Yale University Press, 1993.
———. "'And Rose Up to Play': Midrash and Paraenesis in 1 Corinthians 10:1–22." *JSNT* 16 (1982) 78.
Meyer, H. A. W. *A Critical and Exegetical Handbook to the Epistles to the Corinthians*. Edingburgh: T. & T. Clark, 1879.

Mitchell, Margaret M. *Paul and The Rhetoric of Reconciliation: An Exegetical Investigation of the Language and Composition of 1 Corinthians*. Louisville, KY: Westminster John Knox, 1991.

Moffatt, James. *The First Epistle of Paul to the Corinthians*. New York: Harper & Row, 1938.

Moriarty, F. L. "Numbers." In *Jerome Bible Commentary*, edited by Raymond Edward Brown, Joseph A Fitzmyer, Roland E Murphy, 86–100. Englewood Cliffs, NJ: Prentice-Hall, 1968.

Morris, Leon. *The First and Second Epistles to the Thessalonians*. NICNT. Grand Rapids: Eerdmans, 1991.

———. *The First Epistle of Paul to the Corinthians. An Introduction and Commentary*. TNTC. 2nd ed. Grand Rapids: Eerdmans, 1985.

———. *1, 2 Thessalonians*. Word Biblical Themes. Dallas: Word, 1989.

Mounce, William D. *Pastoral Epistles*. Word Biblical Commentary 46. Dallas: Word, 2000.

Muddiman, John. *The Epistle to the Ephesians*. Black's New Testament Commentary. London: Continuum, 2001.

Murphy-O'Connor, Jerome. *The Theology of the Second Letter to the Corinthians*. Cambridge: Cambridge University Press, 1991.

Neusner, Jacob. "The Idea of Purity in Ancient Judaism." *Studies in Judaism in Late Antiquity* 1 (1973) 137–42.

Neyrey, Jerome H. "Witchcraft Accusations in 2 Cor. 10–13: Paul in Social Science Perspective." *Listening* 21 (1986) 160–70.

O'Brien, Peter Thomas. *The Epistle to the Philippians*. Grand Rapids: Eerdmans, 1991.

———. *The Letter to the Ephesians*. The Pillar New Testament Commentary. Grand Rapids: Eerdmans, 1999.

Otto, Rudolf. *The Idea of the Holy: An Inquiry into the Non-rational Factor in the Idea of the Divine and Its Relation to the Rational*. Translated by John W. Harvey. 2nd ed. London: Oxford University Press, 1950.

Parry, Reginald St John. *The First Epistle of the Apostle Paul to the Corinthians*. Cambridge: Cambridge University Press, 1926.

Patrick, Dale. "The Rhetoric of Collective Responsibility in Deuteronomic Law." In *Pomegranates and Golden Bulls: Studies in Biblical and Near Eastern Ritual, Law and Literature in Honor of Jacob Milgrom*, edited by David P. Wright, David Noel Freedman, and A. Hurvitz, 421–36. Winona Lake, IN: Eisenbrauns, 1995.

Pershbacher, Wesley J. *The New Analytical Greek Lexicon*. Peabody, MA: Hendrickson, 1990.

Petersen, Norman R. *Rediscovering Paul: Philemon and the Sociology of Paul's Narrative World*. Philadelphia: Fortress, 1986.

Peterson, David. *Possessed by God: A New Testament Theology of Sanctification and Holiness*. Leicester, UK: Apollos, 1995.

Plummer, A. *An Exegetical and Critical Commentary on the Second Epistle of Paul to the Corinthians*. ICC. Edinburgh: T. & T. Clark, 1915.

Popkes, Wiard. "New Testament Principles of Wholeness." *Evangelical Quarterly* 64 (1992) 319–32.

Porter, J. R. "Holiness, Sanctification." In *Dictionary of Paul and His Letters*, edited by Gerhard F. Hawthorne, et al., 397–402. Downers Grove, IL: InterVarsity, 1993.

Porter, Stanley E. "What Does It Mean to Be 'Saved by Childbirth'?" In *New Testament Text and Language: A Sheffield Reader*, edited by Stanley E. Porter and Craig A. Evans, 160–75. Sheffield: Sheffield Academic, 1997.

Purkiser, W. T. *Exploring Christian Holiness*. Vol. 1. Kansas City, MO: Beacon Hill, 1983.

Rad, Gerhard von. *Deuteronomy*. Translated by Dorothea Barton. OTL 18 (1966) 100.

Raphael, Melissa. *Rudolf Otto and the Concept of Holiness*. Oxford: Clarendon, 1997.

Reid, T.S. "Paul: A Pattern for Pastors, with special reference to the Corinthian Letters." *Irish Biblical Studies* 19 (1997) 65–80.

Renwick, David A. *Paul, The Temple, and The Presence of God*. BJS 224. Atlanta: Scholars, 1991.

Ridderbos, Herman. *Paul: An Outline of His Theology*. Translated by John Richard De Witt. Grand Rapids: Eerdmans, 1975.

Ringgren, Hehner. *The Prophetical Conception of Holiness*. Uppsala: A.B. Lindquist, 1948.

Roetzel, Calvin. "The Grammar of Election in Four Pauline Letters." In *Pauline Theology*, edited by David M. Hay, 2:211–33. Minneapolis: Fortress, 1993.

Rosner, B. "The Function of Scripture in 1 Cor. 5:13b and 6:16." *BETL* 113 (1996) 513–18.

Rowley, H. H. *Worship in Ancient Israel: Its Form and Meaning*. Minneapolis: Fortress, 1967.

Saarinen, Risto. *The Pastoral Epistles with Philemon and Jude*. Grand Rapids: Brazos, 2008.

Sanday, William, and Arthur C. Headlam. *A Critical and Exegetical Commentary on the Epistle to the Romans*. ICC. Edinburgh: T. & T. Clark, 1902.

Sawyer, John F. A. *Isaiah*. Daily Study Bible Series 1. Louisville, KY: Westminster John Knox, 1984.

———. *Reading Leviticus: A Conversation with Mary Douglas*. JSOTS 227. Sheffield: JSOT, 1996.

Schaffer, Francis. *Escape From Reason*. Downers Grove: Intervarsity, 1960.

Schnabel, Eckhard J. "How Paul Developed His Ethics." In *Understanding Paul's Ethics: Twentieth Century Approaches*, edited by Brian S. Rosner, 267–97. Grand Rapids: Eerdmans, 1995.

Schneider, J. "Stauro." *Theological Dictionary of the New Testament*. Edited by G. Kittel and G. Friedrich. Grand Rapids: Eerdmans, 1964–78.

Schnelle, Udo. *Apostle Paul: His Life and Theology*. Grand Rapids: Baker Academic, 2005.

———. *The Human Condition*. Translated by O. C. Dean Jr. Minneapolis: Fortress, 1996.

Schrage, Wolfgang. *The Ethics of the New Testament*. Translated by David E. Green. Philadelphia: Fortress, 1988.

Shedd, Russell Philip. *Man in Community*. Grand Rapids: Eerdmans, 1964.

Shogren, Gary Steven. *1 & 2 Thessalonians*. Zondervan Exegetical Commentary on the New Testament. Grand Rapids: Zondervan, 2012.

Silva, Moises. "Old Testament in Paul." In *Dictionary of Paul and His Letters*, edited by Gerhard F. Hawthorne, et al., 630–42. Downers Grove, IL: InterVarsity, 1993.

———. *Philippians*. 2nd ed. Baker Exegetical Commentary on the New Testament. Grand Rapids: Baker Academic, 2005.

Slater, Thomas B. *Ephesians*. Macon, GA: Smyth & Helwys, 2012.

Smith, Gary V. *Isaiah 1–39*. Edited by E. Ray Clendenen. The New American Commentary. Nashville: B & H, 2007.
Snaith, N. H. *Distinctive Ideas of the Old Testament*. London: Epworth, 1944.
———. *Leviticus and Numbers*. New Century Bible. London: Nelson, 1967.
Spence-Jones, H. D. M. *Isaiah*. The Pulpit Commentary 1. London: Funk & Wagnalls, 1910.
Spross, Daniel. "Holiness in the Pastorals." In *Biblical Resources for Holiness Preaching*, edited by Dunning H. Ray and Neil B. Wiseman, 311–25. Kansas City: Beacon Hill, 1990.
Staton, Knofel. *Timothy-Philemon: Unlocking the Scriptures for You*. Standard Bible Studies. Cincinnati, OH: Standard, 1988.
Sumney, Jerry. *Colossians*. New Testament Library Series. Louisville, KY: Westminster John Knox, 2008.
Swanson, Dwight. "Re-Minting Christian Holiness: Holiness in Genesis 12–50." *The Flame* 65.3 (1999) 4–6.
Sweet, J. P. M. "A House Not Made with Hands." In *Templum Amicitiae*, edited by William Horbury, 371–88. JSNTS 48. Sheffield: Sheffield Academic, 1991.
Talbert, Charles H. *Reading Corinthians*. SPCK: London, 1987.
Tannehill, Robert. *Dying and Rising with Christ: A Study in Pauline Theology*. Berlin: Topplemann, 1967.
Taylor, Vincent. *Forgiveness and Reconciliation: A Study in New Testament Theology*. London: Macmillan, 1946.
Taylor, Willard H. "Ephesians." In *Galatians through Philemon*, edited by R. E. Howard, et al., 9:147–48. Beacon Bible Commentary. Kansas City, MO: Beacon Hill, 1969.
Thielman, Frank. *Paul and the Law*. Downers Grove, IL: InterVarsity, 1994.
Thomas, Gordon J. "A Holy God among a Holy People in a Holy Place: The Enduring Eschatological Hope." In *The Reader Must Understand: Eschatology in Bible and Theology*, edited by K. E. Brower and M .W. Elliott, 53–64. Leicester: Apollos, 1998.
Thrall, Margaret. *2 Corinthians*. ICC 1. Edingburgh: T. & T. Clark, 1994.
Thurston, Bonnie. *Reading Colossians, Ephesians & 2 Thessalonians*. New York: Crossroad, 1995.
Towner, Philip H. *1 & 2 Timothy & Titus*. IVP Testament Commentary Series. Downers Grove, IL: InterVarsity, 1994.
———. *The Letters to Timothy and Titus*. NICNT. Grand Rapids: Eerdmans, 2006.
Trevaskis, Leigh. *Holiness, Ethics and Ritual in Leviticus*. HBM 29. Sheffield: Sheffield Phoenix, 2011.
Vriezen, T. C. *An Outline of Old Testament Theology*. Oxford: Basil Blackwell & Mott, 1962.
Wall, Robert W. *1 & 2 Timothy and Titus*. The Two Horizons New Testament Commentary. Grand Rapids: Eerdmans, 2012.
———. *Colossians &Philemon*. IVP New Testament Commentary Series. Downers Grove, IL: IVP Academic, 1998.
Walters, John R. *Perfection in New Testament Theology: Ethics and Theology in Relational Dynamic*. Lewiston: Mellen Biblical, 1995.
Wannamaker, Charles A. *The Epistles to the Thessalonians*. NIGTC. Grand Rapids: Eerdmans. 1990.
Watson, Nigel. *The First Epistle to the Corinthians*. Epworth Commentaries. London: Epworth, 1992.

Webb, William. *Returning Home: New Covenant and Second Exodus as the Context for 2 Corinthians 6:14—7:1*. JSNTS 85. Sheffield: Sheffield Academic, 1993.
Weedman, Gary. *Philippians-Thessalonians: Unlocking the Scriptures for You*. Standard Bible Studies. Cincinnati, OH: Standard, 1988.
Wendland, H. D. *Die Briefe an die Korinther*. NTD. Göttingen: Vandenhoeck & Ruprecht, 1965.
Westcott, B. F. *The Epistle to the Hebrews*. London: 1892.
Whitehouse, Owen C. "Holiness: Semitic." In *Encyclopaedia of Religion and Ethics*, edited by James Hastings, John A. Selbie, and Louis H. Gray, 751–59. Edinburgh: T. & T. Clark, 1913.
Whiteley, D. E. H. *The Theology of St. Paul*. Oxford: Blackwell, 1964.
Wilson, Earle L., Alex R. G. Deasley, and Barry L. Callen. *Galatians, Philippians, Colossians: A Commentary for Bible Students*. Indianapolis, IN: Wesleyan, 2007.
Windisch, Hans. "ζύμη." In *Theological Dictionary of the New Testament*, edited by Gerhard Kittel, 2:902–6. Grand Rapids: Eerdmans 1964.
Winter, Bruce W. "The Achean Federal Imperial Cult II: The Corinthian Church." *Tyndale Bulletin* 46.1 (1995) 169–78.
―――. "Civil Litigation in Secular Corinth and the Church: The Forensic Background to 1 Corinthians 6:1–8." *NTS* 37 (1991) 559–72.
―――. "Responses to Religious Pluralism—1 Cor. 8–10." *Tyndale Bulletin* 41.2 (1990) 207–26.
―――. "Theological and Ethical Responses to Religious Pluralism—1 Corinthians 8–10." *Tyndale Bulletin* 41.2 (1990) 208–26.
Witherington III, Ben. *1 and 2 Thessalonians: A Socio-Rhetorical Commentary*. Grand Rapids: Eerdmans, 2006.
―――. *Community and Conflict in Corinth: A Socio-Rhetorical Commentary on 1 and 2 Corinthians*. Grand Rapids: Eerdmans, 1995.
―――. *Grace in Galatia: A Commentary on Paul's Letter to the Galatians*. Grand Rapids: Eerdmans, 1998.
―――. *Paul's Narrative Thought World*. Louisville: Westminster John Knox, 1994.
Wright, Christopher J. H. *The People of God: The Relevance of Old Testament Ethics*. Leicester: InterVarsity, 1983.
Zaas, Peter S. "Cast Out the Evil One from Your Midst." 1 Cor. 5:13b. *JBL* 103 (1983) 259–61.
Zehr, Paul M. *1 & 2 Timothy, Titus*. Believers Church Bible Commentary. Scottsdale, PA: Herald, 2010.
Ziesler, J. *The Meaning of Righteousness in Paul: A Linguistic and Theological Inquiry*. SNTMS 20. Cambridge: Cambridge University Press, 1972.

Index of Biblical References and Other Ancient Literature

HEBREW BIBLE

Genesis

6:9	129
17:1	114, 130

Exodus

4:22	16
6:10–15	9
12:18–20	55
15:11	23
19:1–36	18
19:3–8	11, 66
19:4–6	34
19:5	53, 65, 76, 153, 160
19:6	12, 41, 53, 65, 76, 105, 153, 160
19:10, 14, 22	46
19:10, 14–15	9
20:5	9
22:30	34, 100
22:31	53, 100
23:25a	11
23:30	53
29:16–24	9
29:30	35
29:37 (LXX)	103
29:37–38	102
30:20	35
31:13	143
34:14	9

Leviticus

1:3, 10	127
3:1, 6, 9	127
4:12	79
5:6	13
6	34
6:11	79
10	7
10:1ff.	5
10:1–3	5
10:3	5
10:6, 9–11, 12–15	5
10:11	5
10:17	34
11:36	79
11:44	8, 105, 160
11:44–45	14, 41, 65
11:45	100
12:8	79
13:13, 17, 37	79
18:1–5	5
18:4–30	5
18:29	13, 54
19	76
19:1–37	17
19:2	8, 15, 34, 41, 53, 100, 160
19:2, 11, 13, 15–16, 17–18, 33, 35–36	15

Leviticus (continued)

19:2—20:7	15
19:12b	6
20:3	7, 14
20:7	15, 41, 47, 160
20:7–8	13
20:7, 10, 11, 13, 14, 17, 19–20	15
20:7, 26	53, 105
20:8	6, 14, 15, 143
20:9	13
20:11	54
20:22–26	5
20:23	14
20:24, 26b	53
20:24–27	14
20:26	8, 14
21:6	14
21:8	6, 8, 15, 143
21:22	34
22:2–4, 10–14	34
22:2, 32	7
22:9	5, 143
22:9, 31	15
22:20–25	37
22:31	14
26	13
26:1, 11–12	80

Numbers

3:6, 31	35
4:3, 9, 12	35
5:1–4	18
6:14	103
8:12	79
9:2	103
9:13	79
16:16 (LXX)	9
18:11, 13	79
20	7
20:3–5	6
20:12	5
20:13b	7
27	7
27:14	5
28:16–17	55

Deuteronomy

1:15–16	58
4:5–24	9
4:20	9
5:9	9
6:7	53
7:6	9, 12, 16, 20, 38, 41
7:6–8	11, 108
7:9–14	12
7:11	12
10:8	35
12:13–14	70
14:1	12, 15
14:1, 21	38
14:2	9, 12, 53
14:2, 21	16, 41
16:3–4	55
17:2	35
17:7	54, 55
18:13	129
19:19	55
22:21	55
24:7	55
26:1–19	16
26:16	16, 53
26:18–19	38
28	16
28:9	16, 38, 53
32	7
32:1–7	16
32:4	130
32:19	79
32:51	5

Joshua

24	9
2:10–34	70
7:13	9
24:14	9
24:19	8
24:23	9

Judges

5:11	22

INDEX OF BIBLICAL REFERENCES AND OTHER ANCIENT LITERATURE

1 Samuel

6	10
2:2	8
6:19–21	8
7:1	10
16:5a	9
16:56b	9
21:4–5	10
21:4, 6	8

2 Samuel

22	130
6:7	8
7:14	80
24:15ff.	10

1 Kings

7:48	36
8:16	11
8:27, 29	11
8:53	20
9:3	11
11:32, 36	11

2 Kings

4:9	9
8:61	129
11:4	129
15:3, 14	129
19:21	79
20:3	129

1 Chronicles

6:32	35
15:2	35

2 Chronicles

3:1	11
29:5, 15, 31, 34	47
30:15, 17	47

Ezra

6:20	79

Nehemiah

12:30	79
12:45	79
13:22	79

Job

2:3	114
4:17	114
9:20	114
11:4	114
12:4	114, 130
15:14	114
22:19	114
33:9	114

Psalms

11:2	157
15:2 (LXX 14:2)	102
15:2ff. (LXX 14:2ff.)	127
17:26	157
18:23 (LXX 17:24)	102, 127
18:23, 24	114
19:13 (LXX 18:14)	127
29:5	157
32:1–2	22
36:28	157
40:6 (LXX 39:7)	36
40:7	37
49:5	157
51:2, 7, 10 (LXX 50)	79
85:2	157

Isaiah

6	23
6:3	76
11:9	10
23:18	11
27:1 (LXX)	11
27:13	10

Isaiah (continued)

30:29	11
35:8	11
43:6	80
43:16–20	1
49:8	75
50:1	79
52:11	79
54:1–6	79
57:19	124
60:3	38
62:5	79, 79
66:18	38

Jeremiah

2:3	2
18:13	79
31:4	79
31:9, 23, 31–34	80
32:31–41	80

Ezekiel

11:9, 12, 17–21	80
11:19	69, 70
22:26	2
36:23–26	70
36:23–28	53
36:25–27	149
36:25–29	58
36:25–38	80
36:26	69
37:14 (LXX)	141
37:23	153
40:46	35
42:14	35
43:2, 4–9	70
44:4	70
44:7–9	51
44:23	2

Daniel

7:18, 21, 22, 25	100
7:22	100

Hosea

1–3	79
11:1	16

Joel

1:14	9
2:15, 16	9

Micah

1:2	11

Zechariah

14:16	38
36:25–29	47

JEWISH HELLENISTIC LITERATURE

2 Baruch

51:5	34

1 Enoch

71:11	34

Philo, *De Fuga et Inventione*

12 §63	105

Wisdom of Solomon

7:25	72

NEW TESTAMENT

Matthew

5:8	129
5:48	106
10:16	114
19:21	129

INDEX OF BIBLICAL REFERENCES AND OTHER ANCIENT LITERATURE 181

Luke

1:75	157
11:41	152

John

3:6	93
15:13	106

Acts

3:12	156
4:2	129
10:2, 7	156
13:5	129
13:38	129
16:12	113
17:13	129
18:6	152
20:26	152
21:26	37
22:16	108
24:16	112
24:17	37

Romans

6–8	23
6	97, 126
8	149
1:1	64, 83
1:3–4	87
1:4	29
1:6	20
1:6–7	20
1:16–3:20	21
1:18	29
1:20	96
1:21	21, 124
1:24	25
1:24, 26, 28	21
1:24–32	147
1:28	124
2:29	29
3:1–20	21
3:1—4:25	31
3:21, 25, 26	22
3:21—4:25	22
3:22, 23, 27, 30	22
3:9–23	21
3:19–21	25
3:21, 24	30
3:21–26	21
3:22, 28	21
3:20	93
4:1–5	22
4:3–4	23
4:5–6	22
4:6–8	22
4:9–12	22
4:13	96
4:13–17	22
5:1	30
5:5	29
5:8	35
5:9	30
5:1—8:39	29
5:16	23, 30
5:18	30
5:20a	25
5:20	31
6:1–11	27
6:1–11, 12–14, 15–23	24
6:1—7:6	27
6:2	24
6:2, 10–11	89
6:3a	24
6:3b	24
6:3ff.	89
6:3–11	97, 131
6:4	24
6:6	24, 94, 95
6:6, 18, 22	90
6:6, 12, 13, 16–18, 20, 22	24
6:8	24
6:10	89
6:11	24, 26, 37
6:11, 12	34
6:12, 16, 19	33
6:13, 16	25
6:14	25, 89
6:18	25, 89
6:19	25, 26, 30, 37, 43, 77, 151
6:19–22	27, 86, 127, 139
6:21	26, 30
6:21–23	89

Romans (continued)

6:22	26, 27, 43, 45, 52
6:23a	24
6:23b	24
7:1	27
7:1–6	89
7:4, 6	52, 90
7:6	29, 30
7:7–13	27
7:7–25	27
7:11, 13	25
7:14–25	27, 28
7:24–25	34
8:1	27, 30
8:1–4	29, 32
8:1–5	29
8:1–17	162
8:1–39	29
8:2	27, 30
8:2, 3	30, 31
8:2, 4, 5	29
8:3	30, 93
8:3–7	141
8:4, 5b, 10	26
8:6, 9	29
8:6–13	80
8:9	37, 52
8:9–11, 15–17	34
8:10, 11	29
8:11	27
8:13, 14, 15	29
8:13–14	35
8:16	29
8:23, 26	29
8:29	33
8:29–30	102
8:33	131
8:33–34	128
11:7	131
11:17	37
12ff.	35
12:1	20, 34, 37, 127, 141
12:1–2	25, 32, 86
12:2	33, 149
12:3	37
13:3, 13, 14	37
13:9–10	35
13:12	77
14:3–5	94
14:10	126
14:20	56
15:1	37
15:15–16	32, 35
15:16	36, 37, 146
15:25–26, 31	20
15:31	37
16:2, 15	20
16:13	131
16:19	114

1 Corinthians

1:1	64
1:1–2, 28–30	83
1:2	38, 40, 46, 62
1:8	127
1:9	45, 149
1:11	44
1:11–31	41
1:18–25	44
1:20–28	77
1:26–31	42
1:28–30	160
1:29	93
1:30	26, 41, 42, 43, 46, 48, 52, 61, 62, 73, 86, 151
2:1	129
2:6	119, 129, 130
2:12	77
2:13–16	73
3:1–3	119, 129
3:1–5	93
3:3	44
3:10ff.	104
3:10–11	44
3:16	62, 143, 160
3:16–17	44, 69, 143
3:17	55, 56, 143
3:19	77
4:15–17	48
4:16	105
5:1	54
5:1–12	72
5:1–13	54, 57, 86
5:1–5	107
5:1–5, 11	48

INDEX OF BIBLICAL REFERENCES AND OTHER ANCIENT LITERATURE   183

5:5	54, 56	7:34	20, 51, 53, 62
5:6–8	55	7:35	51
5:7, 8	54	8–10	59
5:8	54, 72	8:7–13	60
5:9	55	8:12	61
5:9–13	78, 83	9:4	36
5:10, 12–13	77	9:13	36, 69
5:11–13	140	9:14	129
5:12	55	10:1	60
5:13	54, 55, 56	10:2–10	60
6:1, 2	58, 77	10:16–30	61
6:1–3	57	10:21	77
6:1–8	58	10:31—11:1	73
6:1–11	45, 57	10:32	112
6:2–4	45	11:1	88, 105
6:4	58	11:32	77
6:6	45	12:4–12	94
6:7, 9, 13, 15, 18, 20b	48	12:12–27	42
6:9	45, 53	13:1—14:1	35
6:9–11	47, 81, 88	13:5, 7	135
6:9–20	59	14:20	129
6:11	38, 40, 41, 45, 47, 52, 80, 146, 149	15:3–5	87
6:12	58, 59	15:20–23, 44, 51–53	33
6:12–20	3, 52, 58	15:42–43	33
6:13	52		
6:13–18	140	## 2 Corinthians	
6:14	59		
6:15	59	1:1	83
6:15, 17b	49	1:1–2	64, 65
6:15–20	49, 50, 81, 82	1:12	72, 82, 84, 105, 111
6:17	52	2:5–11	73, 135
6:18	70	2:5–12	135
6:19	49, 50, 69	2:6–8	107
6:19–20	70, 141	2:7a	74
6:19, 22	42	2:8	74
6:20	59	2:9	74
7:2	140	2:10	74
7:9, 28a, 36	53	2:17	72, 111
7:12–14, 16	48	3:2–3	138
7:12–15, 31, 33	77	3:17–18	33
7:13	48	3:18	146
7:14	40, 48, 49, 50, 151	4:4	77
7:16	48, 50	4:6	146
7:26	51	4:7–12	75
7:28b, 32a	53	4:10–11	93
7:29–31	51	5:11	27, 75
7:32–34	127, 139	5:11–12	75

2 Corinthians (continued)

5:11—6:2	75
5:11—7:16	75
5:12	75
5:13—6:2	75
5:17	46, 75, 131, 143
5:17–20	83
5:18–19	82, 85
5:18–20	82
5:20–21	67
5:20b	75
5:21	26, 37, 48
6:1	75
6:1–10	75
6:2	37, 75
6:4	75
6:6	67
6:9–10	71
6:11	71
6:11–13	138
6:14	67, 77
6:14—7:1	67, 71, 76, 78, 83, 86
6:14a–16a	72, 80
6:14b–16a	77
6:16	44, 65, 69, 71, 76, 80, 160
6:17	78, 79, 80
6:18	78, 80
6:16–18	77
7:1	77, 80, 81, 161
7:6	83
7:11	154
8:12	37
10–13	78, 83
10:3	93
11:2	x, 67, 68, 79
12:21	140
13:5	78
14:2	83

Galatians

1:1	64
1:1–4	90
1:6	45, 149
1:8–9	107
2:11–20	88
2:16	88
2:17–18	88
2:19	88, 89, 90, 94, 98
2:19–20	88, 91
2:20	27, 73, 86, 90, 94, 95, 161
3:3	93
3:26	52
4:3	77
4:21	92
5:1	92
5:13	92
5:14–15	92
5:16	92
5:13—6:10	92
5:13–24	92
5:16–18	35
5:16–24	141
5:19	25, 140
5:19–21	94
5:22	94, 95, 161
5:22–23	112
5:22–24	49
5:24	86, 92, 94, 95, 98
6:12–13	96
6:13	96
6:14	77, 86, 96, 98

Ephesians

1	124
1:1	100, 103, 104
1:4	20, 100, 102, 107, 108, 131
1:5	99
1:6	146
1:9ff.	124
1:12	103
1:13	103
1:15	103
1:15–23	103
1:19, 20	99
1:22	103
1:23	103
2:1, 5	103
2:1–10	88
2:1–13	124
2:2	77
2:8, 9	22
2:8–10	108
2:11ff.	103
2:12	124

2:13	124	1:9	111
2:15b	103	1:9–11	86, 111, 112
2:19–22	104	1:9b	111
2:20–22	44, 104	1:10a	111
2:21	103, 104	1:10b	111
2:22	104, 160	1:11	112
3:2–3	104	1:17, 18	129
3:4b	104	1:27	112, 113, 117
3:5	104	1:27–30	112
3:6	124	2:1–8	112
3:7	104	2:1–11	113
3:7–8	105	2:5–9	111, 112
3:17	102	2:6–11	87
3:19b	101	2:12–15	80
4:2, 15–16	102	2:14–16	113
4:11–13	104	2:15	102
4:13	102, 129	3:5–10	88
4:17	107	3:6	119
4:18	124	3:8–11	115
4:19	25	3:10	90
4:24	157	3:12	115, 117, 118
5:1	106	3:12–16	112, 115
5:1–4	105	3:13	117
5:1a	105	3:15	115, 116, 118, 130
5:2	37, 106	3:16	120
5:2a	106	3:20	113
5:2, 25	102	3:20–21	33
5:3	107, 140	3:21	33, 146
5:3–4	102	4:8	66, 154
5:3, 27	20	4:8–9	112
5:4	107	4:21	110
5:8	77	4:22	110
5:11–21	135		
5:12	102	**Colossians**	
5:23–24	109		
5:25b	107	1:1–2	123
5:26–27	107	1:2	123, 125
5:26b	108	1:3–14	123
5:27	102, 108	1:5, 12	126
5:27a	108	1:9–10	126
5:27b	108	1:13–14	143
5:27c	108	1:15–20	123
		1:16	123
		1:20	123
Philippians		1:21	123, 124
1:1	110	1:21–22	100
1:4	111	1:21–23	123, 124
1:6	112		

Colossians (continued)

1:22	20, 100, 102, 103, 123, 124, 125, 127, 128, 131
1:23	123, 124, 128
1:26–27	124
1:27	x
1:28	128, 129, 130
1:28–29	128
1:29	128
2:12	125
2:16–23	35
2:8, 20	77
3:1	131
3:1–2	125
3:1–14	125
3:1—4:5	126
3:1—4:6	131
3:5	132
3:5, 8	125
3:9, 10	126
3:9–11	131
3:11–12	135
3:12	65, 131, 132
3:12–17	131
3:14	131
4:3	129
4:5	77
4:12	129, 130

1 Thessalonians

1:6	105, 106, 143
2:10	105, 157
2:10–12	139
2:14	106
3:9–11	138
3:11–13	127, 137, 161
3:12	138, 147
3:12–13	138
3:13	20, 81, 137, 138, 139, 146
3:13a	138
3:13b	138
4:1	143
4:1–2	139
4:1, 10	147
4:1—5:22	138
4:3	139, 160
4:3b	140
4:4	140, 145
4:1–7	86
4:1–8	138, 146
4:2–8	77
4:3–4	151
4:3, 4, 7	137, 139, 151
4:3–7	144
4:3–8	127
4:4–5	141
4:4–8	140
4:5	3
4:6	140, 147
4:7	43, 137, 139, 140, 141, 145, 149, 162
4:7–8	144
4:8	142, 145
4:9–12	138
4:10	143
4:11	144
4:12	55, 77
4:13–18	138
5:1–11	138, 163
5:5	77
5:12–22	138
5:22	138, 140
5:23	137, 142, 144, 145, 146, 161, 163
5:23–24	86, 137, 138, 139, 142
5:23a	142, 144
5:23b	142, 143, 144
5:24	144
5:25–28	138
5:26	142

2 Thessalonians

1:3	146
1:4–6, 8	146
1:7	145
1:11	144
2:1	144
2:10	145
2:11	145
2:12	144
2:13	33, 137, 145, 151
2:13–14	144
2:13–17	145
2:14	146

2:15	145
3:7, 9	105, 106

1 Timothy

1:5	152
1:9	157
2:15	88, 151
4:2	154
4:3	150
4:5	150
4:12	155
5:2	154, 155
5:10	149
5:22	67, 154
5:23	155

2 Timothy

1:3	153
1:9	149
1:9, 14	149
2:19	150
2:20	150
2:21	150
2:22	153, 157
3:5	156
3:9	153
3:14–17	35

Titus

1:5–9	157
1:8	157
1:15	152
2:11–14	112, 153, 157, 158
2:14	153
2:14c	153
2:15	153
3:5	22, 108, 149

Philemon

1:1	133
1:1, 7, 16, 20	133
1:1, 9, 10, 13	133

1:2	133
1:3	133
1:4–7	133
1:5	133
1:7	133
1:8	133
1:17–20	134
1:21	133

Hebrews

6:12	105
9:12–13	152
9:14	37, 102
10:5, 10, 14, 18	37
12:11	84
12:14	109, 121

James

1:4	129
4:8	152

1 Peter

1:16	83
1:19	37, 102
2:4–11	77
2:5	37
2:5–9	83
2:9	35
2:9–10	20

2 Peter

1:3, 6–7, 9	156

Jude

1:24	102

PLATO

The Republic X, 613	105
The Laws, 716cd	105
Theaetetus, 176 ab	105

www.ingramcontent.com/pod-product-compliance
Lightning Source LLC
Chambersburg PA
CBHW031428150426
43191CB00006B/438